T0147191

# LABOR VERSUS CAPITAL *in the* UNITED STATES

## LOUIS PATSOURAS

authorHOUSE®

AuthorHouse™
1663 Liberty Drive
Bloomington, IN 47403
www.authorhouse.com
Phone: 1 (800) 839-8640

Published by AuthorHouse    08/13/2019

ISBN: 978-1-7283-1010-7 (sc)
ISBN: 978-1-7283-1009-1 (hc)
ISBN: 978-1-7283-1020-6 (e)

Library of Congress Control Number: 2019906255

Print information available on the last page.

This book is printed on acid-free paper.

Table of Contents

This work is dedicated to Herbert Teklin, Leon Ancely, Chris McVey and Rev. Ralph L. Young

## Prologue and Historical Background

While the struggles between lower/upper workers and the middle class and the richest 1 percent in the United States of America is sweeping and significant in the formation of the current economic climate, there first needs to be an explanation of the historical background of the contemporary class struggle between labor and capital, as well as its various manifestations.

For hundreds of thousands of years in the Stone Ages, humans lived in small hunting and foraging bands of general equality characterized by mutual aid to ensure individual/group survival. From about 11,000 to 8,000 BCE, humans discovered agriculture (grains and so forth and some domesticated animals). These developments allowed for permanent settlement in villages, which in turn resulted in increased economic surplus/labor division resulting in social stratification in distinct territorial units. Warfare followed. Warrior chiefs and priestly groups emerged, ushering in a religious element, which promoted social cohesion among the larger populations.

Villages gradually coalesced into larger territorial units through marriage/warfare, ultimately leading to the earliest civilizations in Sumer and Egypt c. 3500 BCE. Egyptian social structure, for instance, was characterized by Pharaoh, primary war/religious leader/ administrator, with leading secular/religious supporters (nobility/ priesthood) in a hierarchical arrangement. They ruled a sharply demarcated class society in descending order of merchants, artisans, many small independent farmers, and many farm workers working in the estates of Pharaoh, nobility, slaves, and so forth.

Variations of this society whose economic surplus was primarily based on agriculture have endured in most of the world certainly until the early 20th century. In this paradigm, emperors/kings nobility were the large landowners/tax collectors, usually backed by the religious structure, who appropriated a part of the labor time, principally of farmers, the overwhelming majority of the population, to enrich themselves and to perform the duties of government/religion, the two closely intertwined.

In the west, Alexander the Great constructed a Greek Empire which was eventually succeeded by the Roman Republic and Empire built by war and slavery.

With the fall of the Roman Empire in the 5th Century CE by Germanic tribes, a long period of feudalism/manorialism ensued in which the warrior/administrators of kings and nobility, reinforced by a priesthood, mainly ruled over serfs bound to the soil.

Within the crevices of the feudalistic/manorial structure, with the rise of trade and small cities by the 11th-14th centuries of the CE, an early capitalist class of merchants and bankers arose, especially in northern Italy, but also in France, Germany, England, the Netherlands, Belgium and so forth.

With the voyages of discovery of the Americas, Africa, and Asia by Western Europeans, capitalism quickened during the Commercial Revolution, 1400-1700, in which merchant and banking capital were intertwined in the African slave trade and slave crops of sugar and cotton in the Americas.

Capitalism further advanced with the coming of the Industrial Revolution in England and other Western European areas in the 1750s, and afterward, which led to the rise of extensive urban life and large working classes laboring in capitalist-owned factories.

The Industrial Revolution by the 19th century spread to the North in the United States and Japan. This economic development led to the general end of slavery in the 19th century, although remnants of it still existed in the early 21st century in economically backward areas.

By the middle of the 20th century, the socialist Soviet Union industrialized and relatively soon after World War II, socialist China also did, as did to a degree India, South America, Indonesia, and so forth. By the early 21st century, industrialization/capitalism is ubiquitous with finance capital in the lead.

By the early 20th century, the capitalist class, intermarrying with the king/nobility complex, became the leaders, solidifying their hegemony after World Wars I and II, and today are indisputably the world's leaders. In this respect, even the leaders of the Chinese Communist Party are capitalists as mostly former Communists after the fall of the Soviet Union.

Like the previous dominant classes, the capitalists, as the owners of capital/technology, extracted part of their workers' labor time for themselves in their quest for wealth and profit. Generally in this socioeconomic nexus, a conflict model emerged between capital and labor over wages, job security, and social welfare and so on. To be sure, as capital increases so does its need generally for more workers. Thus it is that since the late 19th century to the present, large labor/socialist parties have emerged to challenge capitalism.

The 20th century witnessed the rise of socialist/union activity in Europe, the Americas, Asia, and Africa. Importantly, two Communist revolutions in the former Russian Empire and China established socialist governments: the Soviet Union and the People's Republic of China, the first imploding in 1991 and the second a hybrid of private and state capitalism.

Today, in the second decade of the 21st century, despite setbacks, large socialist/Communist parties throughout the world have gained many improvements for workers in the form of less work hours, increased social welfare benefits – to name just a few.

But capitalist hegemony is still intact in a world of great socioeconomic inequality which since the 1980s has increased. In this contemporary world, wealthy capitalists enjoy unparalleled luxury while large sections of the working class live in misery.

Labor's exploitation by capital was cogently described by Karl Marx, the principal socialist of the last three centuries, in <u>Capital</u> and other works. He was ably assisted by Frederick Engels, where part of labor time at work in the form of surplus-value was extracted by capital. Furthermore, they envisaged that as workers became more numerous their class struggle against the owners of capital would intensify, leading to a socialist society of general equality. The principal of hope is paramount here, similar to Christian millenarianism.

This work is based on the economic struggle between labor and capital, which is manifest within the political arena where, under present capitalist structures, capital has a decided advantage. Labor must work for capital or descent into abysmal poverty; a worker's existence is often economically precarious; the economic whip is ever present.

# Chapter 1: Increasing Economic Concentration

Since about 1980 to the present, personal/corporate income/wealth inexorably has become ever more concentrated. This is because throughout the world, the neoliberals (conservatives) representing capital have gained ground over workers or labor, represented by social-democratic, socialist and Communist parties. This development witnessed the fall of the Soviet Union, the rise of capitalism in Communist China and the rise of conservativism in the United States of America (U.S.), the European Union (EU), Japan and elsewhere.

This work will examine mainly the state of the class struggle between labor and capital in the U.S., with its impact on various areas like social welfare programs, social mobility and so forth, while also noting capital's ills, like the Great Recession and its deleterious train of unemployment and sheer economic waste.

Specifically, the neoliberal rise in the U.S. is characterized by the Reagan presidency (1981-89), the advent of free trade, rapid technological innovation, anti-union and administrations adversely affecting the working class – in fact, impoverishing it – while enriching the wealthy.

The corporate global sector is dominated by transnational corporations (TNCs) having operational plants in two or more nations. Of the leading 500, 244 are in America; 173 are in the EU, 46 are in Japan, which, in 2015, possessed two-fifths of developed nations' GDP.

In the U.S., circa 2000, the 200 largest corporations had 30 percent of sales revenue, the remainder held by 22 million businesses (a third part-time, a third of a one-person variety). As for market value of publically traded corporations, the leading 500 had 85 percent of it. This economic concentration is related to oligopoly in various sectors of the economy.

Examples of corporate concentration in sales in fractions and percentages in the U.S. circa 2000 are as follows: seven telephone companies have most of it; four airlines, two-thirds; three computer software firms, half; twenty in insurance, half; three in mass merchandizing, three-fourths (Walmart alone, 60 percent); four drug chains, half; ten in pharmaceuticals, including foreign, most; five in automobiles, most; two grain exporters, half; three in beef, 80 percent; 1 percent of farms, 40 percent; four cereal companies, 85 percent; hospitals, one chain alone, 10 percent.

The U.S. banking sector itself is becoming ever more concentrated, a condition that is inevitable under capitalism unless checked politically. From 1980 to 2005, there were 11,500 bank mergers, and as of 2008, the 10 largest banks had 60 percent of bank assets, up from 10 percent in 1990. By 2012, the largest 12 banks had 69 percent of assets held by 6,600 banks. In 2013, U.S. bank deposits were at $10.6 trillion, bank loans at $7.58 trillion. Overall, banks are the largest lenders to business enterprise, including home mortgages, commercial property, and student and car loans.

Increasing economic concentration is also indicated by the following: three banks – JP Morgan Chase, Wells Fargo, and Citigroup – hold half the mortgages and have two-thirds of credit cards. The 500 largest transnational corporations (TNCs) had 40 percent of the world's income in the 2004-08 period and 15 percent of S&P corporations in 2012 garnered 60 percent of its profits. Furthermore, the largest 200 U.S. corporations increased their share of total gross profits of the economy from 13 percent in 1950 to 30 percent in 2008 and increased their share of total business income in the same period from 21 percent to 30 percent in the U.S.

Corporate bigness is also observed in the following 2008 statistics: 99 percent of companies with annual incomes between $10,000 and $10 million have only 17 percent of business income. Two-thirds of workers are employed by companies having more than 100 workers. Companies employing more than 500 workers employ half the workforce and pay 57 percent of workers' salaries.

In the contemporary capitalist era dominated by large corporations, it becomes more difficult for them to beat rivals which also have great economic resources. For instance, in the automobile industry, prices of discrete models are largely similar. Price wars among large car companies would hurt profits. Thus, the favored way for company expansion under these circumstances is through mergers and acquisitions (M&A) via financialization.

This leads to the conclusion that free market capitalism today is largely mythical under the impress of oligopoly involved in monopolistic competition.

Thus it is that the M&A frenzy worldwide in 2014 was the best in the last seven years worth $3.5 trillion; in the last quarter alone, the US total was $375 billion (41 percent) the remainder of the world, $546.4 billion (59 percent).[1]

A brief historical background on the U.S. rich, or top 1 percent: When the U.S. secured its independence from Britain in the early 1780s, they had approximately 15 percent of the wealth because the inexpensive frontier land complex made for much socioeconomic equality, despite large plantations/slavery in the South. But as industrialization/urbanization accelerated, coupled with increased immigration and weak unionism, sharper class divisions arose and by 1929 the top 1 percent had 43 percent of the wealth – the peak so far. The Great Depression of the 1930s and rise of progressive New Deal politics in the 1930s and even beyond increased taxes on the rich and saw a rise in real wages with the rise of unionism, resulting in the richest 1 percent in 1976 having 8 percent of income and 18 percent of wealth.[2]

In 2013, the minimum annual income of the richest 1 percent in the US was $380,000; in 2013, hedge fund managers earn in the $1 billion range. This richest 1 percent circa 2014 owns half of stocks and mutual fund value, about two-thirds of financial securities, three-fifths of business equity, and a third of non-home real estate.[3]

The changes enumerated led to the richest 1 percent becoming ever more wealthy (8 percent of the income in the 1970s and rising to 22.5 percent in 2012). In 1928, just before the Great Depression, their income share was 24 percent. Income and wealth of the richest 1 percent in the recent year of 2007 averaged $1.4 million and $19 million respectively; in 2012. 40 percent of wealth.

The richest 1 percent under Bush II (2001-09) garnered 65

percent of all income gains and 95 percent in the 2009-14 period of tepid economic recovery, increasing their income by 31 percent, the bottom 40 percent losing 6 percent. In fact, under Obama's first term, adjusted for inflation, the earning of the bottom 90 percent fell, those of the poorer third dropping the most.[4]

The richest 1 percent of Americans in total national income percentage have done better than those in other developed nations where social democracy is still strong; in 2000, for instance: U.S., 16; Britain, 12; Germany, 10; France, 8; Japan, 8; Switzerland, 8; Sweden, 6.

While the income gains from 1979 to 2006, adjusted for inflation, tripled for the richest 1 percent, they were 55 percent for the highest income quintile, 21 percent for the middle one, and 11 percent for the lowest one. The income gains below the richest 10 percent are because of longer work hours and the rise of two-income families.

Another estimate, from 1983 to 2013 indicating the widening median household net worth wealth gap among income fifths, the top one, the middle one, and lowest one is as follows: In 1983, $300,000, $94,000, $11,400; in 2013, $640,000, $96,500, $9,300. Percentage changes for the respective three quintiles, up 101 percent, up 2.0 percent, down 18.4 percent (another set of household income figures in 2016 dollars to indicate increased economic inequality. The year 1975: top five percent, $130,000; top 10 percent, $106,000; median, $48,000, and bottom 10 percent, $12,000. In 2016: top five percent, $225,000: top 10 percent, $171,000, median, $59,000, and bottom 10 percent, $14,000, according to Steven Brill, Time, May 28, 2018, p. 30. Conclusion: The wealth gap among these groups is widening, the top increasing its wealth from three to seven times over the middle, and from 300 to over 600 times over the lowest.

As for general gradations of the richest 1 percent, the richest 0.01 percent, the wealthiest one in ten thousand taxpayers, comprising about 14,400 families in 2007, had an average annual income of $4 million in 1974 and $35 million in 2007, their percentage of national income rising from 1 to 6 percent. Below them was the richest 0.1 percent, the wealthiest one of the thousand taxpayers

(144,000 households) who annually earned $1 million in 1974 and $7 million in 2007, increasing their share of the national income during this period from 2.7 percent to 12.3 percent. The remainder of the richest 1 percent had approximately the other half of the 23.5 percent of the income in 2007.

Another set of figures in 2012 of the richest 1 percent of U.S. households with respect to wealth calculated by economists Emmanuel Saez (University of California, Berkeley) and Gabriel Zucman (London School of Economics): The richest 0.01 percent (ultra-rich) have 11.1 percent of wealth; the next richest, 0.099, 10.4 percent; the next richest, 99-99.99 percent has 18.3 percent of wealth, or the richest 1 percent has 39.8 percent of wealth. The next richest 9 percent has 34.6 percent of wealth; thus the richest 10 percent has 74.4 of wealth. On the other hand, the poor or near-poor or the bottom half of households, have 1-2.5 percent of wealth.

Among the most common occupations of the richest 1 percent in the U.S. (in percentages circa 2014): physicians, 16; financial, 14; nonfinancial business, 31; lawyers, 8; engineers, 2.

Among the richest Americans in 2015, in billions of dollars: Bill Gates, 79.4; Warren Buffett, 67.6; Larry Ellison, 50.2; Jeff Bezos, 43.5 (145 in 2018); Mark Zuckerberg, 41.6; Charles and David Koch, 41.6, each; the six Walton heirs (of Walmart), 150, or as much wealth as the poorest 40 percent of Americans.

In 2011, the U.S. had 413 billionaires (worldwide, 1,226) with a net worth of $1.518 trillion or about 10 percent of US GDP. In 2008 (Great Recession year), the Forbes 400 billionaires had an average net worth of $3.9 billion, six times more than in 1985, with an average annual income of $345 million, paying only 16.6 percent in federal taxes. In 2007, for instance, they had as much wealth as the lower half (160 million) of the U.S. population. In 2014, the Forbes 400 average wealth was $5.7 billion. Again, in 2014, the richest 400 Americans owned over $2.2 trillion, more than the bottom 160 million Americans. Meanwhile, about half of Americans have less than $10,000 in savings. According to Bernie Sanders: Bill Gates ($90 billion), and Warren Buffett ($84 billion), had somewhat more wealth than that of the bottom half (165 million) of the U.S. population. (For the last sentence, The <u>Nation</u>, April 16, 2018, pp. 4.)

Globally in 2015, according to Oxfam, the well-known British charity, compiling figures from various business periodicals, the 80 richest billionaires own $1.9 trillion, about the same amount as the lower half of the world's population, 3.5 billion.

Also, the 2014 World Wealth Report of the Credit Suisse Bank has the richest 1 percent with half the world's wealth, with the poorest 50 percent having only 1 percent. Again, according to Oxfam, by 2016 the richest 1 percent will own as much wealth as the bottom 99 percent.

Most of the great wealth, with few exceptions, has been inherited. The rich are able to transmit most of their wealth upon death to their descendants through trusts. Traditionally, trusts had a lifespan of about 100 years. But now there are dynasty trusts, legal in 28 states, which can increase in value untaxed as they pass between generations – forever into eternity. As of 2003, $100 billion was invested in this manner. This will contribute to the ongoing formation and consolidation of the American capitalist oligarchy.

The top annual income earners in the U.S. are hedge funds/private equity funds managers and CEOs of large corporations. In 2009, the richest 25 hedge fund managers earned about $1 billion each; in 2007, James Simon, John Paulson and George Soros collectively earned $9 billion. Top earners in 2013 included Leon D. Black, CEO of the private equity firm of Apollo Global Management, who earned $546.3 million and Stephen A. Schwarzman of the private equity fund Blackstone Group at $452.7 million; Lawrence J. Ellison of Oracle, $96.2 million; Leslie Moonvee of CBS, $60.25 million. Average compensation of the 10 highest CEOs in millions of dollars in 2012 in various industries: media, 30; technology, 24.6; consumer goods, 18.7; healthcare, 17.9; industrial goods, 17.5; financial, 16.9; basic materials, 16.6; in 2014 alone, 25 hedge fund managers earned $25 billion.[5]

Annual income disparity, circa 2012 in the US between a median worker ($25,000) and top media CEOs ($30 million), more than 1,000 to 1; between them and average billionaire, 10,000 to 1; between them and average CEO of large (top 100 companies), 500 to 1. These figures do not include CEO stock options. From 1978 to 2011, adjusted for inflation, CEO earnings rose 725 percent while workers' rose 5.7 percent. Since 2010, the richest 1 percent received 99 percent of income gains.

For economist Paul Krugman, high CEO compensation is related to corporate boards who grant CEO salaries, most of which mainly comprise other CEOs and other high corporate officials whom they largely appoint. This incestuous paradigm leads to high compensation.[6]

Income inequality results in consumption inequality in the U.S.. For Mark Zandi of Moody's Analytics, the richest 5 percent indulge in a third of consumer spending and the richest 20 percent in 60 percent of it; for Jack Rasmus on the left, the wealthiest 10 percent consume 60 percent of it. Also, a 2012 statistic by the Institute for New Economic Thinking has the richest 5 percent indulging in 38 percent of personal consumption expenditure (27 percent in 1992); the richest 20 percent 61 percent in 2012 (53.4 percent in 1992); the bottom 80 percent from 46.6 percent in 1992 to 39 percent in 2012.[7]

According to Krugman, the rising wealth of America's super rich has led them to outspend those of the Gilded Age (late 19th- early 20th centuries) and those of the 1920s, as observed in their many mansions, yachts, private planes, and so forth. For their fabulous lifestyle, read Vanity Fair. For Krugman, this great wealth was acquired by their paying lower taxes; in 1955, the 400 highest earning Americans paid more than half their income in federal taxes, now less than a fifth.

I add that the greater wealth of the U.S. rich was at the expense of workers whose wages were reduced by free trade, computerization/ automation and anti-union legislation/decisions by courts and the National Labor Board. Furthermore, rising federal debt has enriched bond-holders, mainly the rich.

According to the British based Tax Justice Research group, the world's rich in 2010 had $21 to $32 trillion in global tax havens, more than a third by U.S. citizens. Succeeding chapters on the working class, taxes, and Great Recession cover this area also.

Income and wealth are closely related to social class, as the following examination shows.

An outline of annual average household income circa 2012 in fifths and percentiles in the U.S.: bottom fifth, $11,000; second fifth, $30,000; middle fifth, $52,000; fourth fifth, $84,000; top fifth, $246,000; top 1 percent, $1,672,000; top 0.1 percent, $7,850,000. A more detailed examination of this income of the top fifth in 2006: the 80th to 90th percentile, $101,000; the 90th-95th percentile, $132,000; the 95th-99th percentile, $212,000; and the richest 1 percent, $1,200,000. As observed, the income of the richest quintile one, among the highest in the world.[8]

In a capitalist US, only a miniscule group, the "power elite," a term coined by the sociologist C. Wright Mills, run the country. The apex of this oligarchy are the chief executive offers (CEOs) and other high officials of the leading 500 or so corporations who by their company PACs and lobbyists basically control Congressional legislative decisions, but more investigation will be made later.

This oligarchy also includes the presidency and cabinet, U.S. Supreme Court, Congress, state governors/legislators, and military and large city mayors.

I also include the stars of the entertainment industry in the power elite (many of whom are very rich) because they affect emotional/ interior life. The leading figures among the power elite exchange positions from one of its sectors to others: the actor Ronald Reagan becoming president, the actor Arnold Schwarzenegger becoming governor of California, the General Dwight D. Eisenhower becoming president, president William Clinton and wife, Hillary, becoming rich, whose estimated worth is about $50 million in 2013.

Examples of the wealthy also becoming political stars include the billionaire Michael Bloomberg becoming mayor of New York City; the very wealthy Nelson A. Rockefeller becoming governor of New York and Vice President of the U.S. in 1974-77 in the Gerald R. Ford presidency. Another Rockefeller, John D. Rockefeller IV was U.S. senator from West Virginia. I estimate the power elite to number in the several thousands, about 20,000 including chief subordinates.[9]

The leading class subordinates of the wealthy and power elite are the upper-middle class, about 10-15 percent of the people whose income range in 2013 was $130,000 - $380,000. In 2013, 20 percent of households earn over $106,000, 5 percent more than $196,000. The 90th to 99th income percentile, circa 2014, earns about 25 percent of all income. This class comprises many professionals, like doctors, lawyers, middle management, many in two income families – 72 percent of married women have regular jobs. The richest 10 percent had a third of income in 1980, half in 2010. The 95th percentile in income – about the middle of the upper-middle class – in 2010 had an after-tax per capita income, not including capital gains, of $58,600, earning 20 percent more than those in Canada, 26 percent more than those in Britain, and 50 percent more than those in the Netherlands. Why? Primarily because of lower taxes.

To join the upper-middle class, a 4-year college education helps. With respect to wealth accumulation or median real net worth among 4-year college graduates from 1992 to 2013, for whites and Asians it increased over 85 percent, but dropped for Hispanics at 28 percent and blacks at 56 percent. Why? Less likelihood to inherit money; higher college loan debt; job discrimination; substantial debt between whites and Hispanics/blacks; the collapse of housing prices during the Great Recession, all of which adversely affected blacks/Hispanics more so than whites.[10]

More than likely, the wealthiest Americans today had rich ancestors, attended exclusive prep schools, colleges/universities and those of the Ivy League, who are members of exclusive clubs, have high positions in corporations and live in wealthy neighborhoods, apartments. Their children will generally follow the preceding pattern.

The prevalent mindset of the rich basically ensconced in capitalist corporations is to amass as much wealth as possible by "shrewd trading and unscruptulous management," aided by lawers involved in "predatory fraud." Those elements will be later observed in white-collar crime, ever-prevelant in a capitalist America with its posessive individualistic ethos.

U.S. concentration of wealth is so great that it has the most socioeconomic equality among developed nations. This has occurred since the counter-revolution of the wealthy against the 1930s – 1981 New Deal legacy of a moderate social democracy beginning with President Reagan and countinuing under successive Republican and Democratic presidencies.

Income inequality is measured by the Geni coefficient (GC) where zero is absolute equality and one indicates that a single family earns everything. The finding of selected nations.

The most egalitarian societies are in social democratic Scandanavia and Finland, where labor unions are very strong, with a GC of .245 in Denmark, .249 in Sweden, .268 in Norway and .268 in Finland. The GC is higher in social democratic Western Europe: .314 in Germany, .332 in France, .341 in Great Britain, .352 in Italy. But .416 in plutocratic Russia and a high of .450 in plutocratic U.S.

# Chapter 2: Working/Lower-Middle Classes and Poverty

This chapter depicts the economic and other struggles of the lower four-fifths of the American people that has been worsening since the 1980s.

The large majority of U.S. workers are in the lower-middle and working class combination: the former, about 20-25 percent of households; the latter, up to 65 percent. Underneath the upper-middle class in income is the lower-middle-class whose income range in 2013 is in the range of $65,000 – $120,000, comprising about a fourth of households. It includes many older two-to-four-year college graduates, younger professionals, two-income families, various managers and business types like salespeople of small corporations. They are the wealthier workers.

The working class in income generally earns under $70,000 annually; in 2013, the median household earned $51,000.

The working class is comprised of un-, semi-, and skilled blue collar workers (a minority in unions), lower white collar workers in retail and many in the mass professions (K-12 teachers and nurses). U.S. median wage at $25,000 annually, circa 2014, about a third, earning less.

Two-thirds of the working class, the poorest 40 percent of the people, earn less than 12 percent of income and have 1 percent of the wealth in 2013; they earn up to $10 – 11 per hour, are definitely the poor or near-poor, including a seventh of the people wholly dependent on welfare. Another estimate of the poor/near poor by two African American activists, Tavis Smiley, a TV personality and Dr. Cornell West, formerly at Princeton but now at the Union Theological Seminary, includes half the people, or those under the median income of $51,000 in The Rich and the Rest of Us.[1]

The following pages describe the deteriorating socioeconomic conditions of the American working class, especially its lower two-thirds.

The federal minimum wage in 2014, still $7.25 an hour in 2015 (higher in some cities and 29 states), in a 40-hour week annually earns $15,080, a fourth higher than the $12,000 a year poverty line for an individual, $23,000 for a family of four.

Low-wage workers include those with median wages of $9 per hour in fast food, $10 in home care, $9 – 11 per hour in retail (Walmart, $9 minimum, and Costco, an exception, at $20 per hour). These workers generally have no company health coverage, sick pay, pensions, and many qualify for welfare in food stamps and Medicaid.

Workers living below the poverty line typically work part-time and are often unemployed or chronically ill. Many are younger, unmarried mothers (30 percent of women are pregnant by age 19). Those in official poverty include 11 percent of whites, 22 percent of Hispanics, and 25 percent of Blacks, circa 2014.

The cohort above them in income earns $15,000, $25,000, $30,000 annually usually share the vicissitudes of the poverty group, living from paycheck to paycheck. Educationally, these two groups are high school dropouts, often ill, many without any family support.

The 2014 Obama proposal to raise federal hourly income from $7.25 to $10.10 would lift about 1 million workers out of poverty and also raise the wages of workers earning $7.26 - $10.09 hourly for up to 30 million workers, or 20 percent of the work force. It may or may not lead to higher prices and slightly more unemployment, for instance, in fast food, but overall it would be beneficial to lower-wage workers, half of whom are over the age 25.

The poverty line devised in the 1960s for a family of four (two adults and two children) should be doubled from $23,000 to $40,000 – 45,000, especially because of the high cost of living in many cities. This modest income includes renting an inexpensive two-bedroom apartment and spending $1.50 per person per meal. To achieve this goal, it would take 1 2/3s full time workers earning at least $12 an hour, 40 hours per week, circa 2013.

This cohort and the median group of $57,000 have been severely savaged in the 2000-12 period by rising combined health care and four-year state college costs for their children of 80 percent, adjusted for inflation.

The federal minimum wage in 2015, still at $7.25 an hour (or $1,250 per month) has lost 40 percent of its purchasing power since 1968. To be sure, other selected and developed nations have a higher minimum wage, monthly earnings: for Luxembourg, $2,500; Netherlands, $2,000; Ireland, $2,000; France, $1,800; Britain, $1,600.[2]

An American family, circa 2011, in the 20th income percentile, earns much less than the same family in Canada, Sweden, Norway, Finland, and the Netherlands. In the 40th income percentile, Norwegian and Canadian families also fare economically better than U.S. ones. In the median (50th) percentile, Canadian families per individual now equal the U.S. at $18,600. From 1980 to 2010, adjusted for inflation, among U.S. household incomes in the lower half of income, have declined but have risen from the 80th income percentile, especially for the richest 1 percent. [3]

In the wealth category, the poorest 40 percent in income saw their average wealth decline sharply from 1983 to 2004 from $5,400 to $2,200. This group of unskilled/semi- skilled workers also experienced ever lower wages and high unemployment in this period.

The Great Recession also resulted in large average wealth loss between 2005 and 2009: whites, $135,000 to $123,000, a 16 percent decrease; Blacks, $12,000 to $5,700, a 53 percent drop; Hispanics, $18,400 to $6,135, a 66 percent decline. For ethnic groups, the average household income in 2012: Asian Americans, $69,000; non-Hispanic whites, $57,000; Hispanics, $39,000; African-American's, $33,000; the last two groups are over-represented in the working class.[4]

To be sure, in average and median income, the U.S. still is among the leaders, only behind Singapore, Norway, Luxembourg, and Hong Kong.[5]

To reinforce the preceding statistics, in the 1999-2012 period, the median household income adjusted for inflation, dropped from $56,080 to $51,017, a 9 percent decline, while median family net worth fell from $126,400 in 2007 to $77,300 in 2010, declining a third, principally because of falling housing prices. The median income of older households, ages 55-64, also fell sharply from $61,700 in 2010 to $56,000 in 2012.

Another set of statistics on falling living standards: the income of non-supervisory blue- and white-collar workers, who comprise 80 percent of the private sector workforce, as percentage of GDP dropped from 31 percent in 1964 to 20 percent in 2010. Also, 4 year college graduates in the 25-34 age group had an average annual income of $60,000 in 2000, $50,000 in 2012; at the same time, their average college debt increased, from $23,000 in 2000 to $29,000 in 2012. Falling/stagnant economic growth until 2014 also has resulted in almost 25 percent of adults aged 25-34 living with parents or relatives, double the 1980 rate.

More studies on increasing exploitation of labor by capital and the widening income gap between average wage workers and wealthy: 1) Average hourly wages, adjusted for inflation, were $21 in 1975 and just under $19 in 2012, while corporate profits, as percentage of GDP, were 7 percent in 1975 and 10 percent in 2012; 2), personal income share of the total by the richest 1 percent, already observed, was 10 percent in 1979 and 22.5 percent in 2012, resulting in an income loss in 2012 for other individuals of $7,015; 3) In the last three decades, the GDP doubled, but the median income of the lowest 90 percent, adjusted for inflation, is lower, according to Robert B. Reich, former President Bill Clinton Labor Secretary and now professor of public policy at University of California at Berkeley.

The hollowing of the "middle class" in the 2000-10 period, is also indicated in the change of median disposable income of selected OECD nations, the developed ones. It increased by 40 percent in Australia, 27 percent in Sweden, 20 percent in Canada, 11 percent in France, 4 percent in Italy, 2 percent in Germany, but declined 4 percent in the U.S.[6]

Indeed, the labor share of wages in the U.S. economy as compared to business profits, according to the Federal Reserve Bank of San Francisco from about 1980 to 2010 and excluding the salaries of the richest 1 percent, has dropped 10 percent. This economic trend is generally true for about two-thirds of the nations throughout the world, including wealthy nations and developing ones like China and India.[7]

More specificity on the deteriorating economic catastrophe befalling American workers from 1970 to 2010: Although men's full time real median wages in 2010 remain near 1970s levels, for unskilled, semi-skilled and part time workers, their wages dropped by 16 percent. Also, for both men and women workers from the 1970s to 2010, adjusted for inflation, averages wages for high school graduates declined by 23 percent, for high school dropouts 25.7 percent, but rose 15.7 percent for four-year college graduates. Part time and contingent workers, earning up to 70 percent of full time workers, are now almost a third of the workforce.

Indeed, beginning workers' wages in manufacturing in the last half decade or so have decreased by half. Average hourly wages of American workers recently are lower than in some Western European nations: U.S. $24.59; France, $28.57; Germany, $37.66. But women's wages in the last several decades have risen, now to 77 percent of men's, but the gap has not narrowed in the last decade.[8]

The preceding falling wages/salaries should be viewed in the light of an 83 percent rise in labor productivity in the 1973-2006 period. Thus, in 1982 constant dollars for Greenhouse, a labor reporter for <u>The New York Times</u>, if annual full time worker wages had kept up with the rise of labor productivity since 1979, they could be earning $58,000 annually in 2007 instead of $36,000. According to the economist Joseph Stiglitz, a typical male worker, in real median wages, earned $33,800 in 1968 and $32,986 in 2011. Another estimate, by Lawrence Mishel of the leftist Economic Policy Institute, reports that median American worker's income, adjusted for inflation, from 1979 to 2014 rose slightly, by 5.6 percent, while GDP rose by 150 percent and labor productivity gained 75 percent.[9]

These factors have seen middle-income workers (75 percent to 150 percent of median income) fall from 61 percent of the work force in 1971 to 51 percent in 2011; in 1971, they had 62 percent of the income; in 2011, 45 percent – almost all of this 17 percent loss going to the richest 1 percent.[10]

Another estimate in annual income range of households in 2014 dollars and their percentage of the people in 1967 and 2013. In 1967:

low income, under $35,000, 40 percent; middle, $35,000 – 100,000, 53 percent; high, over $100,000, 7 percent. In 2013: low, 34 percent; middle, 43 percent; high, 22 percent.

Of note: there are fewer poor (still, as already observed, the bottom 40 percent of the people have only 12 percent of income); bottom 20 percent, 3.4 percent; the middle-income group is significantly shrinking; the top 7 percent grew to 22 percent, in which the richest 1 percent tripled their income share, while the next richest 9 percent also increased theirs. The great gain in the over $200,000 cohort was made possible by two professional income families.[11]

Indeed, younger workers' misery is compounded by an increasingly shabby retirement. For instance, in companies with more than a hundred employees, circa 1980, 84 percent had a pension, but only a third had such a benefit in 2014.[12]

According to Elizabeth Warren, former Harvard law professor and now Democratic Senator from Massachusetts, from the 1930s to the late 70s, 90 percent of all workers shared 70 percent of income gains, but from 1980 to 2012 that 90 percent gained nothing. For Mishel, from 2002 to 2014, the bottom 80 percent of workers have experienced stagnant/falling wages/salaries.[13]

The contributing factors leading to low workers' wages from 1980 to the present (2015) include: 1) The decline of unions and collective bargaining is the first and most significant factor. This in turn is related to free trade, with much of manufacturing going abroad, which then resulted in large middle income job losses and weaker unions; 2) computerization and automation/robotics has led to massive layoffs of workers; 3) add to this, right to work legislation in half the states allows union workers not to pay union dues, which has undermined wages. Also, other anti-union legislation, like the Taft-Hartley Act among others, permits union organizers to be fired (it takes years to resolve this labor dispute) and strikebreakers to replace workers during a strike and afterward; 4) failing to raise the overtime pay threshold for salaried workers; lifting it to $50,000 annually would allow two-thirds of them to receive overtime pay as in the 1970s; 5) a weak social democracy resulting in low taxes on the rich, high sales taxes on workers, lack of universal healthcare system that forces workers to pay high medical costs, no government jobs program for long term unemployed workers, allowing for more job competition among workers, leading to lower wages; 6) legislating for high immigration (an eighth of Americans are foreign born), which cannot but depress wages.

According to Seven Rattner, a Wall Street executive, in 2014 the U.S. has more income inequality than other developed OELD nations because of low federal taxes, presumably on the rich, and less generous social welfare programs. Rattner should have added lower and/or stagnant wages.[14]

Income and wealth inequality result in life longevity inequality, with women in each class/cohort living longer than men because they drink and smoke less, have lower stress levels and work in less polluted work sites. Also, as between the wealthier and more educated and the less so, the latter live in more polluted work places/neighborhoods, have less healthy diets, more stress, smoke and drink significantly more, and have less healthcare coverage.

Average year life longevity: white males, 76; black males, 70; white women, 80; black women, 77. Regarding education: white women with four and more years of college, 83.7; less than high school, 73.5; for white men with a college degree, 80.4; less than high school, 67.5.[15]

Since 1995 to the near present, labor income in the U.S. has declined 8 percent – Tom Hartmann, citing the <u>Washington Post</u>, Free Speech TV, July 5, 2018. Forty percent of American workers earn less than $15.50 per hour, according to the Economic Policy Institute, and 22 percent of college graduates have low-wage jobs, both condemned by neo-liberal economics – Jesse Ventura, Russia TV, July 6, 2018. Forty percent of American workers have two jobs, according to Channel 3, Cleveland, Ohio, July 9, 2018. According to the United Nations, rapporteur, observing the economic conditions of the American workers in 2018, 43 percent of them have inadequate housing, transportation and other vital needs.

Another contributing factor for working class poverty is

increasing corporate shareholder profit. In the 1960s/70s, it was 33 percent of profit, or 1.7 percent of GDP; since the 2000s, 70 percent of it, or 4.7 percent of GDP or 3 percent more of it for the rich. In 2017, $1.1 trillion went to corporate shareholders, who gained $567 billion more or 3 percent of GDP than in the 60s/70s, or $3,500 in wages for all adult workers (Mike Konszal, "Economy in the Stocks," The Nation, Sept. 10/17, 2018, p. 5).

Underlying social welfare is the sociobiological concept of mutual aid developed by the Russian anarchist Peter Kropotkin. It embodies a condition even stronger than love and shows the need among humans to cooperate for survival. To be sure, mutual aid is impaired, even destroyed, in hierarchical/class-stratified societies.

In Western civilization, the Christian religion in a world of strife and inequality was the chief embodiment of mutual aid, to aid the poor and the sick; it established orphanages, schools, hospitals and so on. The Catholic Church, among other religions, played a leading role in this, with its preference for the poor. But in the 20th century, although religion continued to play an important role in social welfare, the modern secular state progressively assumed leadership in this endeavor. Indeed, mutual aid by the 19th century onward also included the general welfare of the population at large, itself leading to anarchism/socialism as final destination.

Traditionally, alongside American religion, American government from its earliest days was also involved with social welfare. Indeed, until the early 20th century, many of the indigent were primarily cared for by county poorhouses which provided for their keep by farming, cooking, and so on.

By the early 20th century, there were also 400 settlement houses, private nonprofit centers of charity in American cities to aid primarily the poor immigrant masses. The first, Hull House in Chicago, was founded by Jane Addams; other pioneers in this movement included Florence Kelley and Lillian Wald; these women were primarily middle-class reformers, and socialists.

Social welfare in the U.S. has constantly lagged behind Western European nations, including Britain, France, Germany and Scandinavia, where the left (labor/socialist parties) were much stronger politically than in the U.S. For instance, by the late 19th and early 20th centuries, these nations had passed legislation to protect workers, with health and unemployment insurance, old age pensions, prohibiting child labor, and so on.

I also add that the U.S. being a frontier nation until the 1890s, having many independent farmers, economically subsisting largely on their own, developed a culture not favoring much government aid to the poor, thus lagging behind Western Europe. In the U.S., circa 1900-1910, there was no federal legislation to protect workers, but states soon passed laws to limit children's work hours: no work before age 12; ages 12-15, 10 hours work per day; after 16, no limit. Before this time, children often worked 12-14 hours daily, at times seven days per week.

Regarding education, by 1900, the majority of states had compulsory attendance laws for six years. In 1900, only a tenth of students attended high school; by 1930, 60 percent, indicating that child labor was still prevalent.

The 19th Amendment to the Constitution (1920), women's national suffrage, also spurred social reform because women, as principal caregivers of children, are more receptive to social welfare than men.

The 1900-1920 Progressive Movement led by President Theodore Roosevelt, the socialist Eugene V. Debs, state governors like Robert M. LaFollette in Wisconsin and mayors like Tom L. Johnson in Cleveland, Ohio, among others, was a step forward to social reform. They were aided by the muckrakers, fearless journalists like Lincoln Steffens and novelists like Upton Sinclair in exposing socioeconomic inequalities and political corruption.

Poverty has always been endemic in American society: in the early 1900s, 40 percent of workers lived thus; in the Great Depression decade of 1930s, up to 40 percent of them were unemployed and living in abysmal poverty. Presently, 40 percent of Americans are poor/near poor.

With the advent of the Democratic Franklin Delano Roosevelt's New Deal that combatted the ravages of the Great Depression in the 1930s, the federal government became massively involved in social welfare legislation to aid the poor and general public.

Hunger relief was provided by the Federal Emergency Relief

Administration. To employ the unemployed and students, there were the Civil Works Administration, the Works Progress Administration, the Civilian Conservation Corps, and the National Youth Administration. Labor union organization was encouraged by the Wagner Act, which permitted collective bargaining between workers and employers. Farmers were rescued by two Agricultural Adjustment Acts.[1]

Social Security enacted in 1935 is the principal government insurance program. It is now funded jointly by employees (7.65 percent of wages) and employers (7.65 percent), totaling 15.3 percent. It includes a retirement pension at age 65 (extended to age 67 if born after 1954), early retirement possible at age 62, with disability insurance (a third of benefits) and survivor's benefits). Employed workers earning up to $118,000 in 2015 contribute. The self-employed pay also 15.3 percent of income of up to $118,000. Its administrative costs, 1 percent.

Eligibility for Social Security retirement benefits requires a 10-year contribution by workers, but not for disability while working, and it is also involved with unemployment insurance/benefits. In 2011, it covered 54.3 million in individual benefits, averaging $1,025 monthly. Its $2.7 trillion reserve fund is fully funded to 2035 and with adjustments, like raising the income contribution to $250,000 or more is viable for 75 additional years or longer. A quarter of citizens over age 65 are almost completely dependent on Social Security and the majority of them derive more than half their income from it.

The average Social Security payouts in 2013: $12,857 for women, $16,590 for men, with women suffering disproportionately than men; poverty rate for whites is 1 in 6, for blacks 1 in 2 and Hispanics 1 in 3.

The second significant push for socioeconomic and political reform occurred under the Democratic Lyndon Baines Johnson administration in the mid-1960s. Its Civil/Voting Rights Acts enfranchised blacks in the South and with the Supreme Court 1954 Brown vs. Board of Education decision ended public school segregation.

The aim to reduce poverty was via the Office of Economic

Opportunity to train/provide work for poor workers and the Volunteers in Service to America assisted them to organize themselves locally in improving their health and education.

Then, the Department of Housing and Urban Development (HUD) of 1965 granted housing assistance to welfare recipients, 2.4 million in 2009. It includes public housing and a 30 percent rent subsidy. Monies for it have shrunk by two-thirds in the last 30 years; still, in 2012, it spent $40 billion. It also aids the homeless with federal funding to local and state governments.

Medicare (1965) provides medical care for Social Security recipients at age 65, eventually age 67. It has an annual budget in 2012 of $550 billion; a fourth of its budget is for treating patients in their last year of life, a third to half of whom spend time in costly extensive-care units. Before Medicare, almost half of citizens age 65 and older had no health insurance.

The very poor and the physically and mentally disabled are covered by Medicaid enacted jointly with Medicare. It is funded 60 percent by the federal government, 40 percent by the states, insuring more than 60 million individuals, including 40 percent of those in nursing homes, at a cost of $356 billion in 2009. Some physicians refuse to treat Medicare, but especially Medicaid patients because of supposedly low government payments.

The Department of Veterans Affairs (VA) provided assistance to 5 million military veterans in 2012 in various programs, including free medical/drug care for uninsured veterans and disability payments. Government aid to veterans began with the American Revolution in 1776. Also, the Great Society included funds to states aiding poor students and for providing legal assistance to the poor. President Nixon to his credit continued the Great Society programs, as did Presidents Ford and Carter.

A government job program at a living wage for the unemployed would be a step forward in welfare. If effected, it would also result in higher wages of employed workers because it would lessen the number of workers competing for wages in a capitalist labor market. It was part of the Democratic Party platform from the 1930s to 1984, killed by the President Ronald Reagan's reactionary New Federalism in the 1980s.

Reagan also eliminated public service jobs, food stamps, and reduced unemployment benefits: in 1980-81, Reagan welfare spending was cut by $101 billion. By 1992, adjusted for inflation, there were 82 percent cuts in subsidized public housing, 63 percent for job training, and 40 percent for community services. Simultaneously, military spending greatly increased, the bogus Soviet threat being an excuse, a form of military Keynesianism.

For poor mothers not eligible for Social Security, there is the President Bill Clinton Temporary Assistance to Needy Families program. In 2008, it covered 4.4 million individuals (70 percent children) in 1.8 million families receiving $20.8 billion from the federal government in block grants to the states, including Medicaid, money assistance for up to five years, many states granting much less. This program replaced the more generous federal one of Aid to Families with Dependent Children (AFDC), children eligible for coverage to age eighteen, part of the 1935 Social Security Act, rejected by Clinton, the Republicans and half the Democrats in Congress.[2]

In 2014, the U.S. spent 18 percent of its GDP or $3 trillion on health care. It is the only OECD nation, except for Greece (no health care coverage after a year's unemployment), not to have universal health care insurance. For comparison, circa 2014, other nations spending as percentage of GDP on health care: Britain, 8.4; Germany, 10.4; France, 11; Canada, 10.1; Japan, 8.1. According to the World Health Organization (WHO), France has the best health care, the US ranked 37th.[3] A number of nations insure their citizens through private non-profit insurance companies, like Germany and Switzerland, insurance being compulsory.[4]

Although universal health care is favored by the majority of the people, including physicians and nurses, privately-owned health insurance and pharmaceutical companies and hospitals, through PACs and lobbyists in Congress, have successfully opposed its full implementation, spending $1 million daily on lobbying Congress. Why? It would eliminate their high income and profit considerably.

The principal factor allowing for high U.S. health care costs is due to privately-owned health insurance companies like Aetna and United Healthcare having high administrative costs (high salaries for executives, dividends to investors, advertising) totaling 25-30 percent. For instance in 2009, the CEOs of the 10 largest health insurance companies had a total compensation of $228.1 million. In contrast, total costs to administer Medicare's 50 million insures are 2.2 percent. The Affordable Care Act (ACA) itself extends to 2034 Medicare's solvency. Tragically, of $551 billion in 2012 of Medicare benefits, 15-30 percent are wasted because of weak government oversight of doctors and arcane hospital bills, hospitals pressuring doctors to increase patient admissions, and by outright cheating by physicians. The 13 million workers in the medical field, including the capitalist insurance drug companies, are a strong political force to be reckoned with in maintaining the status quo.

A most egregious example of health care profiteering was by the Columbia HCA hospital chain, which overcharged Medicare/Medicaid billions of dollars. The company later admitted to 14 felony charges and paid the federal government over $600 million. It was the largest fraud settlement in U.S. history. Its CEO, Richard Scott, was forced to resign, but was elected governor of Florida in 2010.

In 2015 the Department of Justice began investigating Blue Cross/Blue Shield for alleged price fixing. This provider insures more than 100 million people.

Furthermore, two reports published in June 2015, in Health Affairs and by the Centers for Medicare and Medicaid Services, indicate very high health care costs, especially charged by for-profit hospitals, most of which were located in the south. Their high list prices were reduced by private insurance, Medicare and Medicaid, but despite this, final prices paid by patients were outrageously high. The remedy: universal health care.

Medicare Part D enacted under Bush II in 2004 to cover prescription drugs did not allow the federal government to negotiate prices with drug companies, resulting in American drug prices being double those in Western Europe and Canada, adding $50 billion to annual drug costs. The VA settles prices with drug companies, paying much less than Medicare. Drug costs are 10 percent of health care; they should be 5 percent, following the European Union.

Health insurance costs for a working family of four in 2009 are $15,000, and it pays $4,127, the employer the remainder whose costs are tax deductible, thus subsidized by taxpayers. In 2009, nursing home costs for a bankrupt patient on Medicaid was $87,000.

To be sure, the annual private insurance costs for the very rich are in the $40,000 range with such benefits as private rooms, special clinic care and other amenities.

Private-sector (outside the Veterans Administration) health care costs/insurance are usually double the rate of inflation. Also, if unemployed, this insurance is terminated. About a third of workers under age 30 (many part-timers, circa 2010) are uninsured versus 15 percent in 1988. Regarding workers with a high school education, only 29 percent had medical insurance in 2009.

I add that government (local, state and federal employees) numbering about 22 million are favored over private sector employees in that they have health coverage in addition to pensions, although their wages are lower than private-sector workers in similar occupations.[5]

The ACA proposed by the Democrat Obama and passed by a Democratic Congress in 2010, becoming fully effective in 2014, was a large step forward to universal health care.

Its major provisions include compelling health insurance companies to spend at least 85 percent of their premiums on patients (previously 75 percent), mandates health care coverage for those insured with pre-existing health conditions, covers 2.3 million dependent children to age 26, and lowers drug costs.

By early 2015, the ACA enrolled about 20 million uninsured people, about 9 million in federal exchanges, 3 million in state ones, and 4 million in expanded Medicaid, fully funded by ACA from 2014 to 2016, then at 90 percent, states 10 percent. Uninsured citizens fell from 20.3 percent to 13.2 percent in 2015. It forces citizens to enroll in it, the very poor exempted. Twenty-one Republican states as of

2015 have not accepted Medicaid expansion, many millions of poor yet uninsured; 80 percent of these uninsured are in Southern states which have the legacy of slavery and racism.

The ACA hit the wealthy with higher taxes, did not subsidize those not in poverty, their paying higher premiums as healthcare costs rise, but so do the subsidized – again, healthcare costs outstripped inflations, doubling in 2010-15.

On the whole the ACA increased the federal budget by 3 percent, this cost offset by overall lower healthcare costs, although in 2015 opinion polls only 5 percent thinks so. I blame the capitalist media for this discrepancy. Overall, the ACA has been successful, the recently enrolled satisfied with their insurance. It has eliminated co-payments and deductibles for preventive care like mammograms and provides discounts for heavy users of prescription drugs. Also, it puts limits on patient spending per year and over a lifetime.

To be sure, the ACA by 2015 has partly remedied the abysmal state of US health care in 2012-13. According to the Common Wealth Fund and World Health organization in this period, 37 percent of ill-Americans did not avail themselves of doctor-recommended health care, saw a doctor when sick, or filled prescriptions because of costs as opposed, for instance, of 4 percent in Britain. Almost a quarter of Americans could not afford to pay a medical bill less than 7 percent in five other nations, the US being last. When ill, less than half of Americans could see a doctor/nurse within two days and a fourth had to wait six days or longer, only Canada being worse in both instances. Inadequate or lack of health insurance coverage in a recent US year resulted in 700,000 or half of all bankruptcies and 45,000 deaths.

The ACA itself closely follows the health care guidelines of the conservative Heritage Foundation, the successful health care law in Massachusetts favored by its Republican governor Mitt Romney (in 2015, 95 percent of its people were insured), and would have been accepted by the Republican Party before the reactionary Reagan Revolution of the 1980s.

Of note: the imperfect ACA only secured passage because it promised more profits for the health care industry via their coverage of more insurees, partly satisfying their PACs and lobbyists. In opinion polls, Republicans/wealthier opposed it two-to-one, while lower income Blacks/Hispanics supported it by an equal margin.

In early October 2013, House Republicans launched an unsuccessful drive to repeal the ACA, partially shutting down the federal government for sixteen days and almost not renewing the federal debt by one day.

Presently, the Republicans/conservatives are attacking the ACA also by the judicial route. The first challenge before the conservative U.S. Supreme Court was partly successful. Although upholding the buying of subsidized health insurance through state exchanges, it did not allow much state expansion of Medicaid for the poor.

The second Republican challenge to the ACA was heard by the Supreme Court in March 2015, King v. Burwell. The conservative plaintiff King charged that the language itself of the ACA does not allow federal subsidies in the federal exchange program and that penalizing monetarily individuals who do not wish to be enrolled in the ACA program is unconstitutional. King lost in June 2015 by a 6-3 vote, allowing the ACA to continue unscathed.[6]

To aid poor working-class households, Congress passed the earned-income tax credit, costing $61 billion in 2012, parent(s) with one child receiving $3,305, $6,143 maximum for up to three children.

Because the poverty/near-poverty cohort is now increasing, food assistance programs are greatly needed for sheer survival. Thus, there is primarily, the Supplemental Nutrition Assistance Program (SNAP), previously called food stamps, and others for school lunches, and for women with children, feeding 48 million people in 2013 (26 million in 2007) who are "food insecure" at $80 billion annually. In 2013, $272 monthly in SNAP assistance goes to an average poor household. Approximately 40,000 private/religious food banks contribute only 5 percent of the amount to feed the hungry, spending $4 billion annually.

The relentless Republican attack against social welfare legislation continued in July 2013 when the Republican-controlled House voted to strip SNAP from the Farm bill for the first time since 1973, which ties it to government subsidies to mostly wealthy farmers/ corporations, and to cut it by $40 billion in the next decade; the Democratic cut would be $4 billion; it was eventually reduced to $8 billion by law.

Stephen Fincher, a Tea Party Republican representative from Tennessee, a wealthy farmer receiving government subsidies in the millions of dollars, justified his voting against SNAP with a New Testament quote that one unwilling to work should not eat; evidently, Fincher forgot Matthew 25:34-36, where we should feed, clothe and house the poor. As it is common throughout the world, specifically in westernized countries, workers must work for the simple reason of sheer economic survival, that the only people not working are the disabled, the unemployed, and the idle rich, that 5 million mothers with children on welfare are required to work, and that for every job opening in 2014 there are on average two job applicants. Fincher's views are typically Republican.

Furthermore, of the 23 million households receiving SNAP assistance, 45 percent are children, 41 percent working parents not adequately feeding their children, the remainder poor, elderly and disabled.

To be sure, Republicans after Reagan attempted to reduce or either eliminate social welfare. For instance, in Republican dominated states ca. 2015 funding for social welfare and schooling was greatly reduced. Also, House Republicans in 2015 wish to privatize Social Security, Medicare, repeal the ACA, reduce funding for SNAP, college Pell Grants for poor students, job training, and housing assistance.[7]

The EU, contrary to the U.S., is more generous to support children (France, for instance, grants $176 monthly to support a second child), and France, Germany, and other nations have government-run daycare centers; in France, for instance, they cost $17 weekly and are open from Monday to Saturday from 7 a.m. to 7 p.m. In the US, daycare is privately-owned/expensive, often costing more than $100-250 weekly.[8]

Since President Johnson's Great Society to the present, poverty rate percentage rates are in the teens – the two lowest, 11.1 percent in 1973 and 11.3 percent in 2000. In 2012, without social welfare programs, the poverty rate would be 30.5 percent; with them 16 percent. In 2014, the poverty rate was 15 percent.

The elderly, for instance, through Social Security/Medicare, also basically have lowered their poverty rate from 35 percent in 1960 to 9.5 percent in 2012. The programs enumerated have reduced teenage pregnancy of poor women and have aided poor youth to receive more education, improved health, more employment, higher earnings. On the whole, social welfare programs have been beneficial to individuals and society in general.

Of course, families just above the poverty line lose government sponsored benefits. For instance, a family of two parents and two children earning $20,000 annually, after losing welfare benefits and having expenses like daycare for children, higher taxes and so forth, would earn only 30 percent more of an additional dollar earned.

A better alternative to this circumstance would reduce government benefits gradually relative to earnings (the ACA does this in expanding Medicaid and subsidizing private health insurance), but this is only one program. Only a coordinated state/federal program could end the patchwork of programs to aid the poor and provide a sliding scale solution to families just above the poverty line.[9]

Inadequate U.S. social welfare decrees its high children's poverty rate. Statistics for 2013 are as follows: U.S., 19 percent (16 million under age 18); Sweden, 4.2 percent; Norway, 3.4 percent; Finland, 2.8 percent. Of 35 OECD (wealthy nations), the U.S. ranks 34th, while the last is Romania, though Greece could possibly be ranked at the bottom due to current economic situations there. There are also 1.5 million homeless children in the US.[10]

A brief sketch on some of the travails experienced by the poor whose annual income is up to $20,000 annually. To begin, their debt burden from 2000 to 2010 doubled to $26,000. About 12 million poor are also preyed upon by payday lenders charging 15 to 30 percent interest every two weeks, or 500 percent annually, only a seventh of them surviving this economic nightmare. In 2014, the poorest third of the people, carrying an average $5,000 in debt, are often hounded by debt collection companies.

The poor today also face exorbitant fees for cashing payroll and government checks, totaling 2.5-5.0 percent of their income, paying up to $1,200 annually. This cohort and others like it spend 42 percent of income alone on transportation.[11]

Because American social welfare is grossly underfunded, its cash payments for unemployment, disability and so forth are about 10 percent of GDP, as opposed to at least double or more that amount in social democratic European nations with strong labor/socialist parties; but their social welfare is greatly dependent on VAT taxes on consumption in the 18-20 percent range.

With low wages/social welfare payments, an American family in the 20th income percentile ($9,000), in 2010 subsists on less money than Canadian, Swedish, Norwegian, Finnish, and Dutch families – not true 35 years ago.[12] Also, college tuition in the EU is generally free but not so in the U.S.[13]

Vacation time for workers is an important element of their well-being. In the EU, the law requires a minimum of four weeks' vacation after a year of employment, which is usually extended a week or two by agreement. In contrast, the U.S. is the only developed nation with no state or federal legislation mandating paid vacations. In its private sector, it averaged 16 days annually in 2013; the average was 20 days from 1980 to 2000.

Generally in the U.S., after a year of employment, an employee receives a 10 day vacation; after 5 years, 14 days; after 10 years, 17 days; after 20 years, 20 days – but only if the employee works at the same company. Eighty-seven percent of full-time workers get paid vacations, 34 percent of part-time workers, but almost 40 percent of low-income workers have none. On the whole, 74 percent of workers have paid vacations. Indeed, almost 5 days of vacation time in 2013 are unused because of a heavy workload upon return or not being able to afford it and so on.

For selected EU nations, vacation days per year ca. 2015: Italy, 35; Germany, 30; Britain, 25; Norway, 25; Sweden, 25; France, 25. Alan

Grayson, Democratic Congressman from Florida, proposed federal legislation to mandate that companies with more than 100 employees offer, after a year's employment, a week of paid vacation. Regarding maternity leave, federal policy since the 1993 Family and Medical Leave Act mandates that companies with 50 or more workers (half the workforce) grant pregnant women after a year's employment up to 12 weeks of maternity leave with no pay – it covers less than half of working women. Nevertheless, 26 percent of white-collar women get some paid maternity leave in the private sector, less than 6 percent in low-paid retail and fast-food jobs. California, New Jersey and Rhode Island now have mandatory maternity leaves, California is at 6 weeks at 55 percent of wages. Several nations also have paternity leave at child birth.

But in the EU, paid maternity leave is standard; in weeks and percentage of pay in selected nations: France, 16 at 100; Germany, 14 at 100; Italy, 22 at 80; Norway, 35 at 100; Poland, 26 at 100.

As for paid sick leave for workers, it is common in the EU (part of the social safety net), but there is no federal law in the U.S. to cover it, although some states and cities mandate it, like Oregon, Connecticut, and two other states, as well as New York City and San Francisco and others. Forty percent of U.S. private sector workers have no paid sick leave, rising to 80 percent for low-wage ones as in retail and fast food.

Aid to the poor in a Europe of social democracy is more extensive than in the more conservative U.S. Social services as a percentage of GDP are as follows: U.S., 19; Germany, 26; Sweden, 28; Denmark, 30; France, 32. (The Nation, June 20/27, 2016, p. 6).[14]

In January 2015, Obama proposed federal legislation to cover federal workers for seven sick days annually and to receive six weeks of paid leave for pregnancy or adoption.[15]

Another proposal in January 2015 by Democratic representative Chris Van Hollen of Maryland would tax Wall Street trades and raise taxes on the richest 1 percent for a "paycheck bonus credit" for couples earning annually under $20,000. At the same time, Senator Bernie Sanders, Independent Democratic Socialist from Vermont, who caucuses with Democrats, in May-June 2015, introduced legislation to expand Social Security/Medicare and federally mandated two weeks' paid vacation for workers.[16] In comparing social welfare benefits including food, health care, housing, education and cash, Obama's first-term presidency spent 17 percent of the federal budget on them versus Clinton's 12 percent and Carter's 8 percent, or (in dollars) $13,731, $8,310, and $4,431 per person respectively, adjusted for 2014 dollars. The Obama administration is the most pro-welfare one since the New Deal. The ACA, of course, contributed greatly to this increase.[17]

Federal means-tested programs in 2010, already observed (Social Security/Medicare is not means-tested) were funded at $585 billion recently, higher in 2015 because of ACA. They are under 5 percent of a $17.5 trillion US GDP in 2015 – they should at least be doubled.[18]

On balance, corporate pillage of society (government and public) far exceeds social welfare spending on the poor and disabled. (Poor workers, super-exploited by capital, more than pay for their welfare costs).

Why is the U.S. behind Europe relative to social welfare programs? Voters in the United States are more conservative than their European counterparts, especially following the Conservative Revolution under President Reagan in 1980. This was largely the result of the South massively voting Republican after the passage of the Civil Rights/ Voting Rights acts in the mid-1960s, which legally ended segregation in the South and enfranchised African Americans. The obvious conclusion: Present American opposition to social welfare is largely because of the legacy of slavery. The semi-caste South is against such progressive measures that would mitigate poverty, such as increasing minimum wage, and imposing taxes on the rich/corporations, and workers' unions, among others. The tragedy: a divided working class, especially in the South where it is white against black, recent immigrants (outsiders), and the poor, all of whom suffer.

To begin, 65 percent of black children reside in very poor families living 200 percent under the poverty line versus 30 percent of white children. Also, 80 percent of black children are in an environment of neighborhood poverty replete with high unemployment, racially segregated, inadequate social welfare benefits which should be markedly increased, and with 72 percent of families with only a single mother (U.S. generally 41 percent). Black children are especially educationally-challenged by this family poverty, stress levels and their ill consequences triple that of average and higher-income families.

Also, not surprisingly, black premature births are double the white rate and their children are under-examined for psychological and other disabilities like speech impairment and health issues in general. The brain and health development of black children is also affected by high lead levels in their bodies, 36 percent having this condition while only 4 percent in suburban white communities. With the blight of many industries going abroad (China, Mexico) and technological advances, many unskilled and semi-skilled jobs have been lost affecting especially Midwest cities with large black populations, like Detroit and Cleveland, among others. Also, black areas are largely devoid of small business which can provide employment.

Thus it tragically is that blacks commit half the murders in the U.S. (mostly in black areas), are half of the incarcerated, with a third of their adult males having a felony record, hampering the possibility of having a decent-paying job, resulting in more criminal activity and ultimately a high recidivism rate.

The annual cost to place every American poor individual above the poverty line is $193 billion. A 1 percent wealth tax on the richest 1 percent ($23 trillion in assets) would generate $230 billion. Average annual stock returns since 1928, 11 percent. The rich will scarcely suffer.

Sixty five percent of black children are currently in poverty/inadequate social welfare. Newborn U.S. children today have a lower lifespan than those in Britain, France, Germany, Scandinavia, Italy, Netherlands, Spain, Japan, Switzerland and South Korea among other nations, according to Eduardo Porter in The New York Times, May 30, 2018.

Chapter 4: Social Mobility/Education

This chapter examines the decline of upward social mobility in the U.S. since 1980, a process that was ultimately a manifestation of weakening working class political activity, which allowed for the rise of a plutocratic oligarchy.

The traditional myth of America as the land of opportunity and upward social mobility is not as true today as it once was. When there were free and inexpensive land and scarcity of labor (slavery in the south) in an expanding frontier, opportunity was plentiful. Combined with the higher paid labor in the North, encouraging large scale immigration and lifting the earlier immigrants up the social ladder, the famed upward social movement of all was in many respects true.

But in contemporary America, upward and downward social mobility is lower than in many Western European nations and Canada, especially after 1980.

The basic reasons why the U.S. has less social mobility than, for instance, Western European social democracies, are its legacy of slavery and racism, a less generous social welfare system, high college tuition costs, lower taxes on the rich, lower and stagnant working class wages, weaker unions, and more conservative political parties unduly influenced by the wealthy.

From a general perspective, the children of the poor and near-poor have much more difficulty achieving upward social mobility than those of affluent parents, whose wealth generally protects their social class status.

Concrete examples on social mobility: An American born in the top fifth income quintile has a 62 percent chance to remain in the top two income quintiles, while one raised in the bottom income quintile has a 65 percent probability to remain in the lowest two income quintiles. One born in the bottom income quintile also has only a 6 percent chance to be in the top income quintile and a 1 percent probability to be in the top 5 percent of income earners. A child born in the middle income quintile has a 20 percent chance to climb into the highest income quintile. A father's income level being equaled by a son is half in the U.S., but a fifth in Canada, indicating its greater social mobility. As for entrance to the top 1 percent in income in a recent 10-year period, 70 percent were from the top 5 percent cohort.

To be sure, there are extremely rare instances of members of the middle class Bill Gates and working class Steve Jobs and Jeff Bezos becoming fabulously rich, who are then greatly celebrated by the media as "The Only in America" shibboleth.

Christopher Hayes in The Nation cited two massive studies in American social mobility conducted by FRB economists in Boston and Chicago: The first reported rising upward social mobility from 1950 to 1980 before a sharp decline; the second indicated than an individual remaining in his/her income tenth was 36 percent in the 1970s and 40 percent in the 1980s. The conclusion of both: declining social mobility.

On the other hand, professors Raj Chetty of Harvard and Emmanuel Saez of the University of California, Berkeley (both economists) and three others conducted a massive study which found that upward social mobility of American children born in the 1980s was largely similar to that of children born from 1952 to 1975. But the authors also admitted that American children had half the chance of leaving poverty as those of the highest upward mobility nations like Denmark. Also, Chetty stated that low social mobility in the U.S. posed a significant problem.

Generally, the developed nations with the highest social mobility are Denmark, Norway, Canada, and Finland; those in the middle range include Germany, France, and Sweden, and those in the bottom include the U.S., Britain, and Italy – with the U.S. being last. Where social democracy is in place, with the exceptions of Italy and Britain, there is more social mobility than in the politically conservative U.S., where the social safety net, as already observed, is greatly inferior to many of the preceding nations.

Since 2003, U.S. military spending is greater than that on education from K to 12; annually in the 2009-12 period, the average spending for the former is $711 billion; for the latter, $613 billion. Less priority on education results in less upward social mobility.[1]

For upward social mobility or simply to maintain present class position if in the broad middle class, a two-year or four-year college degree, if not a post-graduate degree, are now required, as it certainly allows a greater likelihood for employment and a middle-class salary. The U.S. lags behind a number of nations in two-year/four-year college degrees in the 25-34 age group: Korea, 64 percent; Japan, 59 percent; Canada, 57 percent; U.S., 43 percent. The OECD average is 39 percent.[2]

College education now is many times more expensive than before, especially in state schools where tuition was essentially free in the 1950s and early 60s. In 2012, tuition alone averages $3,000 in two-year community colleges, $8,500 in the state four-year group, and $28,500 in private ones. Today, in public higher education, 80 percent of tuition costs are borne by students; before the Reagan Republican Revolution of the 1980s, that figure was 20 percent. If college room and board costs are added, private college costs are usually in the $50,000 – 70,000 range; state college costs are in the $20,000 range – which does not include books and supplies.

Two-year community colleges, with 44 percent of college enrollment, are now experiencing financial difficulty because their budgets, adjusted for inflation, have been static since 1979, driving up college costs for working-class students.

In the more expensive/prestigious four-year colleges, only 5 percent of their students come from the lowest income quintile, another indication of American social rigidity.

The high tuition of a college education necessitates more debt; thus for a bachelor's degree student in 2014, its average is approximately $33,000, and many times more for graduate school/professional degrees. For lawyers, that amount can reach as much as $100,000 and $150,000 for physicians. But one-third of college graduates, those from wealthier families, emerge from college debt free.

As 60-71 percent of students borrow, student loan debt climbs. In 2013, loan debt exceeded $1.2 trillion, passing credit cards and car loan debts. In 2018, 44 million college students owe $1.5 trillion for their education.Only mortgage debt is higher. From 1985 to 2013, college tuition has increase 559 percent. Interest in 2015 on student college loans is high: federal loans, 4.6 percent and an origination fee of 1.1 percent; federal loans to parents of college student with good credit, 7.2 percent and an origination fee of 4.3 percent; for bad credit, co-signers for their college student must turn to private lenders who charge up to 12 percent. Of interest, in 2014, a third of student college loans are in default. These loans must be paid, even if bankruptcy occurs. Comparatively, car loans are about 3 percent and mortgages are 3.5 percent.

In 2009, the Obama administration permitted low income college student federal borrowers to repay their loans for 25 years at 15 percent (10 percent from July 2014) of their income, or 10 years if in public service.

In January 2015, Obama proposed extensive aid for two-year part/full time college students, essentially free tuition in community colleges.

It is common knowledge that a college education opens doors and improves one's quality of life in several ways, but there are additional advantages. New technologies and free trade have led to lower wages for blue collar workers, but college graduates (or the "cognitive class"), needing to serve the new technologies, enjoyed lower unemployment and higher wages than the less educated since the 1980s.

But in the 2001-13 period, average hourly wages for workers with a bachelor's degree have basically remained the same: men in 2001, $33.60 and $33.71 in 2013; for women in 2001, $25.33, and $25.35 in 2013 – both in 2013 dollars. Why? Because they simply replaced less educated workers performing the same job in many fields.

Nevertheless, a college bachelor's degree is invaluable for economic survival, including regular employment. In 2007, annual earnings for men with a bachelor's degree was $57,000, and for women, $36,000. For high school graduates, that figure was $31,000 for men and $18,000 for women. In 2013, median wages for those with a bachelor's degree was $45,500, but only $28,000 for high school graduates, a $17,500 gap. The conclusion is plain: the gap between the educational attainments of the groups mentioned is becoming wider because new technologies require more education.

Lifetime earnings show a broader, but no less disturbing, picture: less than a high school, $1 million; high school graduate, $1.4 million; some college, $1.6 million; bachelor's degree, $2.4 million; doctoral degree, $3.5 million; professional degree (physician, lawyer, and so forth), $4.2 million. As for the income gap between high school graduates and those with bachelor's degree, 50 percent, in 1975, and 77 percent in 2011-12.

This discrepancy in salaries has led more students from average and even poor families to seek a college education despite its high cost. After all, the norm of individual success for most is to have a college education. In this endeavor, there are Pell Grants to aid students from low income families to attend college; under Obama, they have increased from $14.6 billion in 2008 for 6 million students to almost $40 billion for 10 million students in 2012, more of them attending two-year college programs. Nevertheless, the high cost of a college education still discourages many low-income students from attending a four-year university.

As of now, 20 million students attend college (four-fifths public, a fifth private), including many older ones from Black and Hispanic families in two year community colleges. In the 18-24 age group in 2008, 41 percent of whites, 32 percent of blacks, and 26 percent of Hispanics attended college. Also, by 2008, 87 percent of students by age 25 have graduated from high schools. In 2013, 33.5 percent of Americans in the 25-29 age group have a four-year college bachelor's degree versus 24 percent in the 50-69 "boomers" age group. Also, 43 percent have a two-year college associate's degree. But the average income, as already observed, of a four-year college graduate in the 25-34 age group has fallen and their college debt has risen. Also, unemployment for the 20-24 age college group in 2013 is a high 12.8 percent. The preceding statistics spell lower income for many college graduates.

Low upward social mobility for poor children is also because their educational milieu is confronted by the ills of poverty itself, with its socioeconomic and cultural deprivations and attendant ever-present social and psychological stresses, three times higher than in other families, which in turn severely affects language skills. In 2012-13, New York State Regents exams, a fourth of New York City students failed to qualify for college work; only 11 percent of Blacks and 13 percent of Hispanics – whose poverty rate was double of whites – qualified.

A brief sketch on the socioeconomic and psychological milieu of poor children, focusing mainly on African-Americans. To begin, there is pervasive economic insecurity characterized by low-wage jobs along with high unemployment related to inadequate housing and other amenities of life.

Crime and fear/stresses contribute heavily to the overall quality of life for many African-Americans. For instance, in 2009, African-Americans, with an eighth of the population, were 38 percent of inmates in state and federal prisons and young/poor black males are killed by guns at eight times the rate of their white counterparts. Furthermore, the poor are angry because they cannot have the plethora of goods of a consumerist society displayed in the media, principally TVs. In turn, they respond with criminal activity to acquire what they what.

In this world of poverty/crime, 72 percent of black and a quarter of white women have children out of wedlock, usually in vulnerable short-term relationships (married couples in general also have a high divorce rate, about 50 percent in first marriages). Overwhelmingly, these women are from poor families who know that their socioeconomic futures are bleak and invariably condemned to low-wage menial work.

Because most individuals have a propensity for sexual intimacy/ companionship, without which there is often an inner loneliness, poverty usually decrees short-term relationships and unwanted pregnancies (80 percent of teenage pregnancies are unintended). Poor men, not having the economic means for marriage, are involved in serial sexual relationships.

Poor children are also victimized by attending under-funded

schools in low-property tax districts (American education is primarily funded locally, not nationally as in most developed nations). They are characterized by crowded classrooms, antiquated textbooks, little to no instruction in art and music, and teachers often supply students with materials from their own monies. And with the rise of private charter schools, also financed by the public, public school resources are further depleted. In most U.S. cities, the wealthiest school districts outspend the poorest ones by a 2-1 margin; in some, as in California, the figure is 3-1.

Conservatives primarily blame the teachers for poor teaching results of poor children, but the basic culprit is inherent in a predatory capitalism condemning poor children and their parents to the outer reaches of humanity.

On education expenditures alone, wealthier parents today spend nine times as much as their poorer counterparts on their children's education, enriching their lives by private tutors in various subjects/ recreations, such as music, along with vacations and so forth.

In addition, 3 percent of families (median 2012 income, $147,000) have tax-free college education accounts for their children. These tax breaks (a 529 and a Coverdell Education Savings Account) have no income limits and grant generous contributions. The Obamas, for instance, in 2008 earned $2.8 million, mostly on book royalties, and deposited approximately $248,000 into their 529 for their two daughters.

Obama himself proposed that this tax "giveaway" to the upper-middle class and rich be eliminated and instead be for families earning up to $180,000 annually. As the tax payer makes more money annually, fewer tax breaks would be available.

Congressional Democrats and Republicans alike rejected this proposal because primarily the wealthier classes objected to its provisions.[3]

In summary, the educational problem is closely connected to the social class problem. Dr. Diane Ravitch, a well-known progressive educator affirmed:

> If every child arrived in school well-nourished, healthy
> and ready to learn from a family with a stable home and

a steady income, many of our educational problems would be solved. And that would be a miracle.[4]

In fact, in the latter part of 20th-century America, wealthier students also had a 9-1 advantage over poorer ones to attend graduate/professional schools.[5] I doubt that this statistic is very different today, again indicating a society of great and rigid class divisions between the upper- and middle-class and the underlying majority.

This sharp class division is manifested in test achievement scores where rich children perform almost twice as high as their poor counterparts; the white/black divide traditionally was of the same magnitude but has since narrowed to being half the class gap.[6]

Again, sharp class division in the U.S. is indicated in international educational tests of 15-year-olds in 65 rich/poor nations in which Americans placed 17th in reading, 23rd in science, and 27th in math, much below other advanced nations.[7]

Aware of low upward social mobility and widening income gap between the rich and the rest of the people, President Obama in December 2013 pledged to the American people that he and the Democratic Party will attempt to correct these inequities.[8]

Because of Republican recalcitrance, Obama/Democrats have not succeeded in these endeavors. In fact, the 2014 elections resulted in huge Republican electoral victories, whereby they gained control of both Houses of Congress – a result led, in part, to gerrymandering of electoral districts and low voter turnout of the poor and youth.

Ultimately, only a socialist society can resolve the inequality of education related to class inequality. But in the short run, a vigorous federal job program for the poor/unemployed and increased school funding for poor children should lead to less educational inequality.[9]

Final remarks on education and the importance of socioeconomic environment on general cultural intelligence. In a French study of working-class infants adopted by bourgeois parents, the children averaged 16 points higher on IQ tests than siblings raised in a working-class environment. In similar studies in the U.S., the general consensus was similar.[10]

Chapter 5: The Great Recession in the United States

Capitalist economies, even with Keynesian government intervention, are characterized by boom and bust, the latter phase resulting in economic contraction and rising worker unemployment with its accompanying socioeconomic misery. Even of this writing (2015), although the U.S. is not in recession, much of the European Union (EU) is in a Depression/Recession phase – especially Italy, Greece, Spain and Portugal.

The U.S. was mired in the Great Recession from December 2007 to June 2009 as unemployment rose to 10.1 percent (up to 30 million workers were unemployed/underemployed, a fifth of the workforce – even in 2013 this group comprised 24 million or a sixth of the work force). Industrial production dropped by a third (in 2013, 20 percent of industrial capacity was still unused). The Dow Jones Industrial Average plunged from 14,153 on October 9, 2007 to 6547 on March 9, 2009, decreasing by half. Then, too, household median wealth fell by a third (a $7 trillion loss from 2006 to 2011) as housing prices fell by a third, with at least 14 million foreclosures by 2012 and a fifth of home mortgages (12 million) "underwater," their value dropping sharply since purchase. Home ownership itself dropped from 69 percent in 2006 to 65 percent in 2013. Not surprisingly, consumer spending (70 percent of GDP) dropped sharply and the financial system was on the verge of collapse.[1] Except from 1948 to 1972, there has been a financial crises in the U.S. every decade.[2]

Some background on what triggered the Great Recession: To prevent financial speculative excesses, the Glass-Steagall Banking Act of 1932 drew a sharp distinction between commercial and investment banking, with the former relying on depositors' money which made loans to homeowners and business, and the latter started new enterprises and sold stocks, bonds and derivatives, and bet on future commodity prices, like oil and wheat.

A series of laws overturned this model. In 1999, the Financial Services Modernization Act allowed commercial and investment banks to merge, overturning Glass-Steagall. In 2000, the Commodity Futures Modernization Act deregulated the derivatives market, permitting banks and hedge funds to trade complex derivatives over the counter and the right to purchase insurance on them (hedge bets), a trading called a credit default swap (CDS).

In turn, the CDSs became collateralized debt obligations (CDOs), complex derivatives of various loans to business and consumers, including residential and commercial mortgages, a mixture becoming an asset-backed security (ABS). Combine many ABSs and there is a single CDO. Then, link this CDO with many others and it becomes a CDO of the second degree; repeat this process and it becomes one of the third degree, and so forth – from the second degree on, CDOs are "synthetic." This Wall Street betting casino is infinitely complex, opaque, and risky. Two-thirds of derivative trading is inter-bank, 90 percent over the counter, 10 percent via exchanges. Wall Street also earns money because it knows every side of financial transactions, making its own bets on them.

Mortgages on real estate were an important part of the derivatives market (by 2000 they were the majority of bank loans). Globally, the derivatives market expanded rapidly, from almost $200 trillion in 2003 to $615 trillion in 2008 to $700 trillion in 2012, banks were allowed to increase leverage (borrowing) to more than twenty-times their assets, adding to more financial vulnerability, especially in an economic downturn. Warren Buffett, a successful market investor, noted that derivatives are "financial weapons of mass destruction," akin to a house of cards, inherently unstable financial instruments, deceptive, employed to avoid national regulations and taxes.

Since the 1990s, banks could also own commodities like oil and aluminum and speculate on them, like withholding them from the market and entangling them with complex derivatives, driving up prices and profits but also leading to more economic instability.

The laws and financial practices just mentioned, overwhelmingly supported by Wall Street, were passed by Congress and signed by President Clinton. They reflected the unrestrained laissez-faire free market philosophy of Milton Friedman, a conservative small-government economist; Alan Greenspan, former Chairman of the Federal Reserve Bank (FRB) from 1987-2006, was an acolyte of his and of Ayn Rand, a novelist and exponent of "objectivism," promoting a selfish individualism, which views government as an unmitigated evil which stifles creative capitalists and condemns the poor to the charities of the rich. Greenspan's successor at the FRB, Ben Bernanke, a conservative monetarist, chastened by the Great Recession, approved of government regulation and intervention to stimulate the economy, but still allow for complex derivatives.

Art Laffer, a conservative Republican, a favorite of President Reagan, promoted a theory of supply-side economics of lower taxes on the rich and corporations, higher regressive sales taxes on consumption, hitting workers the hardest. These measures would lead to economic growth, he said, although leading to more socioeconomic inequality between the rich and workers – to be remedied by higher economic growth. Laffer's economic policies basically continue today, resulting in lower economic growth, increasing inequality, evisceration of the middle income quintile and increasing poverty among the poor. Another result was too much capital relative to consumption, much of it going to tax havens and the lower income quintiles consuming less or borrowing more money.

The immediate cause of the Great Recession was the collapse of the housing market as home foreclosures increased with a concomitant fall in housing prices, triggering the plunge in CDOs having subprime tranches (portions) in them. This development was exacerbated by broker fraud, earning them high commissions in selling sub-prime home loans to poor black and Hispanics at adjustable high interest rates – "NINJA" loans, or "no income, no Job, and no assets." This practice is related to robo-signers (company employees) illegally signing the names of the foreclosed owners. Lender Processing Services, a company which employed many robo-signers, was prosecuted in Nevada and Missouri for this practice.

These frauds were aided by the three major credit agencies: Moody's Investor Services, Fitch, and Standard and Poor's, all of which succumbed to economic pressure from Wall Street to earn high commissions by giving triple-A ratings to risky CDOs having subprime mortgages in them. They were insured by American International Group (AIG) whose top executives earned huge commissions in these transactions.

Freddie Mac and Fannie Mae, private for-profit corporations backed by the federal government which guaranteed mortgages of lower-income buyers, in 2005 joined Wall Street banks and Countrywide Bank in the subprime hunt.

With the advent of the housing bubble and collapse of the subprime housing market, the price of CDOs fell sharply because Wall Street did not know which of the triple-A CDOs had toxic subprime trances, freezing inter-bank borrowing. These are the fruits of the so-called free market, one controlled by the large banks and their cohorts. This casino-type gambling and fraud is augmented by the high-speed trading of stocks/bonds in milliseconds, profit made on small price variations. That bank fraud was pervasive in the subprime CDOs was evident as 16 banks, including Goldman Sachs and Bank of America, settled with the federal government paying almost $18 billion in penalties. Two banks, Nomura Holdings (Japanese) and the Royal Bank of Scotland, refused to pay a penalty and were found guilty for fraud in early 2015, but both are appealing.[3]

Bill Black, a former President George W. Bush appointee as a financial federal regulator and now an economics professor at the University of Missouri, Kansas City, claimed that bank regulators under Bush were lax in enforcing rules, that financial fraud is prevalent on Wall Street and that business schools are fraud factories.

To buttress Black's contention of pervasive fraud in the financial sector, three economists, Luigi Zingales, Adair Morse (both University of Chicago professors) and Alexander Dyck (University of Toronto) claimed in a study that in any given year, from 11 to 13 percent of large American corporations committed business fraud. Another work by economists Paul Romer and George Akerloff averred that in banks too-big-to-fail, their executives inevitably pillaged them.[4]

The FRB now intervened by pouring $116 billion into Fannie Mae, $72 billion in Freddie Mac, and underwriting their $500 billion in home loans, in effect their becoming government-owned corporations. Then it purchased $180 billion in stock to shore up a failing AIG, transforming it to a basically government-owned corporation, and assumed its CDOs owed to Wall Street at 100 cents on the dollar. This government welfare to the banks prevented another Great Depression. When in economic need, laissez-faire capitalists beg for economic rescue from government.

The financial malaise was so pervasive that money market and commercial paper funds fell sharply: the former, a $4 trillion industry, the latter a lender of $1.4 trillion. Again, the federal government stepped in to guarantee their viability.[5]

Within months, according to Roubini and Mihn, "Wall Street had been utterly transformed, with all five independent banks destroyed, absorbed or temporarily muzzled." This included the fall of two venerable banks, Bear Stearns and Lehman Brothers, and Merrill Lynch (stock brokers) absorbed by Bank of America.[6]

The stock market itself is mainly comprised of wealthy investors, hedge and pension and mutual funds and university endowments. Thus, Wall Street fraud and manipulation affected these groups adversely. Hedge funds specifically comprise only 5 percent of stock market assets.[7]

The financial crash, the immediate cause of the Great Recession, which began in the U.S., became in varying degree into a worldwide financial meltdown; this was so because approximately half of Wall Street subprime CDOs were purchased abroad. Thus, there were bank failures in Britain, Ireland, and Iceland, among other nations, many of which, like Ireland, had their governments guarantee their deposits and assume their debts. These developments led to the Great Recession engulfing many nations, indicating that the world's financial system is deeply intertwined.[8]

To stanch the financial crash and economic free fall, President Barack Obama and the Democratic Party passed the Recovery and Reinvestment Act in 2009 (it included aid to banks passed under Bush II in 2008), a federal government program of $1 trillion. It gave $340 billion to banks through stock purchases in them; $80 billion to the almost bankrupt General Motors and Chrysler by also buying their stock; $260 billion to economically beleaguered cities and states to maintain their workforce; $237 billion in tax cuts to individuals to spur consumption; and $100 billion to rebuild infrastructure (to 2012, half has been spent).

Furthermore, a second stimulus package of $800 billion was passed in late 2010, which extended the Bush II tax reductions and cut $110 billion from Social Security taxes to provide tax relief to individuals earning under $110,000 annually. In addition, in 2011, tens of billions of dollars aided small business to encourage employment. Obama also proposed in 2011 more funds to rebuild schools/infrastructure and rehire teachers, but the Republican-controlled House rejected them, sabotaging the stimulus effort.[9]

On the whole, government actions to aid economic recovery created jobs, saved the auto industry and allowed the six largest American banks to earn a $75 billion profit in 2010. Without Keynesianism, there would inevitably have been a repeat of a worldwide Great Depression.[10]

The financial crisis, which triggered the Great Recession, indicates the importance of the financial system (finance, insurance, real estate, or FIRE) in the economy. For instance, financial domestic profits as percentage of GDP were 15 percent in the early 1960s, 44 percent in 2002, 31 percent in 2009, and 34 percent in 2010. Indeed, pre-tax corporate profits recovered rapidly after the Great Recession, the low in 2008 at $1.38 trillion, to $1.85 trillion in 2011 and to $2.19 trillion in 2012.[11]

The volatility of the massive financial system which overlays the productive sector, as in its $700 trillion derivative sector, the up to $34 trillion in tax havens and increasing economic concentration, are a Sword of Damocles hanging above the world's economy. This explosive mixture is based on quick and great profit, relentlessly circling the globe.[12]

Oligopolistic U.S. industry via free trade, computerization and automation and anti-union activity, with resultant weaker unions, since the 1980s has taken all of the productivity gains, impoverishing workers, leading to lower consumer demand, another significant factor in economic downturn.[13]

To shore up the U.S. and world economy, the FRB secretly lent $16 trillion at low-interest rates to large American and foreign corporations to stabilize world stock, bond, and other markets. This was revealed thanks to the efforts of the social-democratic Senator Bernie Sanders of Vermont and others.

An example of how this aided large banks: the FRB would lend money to them at 0.5 percent interest, which they in turn would purchase U.S. Treasury Bonds at 2-3 percent interest, earning a tidy profit.[14]

FRB's primary function is to rescue banks in a financial crash and to help them and shadow banks (hedge funds, private equity firms, mutual funds, etc.) with Quantitative Easing (QE) to be soon examined. Its secondary function is to manage the money supply (tied to QE).

Then there is the matter of "toxic" assets, almost worthless, helped by banks valued at $1.4 trillion. To secure them, the federal government established a Public-Private Investment Program. It would lend money to investors of "toxic" assets at low-interest rates, which if not profitable, the government would make up the difference. So far, because they are basically worthless, only a few speculators are interested. In fact, the money lent by the FRB to this and other programs is not added to the federal debt; it's on another ledger.[15]

My socialist solution: nationalize the banks, let them become a public utility to aid in rational economic planning, an impossibility under a now-dysfunctional capitalism.

Fraud on Wall Street is prosecuted by the Securities and Exchange Commission (SEC) and Department of Justice (DOJ). If tried, defendants almost invariably pay fines, which are tax deductible; they do not admit guilt, which would open the gates to civil suits against them. Examples of such fraud include Citigroup, which sold derivatives, but then bet against them, earning $160 million in profits, while the client lost $700 million. The SEC fined Citigroup $95 million and forced it to surrender its profits. But the buyer of the derivatives was not compensated.[16]

Another instance of bank malfeasance involved Goldman Sachs, which sold $10 billion in mortgages to a client and then bet that they would fall in price, which in turn earned the company a large profit. The SEC fined Goldman Sachs $550 million, and again clients were not compensated.

In 2012, a major banking scandal involving many banks emerged – the LIBOR or London Interbank Offered Rate – a daily, three-month and yearly interest rate used worldwide in interbank lending and negotiated by a group of London banks. This, in turn, determines interest rates charged to consumers, corporations, government institutions, and so forth. Government banking regulators in Britain, the U.S. and elsewhere are now looking at LIBOR malpractices to manipulate interest rates higher or lower for more profit or to reduce losses, or to report artificially low interest rates to demonstrate economic viability.

Barclays, a large British bank, was caught in late 2012 by bank regulators after it submitted false LIBOR rates to disguise its financial weakness. It was fined $450 million and dismissed of top executives.

In late 2012, a series of lawsuits by investors, insurers and regulators which amounted to many billions of dollars were filed against Wall Street for duping clients into purchasing worthless mortgage securities. If banks lose these cases, they could lose up to $300 billion. But this is not all. The Swiss HSBC bank was found guilty of allowing Columbian and Mexican drug cartels to launder $881 million and other illegalities in December 2012. For this, it paid a fine of $1.9 billion, a paltry sum, almost 10 percent of its pre-tax 2010 profits; none of its employees were jailed.

In January 2013, 10 banks, including JP Morgan Chase and Citigroup, negotiated an $8.5 billion settlement with federal regulators to correct foreclosure abuses like robo-signing on forged documents. It covers 3.8 million households, payments to them ranging from under $1,000 to $125,000.

In early February 2013, the DOJ, joined by many state prosecutors, charged Standard and Poor's in a $5 billion civil suit for committing fraud by misleading bond investors with its ratings of bond grades in risky residential mortgages. S&P and other bond rating agencies are paid by Wall Street banks to rate bonds, undoubtedly contributing to inflating their ratings.[17]

In November 2013, JP Morgan Chase and the DOJ reached a $13 billion settlement. The largest part – $6 billion to compensate pension funds – was for losses in fraudulent mortgage securities; $4 billion for struggling homeowners on their mortgages, and $3 billion in tax deductible fines.

In January 2014, Wall Street insiders told The New York Times that Wall Street banks may have to reimburse homeowners with mortgages with cash and reductions on them totaling $50 billion. The two leading banks holding mortgage securities are Bank of America ($637 billion) and JP Morgan Chase ($460.4 billion); others include Wells Fargo ($151.4 billion) and Goldman Sachs ($121.2 billion), nine others having less than $100 billion. In comparison, large U.S. bank profits in 2012 ($100 billion).

In June 2014, BNP Paribas (a French bank) dealt with designated terror states like Iran and Sudan to launder money. The bank was later fined $8.9 billion. In July 2014, Citigroup was fined $7 billion for mortgage deception. In August 2014, Bank of America was again fined $16.65 billion for mortgage deception. What this bank actually paid to the government was less. For instance, the government announced a settlement of $16.65 billion, but received $8.03 billion, with the remainder in consumer relief and company tax deductions.

In the 2001-11 period, the SEC issued 350 bank waivers, mostly to Wall Street, including selling stocks and bonds without its approval, allowing banks to avoid litigation. A case in point is JP Morgan Chase which the SEC charged six times in the last decade with customer fraud, but granted waivers.

All in all, the SECs lenient treatment of banks indicates their great political influence of PACs/lobbyists on Congressional and government regulatory agencies. In fact, many SEC employees leave it for lucrative employment in banks.

Bernard Madoff and his crew perpetuated a Ponzi pyramid scheme that lasted many decades, duping 4,000 investors worth $64 billion in paper losses. He was arrested in December 2008, tried, and later convicted for fraud. He is serving a 150-year prison term. A number of his accomplices are also in prison or awaiting trial. Some of the money lost to Madoff by investors will be recovered, but the amount is paltry.

For Neil Barofsky, former Treasury Department Inspector General, the revolving door between Wall Street and government has led to an incestuous relationship in which the bankers who caused the crash also conducted its bailout. And since Wall Street is "too big to fail," another crash is inevitable.

Although hundreds of bank officials were imprisoned in the savings and loans debacle in the late 1980s and afterward, the Obama Presidency, with its SEC and DOJ, refused to prosecute and imprison bank and other financial executives for fraud and malfeasance on the dubious grounds that it would weaken the financial system. As small reassurance, some stiff fines were issued.

In January 2015, S&P reached a settlement with the SEC for inflating credit ratings, paying a $1.37 billion fine. In February 2015, HSBC was again investigated for aiding wealthy clients from many nations to avoid paying taxes before 2007. Some of these taxes are now being paid because a former disgruntled HSBC employee made the list of tax evaders to various governments.

In April 2015, Deutsche Bank, Germany's largest, paid a $2.5 billion fine for colluding to manipulate LIBOR Worldwide interest rates. This was criminal behavior by the banks, but no one was criminally charged, though some employees were dismissed. In May 2015, JP Morgan Chase, Citigroup, Barclays and Royal Bank of Scotland were charged with fraud and anti-trust violations. They pleaded guilty to these felonies and paid a fine of $5.6 billion. No bank official will face imprisonment. By the middle of 2015, no banker has been imprisoned by the federal government for fraud, but several employees have been dismissed. Fines paid by banks to the federal government by March 2014 were in the $100 billion range, and by 2015 the amount increased.[18]

Because of repeated Republican Congressional obstruction

to stimulate economic recovery with fiscal Keynesianism (jobs programs, rebuilding a crumbling infrastructure and so forth), Bernanke employed the monetary route, QE and discount rates to banks at 0.25 percent from 2012 to 2015. These measures have had some success: by late 2014, annual GDP growth was at 3 percent and the unemployment rate fell to 5.6 percent. Earlier, 2009-13, GDP growth averaged an anemic 2.3 percent.

From 2009 to October 2014, QE purchased $4.48 trillion in treasury-backed bonds and mortgage securities (many sub-prime) adding 46 percent to the money supply. The stock market almost tripled during this period. Keynesianism technically applies to fiscal policy, but I see no reason to now also apply it to monetary policy, especially in the preceding scenarios. This QE maneuver has primarily enriched the bond/stockholders.

Incidentally, the QE securities will be held by the FRB for at least the near future because when they mature it will roll over the proceeds to purchase new securities.

QE has also aided speculators of commodities, like food products and oil, who borrow at low interest rates to drive up their prices, making large profits.[19] In oil derivatives, for instance, speculators, who control 70-80 percent of its market, have driven oil prices of up to 40 percent where they should be as of May 2012. In fact, 70 members of Congress in March 2012 asked the commodities Futures Trading Commission to investigate these high prices, with no results.[20]

In the midst of the Great Recession in 2008, $32.6 billion in bonuses were awarded to employee-traders at these banks: Merrill Lynch (bought by Bank of America), Bank of New York Mellon, Wells Fargo, State Street, and JP Morgan Chase. But simultaneously these banks reported $88 billion in losses, allowing them to receive $165 billion in government bailouts. While workers suffer economically in the downturn, Wall Street waxes fat.[21]

The Dodd-Frank Bank Act of 2010 began the process to control derivatives trading through the Volcker Rule (VR), a weaker version of Glass Steagall. Nevertheless, in 2012 JP Morgan Chase lost $6.2 billion in a poorly formulated derivative.

By May 2013, 90 percent of the VR was completed, but of the Bank Act itself only 153 of its 398 rule were finished. The VR now requires that derivative trading be somewhat regulated because banks must offer price quotes over the phone. But the commodity Futures Trading Commission would still allow JP Morgan Chase, Citigroup, Bank of America and Goldman Sachs to control 90 percent of the $700 trillion derivatives market.

Dodd-Frank empowered the federal government to designate "systemically important financial institutions," which might create a financial crises, to be under special scrutiny/regulation. Companies like MetLife are attempting to stay off the list. Also, Dodd-Frank allowed government to seize large financial companies in an economic crisis and established the Consumer Financial Protection Bureau to protect consumers against bank predatory lending resulting in many individual bankruptcies.

A final version of the VR was approved by regulators in December 2013: it would prohibit banks from most forms of "proprietary trading," i.e. trading for their own profit in derivatives and so forth, although allowed to do so in U.S. treasury bonds and municipals; but there are still many gray areas in trading to allow banks to game the rules. The VR was to be enforced beginning July 2015.

In the 2014 elections, most Wall Street money went to Republicans wishing to repeal the VR, which would lessen financial gain and help prevent financial instability.[22]

The regulated derivatives at first were not insured by the FDIC, but the December 2014 federal omnibus bill passed by Congress and signed by Obama insures them, indicating the lobbying success of banks. Is this a harbinger of an approaching economic downturn?

Financial speculation/fraud was the immediate cause of the Great Recession, but the underlying one was debt: of consumer household (it propels 70 percent of the economy), corporate and government. The debt crisis as percentage of the GDP is as follows: federal government debt in 2011 (100 percent); private debt in 1981 (123 percent), in 2008 (290 percent); financial services debt in 1981 (22 percent), 2008 (117 percent). Overall, in 2008, government, corporate, and household debt in the US was 350 percent of GDP, or $48 trillion, $6.3 trillion less than the world's GDP, the world's highest debt.

To be sure, household debt reached its peak in 2009 at 97.5 percent of GDP, falling in 2012 to 85 percent of it, still higher than 65 percent of it in 2007. For Krugman, among other economists, stagnant household debt is the main reason for slow economic growth which he relates to rising economic inequality and lower consumer consumption for the bottom 90 percent of households who are now poorer than before the Great Recession. In fact, this reality was mainly caused by decreasing GDP growth rates; annually, from 1945 to 2000, 3.2 percent, while since then to 2012 and for decades afterward projected at 2.2 percent. Of note: 2014 GDP, $17.5 trillion; federal debt at $18 trillion.[23]

To be sure, household debt is related to increasing capitalist exploitation of labor: between 1979 and 2013, labor productivity rose 64.9 percent while hourly wages of production and non-supervisory workers were stagnant. Thus it is that capital since about 1980 has made further inroads against labor.

Indeed, as the economist Thomas Piketty avers in <u>Capital in The Twenty-First Century</u>, in stagnant developed economies, capital growth increases more than the GDP, which includes the wages of workers.

Trade deficits also weaken the U.S. economy. U.S. global trade, for instance, in 2008, was 14 percent exports, 17 percent imports totaling at 31 percent, compared to Germany's 44 percent, the highest of developed nations.

Free trade (WTO, NAFTA) imports has resulted in huge trade deficits for the U.S. Examples include $712 billion in 2008; $738 billion in 2011; $500 billion in 2014. The largest trade deficit is to China, about $300 billion annually since 2014. Since NAFTA to 2014, trade deficits total $11 trillion. To be sure, U.S. TNCs operating in China have accounted for half of the China trade deficit. Trade deficits have allowed foreign investors to own 15 percent of American industry. These dismal statistics obviously weaken Keynesian economic stimulus.[24]

Furthermore, workers' declining real wages since 1970 have resulted in under-consumption as capital has increased its strength over labor. Thus it is that U.S. citizens have approximately $12 trillion in tax havens circa 2015. Then, U.S. corporate buy-backs of stocks because of huge cash reserves, total in the many billions.[25] Indeed the St. Louis FRB has U.S. corporations in 2013 holding $4.75 billion in cash and short term bonds, another brake on economic activity. Add to the preceding lower spending by local and state governments; 49 of 50 states have balanced budget constitutional amendments.[26]

The Great Recession itself was exacerbated by private equity firms buying companies with weak sales but large reserves, burdening them later with large debts and resulting in workers' layoffs and lower wages.

A larger perspective on excessive financial capital because of low taxes and super-exploitation of workers: Bain and Co. estimates that by 2020 worldwide, $900 trillion in financial assets will be invested in a $90 trillion world GDP.[27]

The military-industrial complex (MIC) is also a wasteful institution (military Keynesianism) relative to economic development and government debt. It employs six million workers, many of whom are involved with research and development (R&D) to modernize continuously weapons' system; its average employee earns $60,000 annually. The MIC has significant political influence because its suppliers are in 69 percent of Congressional districts.

To be sure, there are spin-offs of MIC R&D for the household consumer market, but would it not be more cost effective to reduce the bloated military budget and develop more civilian R&D where average salaries are in the $50,000 range and which generate more jobs and taxes? For instance, $1 billion in federal spending results in 11,200 in the MIC sector, 16,800 in clean energy and 26,700 in education. The MIC itself is responsible in making government into its cash cow with huge overruns and fraud.[28] All in all, however, government military spending somewhat counters economic downturn because it is a significant part of its total GDP in 2009 of 4.2 percentage.

In 2013, the federal government recouped its losses from the bank bailout, but will lose about $12 billion in the auto bailout. AIG repaid the government bailout of $180 billion, with the government earning a $22 billion profit. Freddie Mac and Fannie Mae are still solvent with $200 billion in government subsidies, and more than $1 trillion in toxic assets are still held by banks.[29]

The GDP losses of the Great Recession and its aftermath are immense: According to the CBO, by 2017, $7.5 trillion; for the Dallas FRB economists, by 2023, $6-14 trillion, its most pessimistic account being $25 trillion. But corporate profits continue to soar into the $2 trillion range in 2014.[30]

Republicans in 2013 still insist that the Great Recession was basically caused by the collapse of the housing bubble which they blame in lax government standards, but this catastrophe occurred under a Republican-controlled Congress. In fact, government did not mandate that banks lend money to the poor to purchase homes, but banks did so for quick/fraudulent profit.

Furthermore, during this period, the Republicans averred that federal government deficit spending would reduce job growth because it would impinge on private business investment to create jobs and that the federal budget deficit should shrink to keep interest rates low. To be sure, these Republican proposals would have led to repeating the Great Recession. For Krugman, these Republican views are "zombie ideas" that have been disproven but serve the Republicans politically.[31]

Some general remarks on the Great Recession from the statistics presented from a class perspective regarding the working class and wealthy: the big losers were the former in unemployment, home foreclosures, smaller retirement savings, and small businesses becoming bankrupt. The latter saw their stock/bond investments fall by more than half, but within several or more years they recouped their losses and made more gains; they continued to live well in a parallel world of conspicuous consumption, aided by a government which poured huge sums of money to rescue the banks, but which paid scant attention to working class misery.

Economists now are debating whether high government debt reduces economic growth rates. Carmen Reinhart and Kenneth Rogoff, two Harvard economists, claim that central government debt above 90 percent of GDP, annually reduces GDP growth by 0.1 percent. But two economists, Michael Ash and Robert Pollin, backed the findings of Thomas Herndon, their graduate student at the University of Massachusetts, indicated that nations whose debt ratio was at 90 percent of GDP in the 2000-09 period, had GDP growth rates comparable or even higher than those whose government debt was between 30 percent and 90 percent. But Japan whose government debt is 200 percent of GDP has experienced practically no economic growth in the last several decades, although stimulative policies in 2013 have brought some gains. But by late 2014 Japan was again in recession.[32]

As long as capitalism survives, I favor its Keynesian variety, which asserts that government should play the principal role in correcting economic downturns through massive fiscal deficits to increases, employment and consumer demand, and ultimately government revenues. Among the major Keynesian economists are Joseph E. Stiglitz, Nobel Laureate in Economics, professor of economics, Columbia University; Paul Krugman, Nobel Laureate in Economics, professor of economics, New York University and columnist for The New York Times; Nouriel Roubini, professor of economics, New York University, Stern School of Business; Stephen Mihm, associate professor of history (economic history), University of Georgia; and Richard Duncan, author of Dollar Crisis, which predicted the Great Recession.

A composite of their views to end recession/stagnant economic growth follows: rehire local and state workers laid off by recession, lower interest rates generally and on "underwater" home mortgages, rebuild a crumbling infrastructure which the American Society of Civil Engineers has given a D+ average and requires $3.6 billion by 2020; US spending on infrastructure is 1.7 percent of GDP, whereas the European Union is 5 percent.

Furthermore, they would promote clean energy (wind, solar,

and so forth), start new industries like electric automobiles and nanotechnology, extend unemployment benefits and raise taxes on the rich and promote unions to increase workers' wages/consumption/tax revenue; also, jobs retraining for unemployed workers, tax credits for companies hiring the unemployed and a government-run jobs programs.

Even the super-capitalist bond traders of PIMCO, Mohamed El Arian and Bill Gross, affirm that economic inequality is stifling economic growth and urge more government spending on infrastructure and clean energy.[33]

In contrast to the Keynesians, the Republican Party now largely captured by its Tea Party right wing like Rand Paul in the Senate and Paul Ryan (Romney's vice-presidential running mate in the 2012 elections) in the House, would even reject the Federal Reserve's shoring up failing banks financially in the event of depression to prevent a sharp drop in the money supply as was done by Bernanke.

Instead, Paul and Ryan supposedly follow closely the dictates of the pro-capitalist Austrian-born economist Friedrich Hayek of The Road to Serfdom fame (itself for much social welfare), who essentially argued that once depression engulfed a nation, it should be allowed to run its course without any government interference – despite the pain of widespread bankruptcies and unemployment.[34]

Worldwide, much of capitalism is in economic crisis in 2015: the Eurozone mired in stagnant economic growth (0.6 percent) and high unemployment (11.5 percent), with Greece and Spain at over 25 percent unemployment. Russia, with the large drop in oil prices, is in recession. Japan, after some economic growth in 2014, is now in recession. Brazil, the largest economy in South America, is in recession. Chinese economic growth, before at 10 percent of annual GDP growth, is now in the high 6 percent range.

The U.S. and Germany continue to have some economic growth. But the U.S. has these weaknesses: real wages for 90 percent of its workers continue to fall and the strong dollar will hamper its exports, both contributing to economic slowdown. Furthermore, bank and other speculation continue, leading to financial instability in the U.S.

and elsewhere. The U.S. stock market, helped by corporations buying their stock and QE, is perilously high, the Industrial Dow Jones stock average at 18,000 in June 2015, almost triple its March 2009 low.

Also, in the first half of 2015, there is a boom in mergers and acquisitions (M&A) of $775.8 billion, 50 percent higher than in 2014. M&A includes buy-backs of company stock to increase its market price; this excess cash should have been in the hands of workers to increase consumption. This is occurring in the context of increasing corporate revenue growth. Of course, technological innovation and other cost-cutting has made this possible.[35]

Every seven to ten years, U.S. capitalist economic downturns occur. Thus, I forsee one in 2019. The danger signs are obvious: In August 2018, the Down Jones Stock Average reached about 26,000, an all time high. Worldwide debt is now much higher than its DGP. Again, a derivatives time bomb may spurn the next downturn.

Chapter 6: Unemployment

Unemployment is both inevitable and common in capitalism because workers are viewed as a commodity in the making of profit. In this equation, workers usually have scant input concerning employment and are, inevitably, victims of the markets.

To be sure, unemployment itself is measured in three ways: those unemployed workers wishing for employment, those part-time workers wishing employment and discouraged workers.

Unemployment itself varies according to capitalist economic cycles. In recessions/depressions it is very high: in the height of the Great Depression in the 1930s, it was 25 percent (50 percent in the cities); in the Great Recession of 2007-09, the rate peaked at 10.1 percent.

Working class power increased in the 20th century with lower unemployment: with the rise of a socialist Soviet Union as a result of the 1917 Communist Revolution in the Russian Empire; in the 1930's New Deal, government jobs programs employed the unemployed; and with the rise of social democracy in Western Europe with extensive nationalizations of the economy and comprehensive social welfare benefits and job opportunities.

But beginning generally in the 1980s, the capitalist counteroffensive against labor, with the election of the Republican Ronald Reagan as president in the U.S. and of the Conservative Margaret Thatcher as British prime minister, social welfare was reduced and unemployment increased. Also, the fall of the Soviet Union in 1991 could not but strengthen the capitalist project by invariably weakening labor and increasing unemployment. The Soviet Union itself had a full employment economy; work was guaranteed to all workers, who, if they lost jobs, were retrained for new ones.

Contributing factors for high U.S. unemployment now include: 1) the Great Recession and consequent economic stagnation as wages remain stagnant with consequent consumer demand; 2) Free trade (GATT, WTO, and NAFTA), allowing many American jobs going to low-wage nations like Mexico, China, Vietnam, India, Bangladesh, and others (U.S. tariffs now are under 2 percent, but 30 percent previously); 3) technological innovation, like computers and automation, replacing many workers (referenced later); 4) deregulation of industry allowing more laissez-faire and thus fewer jobs; 5) Green Card foreign workers allowed to work; 6) increased corporate economic concentration as in fast food chains, home building supplies, and so on resulting in closing many small retail outlets, an ongoing market phenomenon.

And so it goes – the large fish devouring the small fish.

Unemployment that resulted from the preceding phenomena led to lower average workers' wages since ca. 1980. Unions themselves under capitalism are powerless to prevent unemployment or prevent wage decreases in the long run.[1]

In GDP terms, manufacturing in 1959 was 28 percent of it and 12 percent in 2012, while its output tripled because of automation. As for workers employed in manufacturing, 16 million in 1953 (a third of the non-farm work force), 12 million in 2012 (a tenth of it), a third of this in management, sales, and technical support. Output per hour from 1980 to 2012 in manufacturing increased by 189 percent, but workers' wages remained stagnant with great job losses. From 2000 to 2014, 6 million jobs were lost and 63,000 factories closed their doors.

Half of the manufacturing job losses alone are due to advances in technology, half to American companies seeking low-wage workers abroad; 60 percent of Chinese exports to the U.S. are by American TNCs, which from 1999 to 2009 reduced their domestic workforce by 2.9 million and increased it abroad by 2.4 million. Some American TNCs employ more workers abroad than at home: in 2010, GE employed 133,000 at home and 154,000 abroad; Caterpillar, 47,000 domestically and 57,000 abroad; Oracle, 39,000 at home and 66,000 abroad.

The most notorious American corporation employing overseas labor under the free trade banner in low wage nations like Vietnam and Bangladesh is Nike. A third of its overseas work force is in Vietnam where workers earn 60 cents an hour, and even less in

Bangladesh. Nike employs a million workers in Asia and 28,000 in the U.S. Its business model is predicated in hiring cheap foreign labor in poor nations and selling products in the U.S., a developed one, at current high market prices and resulting in huge profits. Its co-founder, Phil Knight, is a billionaire.

A million American jobs alone have also been lost because of NAFTA. To be sure, since the advent of free trade, China is the main TNC supplier of cheap labor for the U.S. market. United States TNCs employ Chinese youngsters from rural areas migrating to the cities. Chinese factory monthly wages average $300 to $500 month, whereas in the US those figures are $2,700.

The loss of manufacturing jobs has hurt domestic job creation because each new manufacturing job creates four others, while each new one in personal/business services adds 1.5 jobs, and each new job in retail slightly produces less than one. Fifty percent of U.S. manufacturing now is located abroad generating 25 percent of its profits.[2]

In the next decade or two, it will not only be unskilled and semiskilled jobs that will be offshored, but according to Alan Blinder, former vice chairman for the FRB and now an economics professor at Princeton University, also skilled jobs as in computer programming and medical procedures are at risk, in most cases moved to China and India. He estimates these job losses in the 37-42 million range or a quarter of the workforce, a phenomenon related to the computer-based information revolution.

Blinder's dire predictions of rising unemployment are repeated by Krugman who asserts that recent advances in robotics, automation, and computers will lead to progressively higher unemployment. There are now humanoid robots, like Atlas in the US and Honda's Asimo in Japan, which can walk and have dexterous hands. In fact, they may soon serve as caregivers, security guards, indeed perform almost any kind of routine human labor.

Indeed, "Watson," the IBM computer system in 2014 is involved in complicated mental labor-like aiding military veterans where to live, purchase insurance and so on. In fact, Frank Bruni in <u>The New</u>

York Times reports that Martin Ford in The Rise of the Robots claims that computers can perform a "legal, pharmaceutical and medical work" as well as "produce journalism."

The preceding phenomena have led to many workers not being regularly employed, many in the "underground" economy of 8 percent of GDP: in 2000, this comprises 10 percent of men, 25 percent of women; in 2014, 16 percent of men, 30 percent of women.[3]

These developments now and in the future also spell higher unemployment of even highly skilled mental labor that spent much time and money to educate themselves. Krugman's solution to alleviate this unemployment consists of a minimum income for everyone and universal healthcare; this suggestion implies political action for an advanced social democracy. I take it beyond: to a socialism based on participatory democracy.[4]

Although more education is now required to service the new technology, Thomas Friedman, a free-trader columnist for The New York Times, warned workers that to secure a middle-class job, the old rules of "just work hard and play by the rules" no longer apply; now the demand is "to work harder and smarter" with "higher skills, passion or curiosity." But government and industry should aid workers by providing at no or low cost, post-high school and continuing education.

In Friedman's new technological/capitalist economy, workers have no job security and must accept the rules of a merciless capitalism: frequent unemployment, loss of seniority, lower wages, and fewer benefits – especially when older. To be sure, a well-educated worker can be retrained rather rapidly and become re-employed, but usually at a lower wage.[5]

Under Bush II, (2001-08), the U.S. unemployment averaged 6 percent, despite 2001 and 2003 tax cuts and wars in Iraq and Afghanistan; indeed, only 1.08 million jobs were added, all in the public sector, while 600,000 were lost in the private one. Since World War II to 2000, every decade saw job growth rising from 22 to 38 percent; from 2000 to 2012, 0 percent growth. In 2013, there are three applicants for every job opening.[6]

A snapshot of U.S. unemployment in the aftermath of the Great Recession in September 2011: 14 million officially unemployed; 9.3 million part-time workers desiring full-time work; 2.5 million discouraged job seekers. (If employed one hour a week or more, the government considers you employed). Many in the last two categories work in the underground economy. The total for the unemployed and underemployed was 26 million workers or 16.5 percent of the workforce. Under Bush II, three-fourths of the unemployed were men, mostly unskilled/semi-skilled; under Obama (2008-12), most were women, many in the reduced public sector of Republican dominated states.

In Septmeber 2015, the U.S. unemployment rate was 7.9 percent or 11.3 million, with 7.9 million part-timers wanting full-time work, and 5.8 million discouraged, equaling 25 million, a sixth of the workforce. A third of unemployed workers did not earn the minimum wage in each quarter to qualify for unemployment benefits (unemployment compensation, if qualified, is at 40-50 percent of the lost job). During the height of the Great Recession, unemployment benefit duration was 99 weeks, then reduced to 73 weeks, and by January 2014 to 26 weeks for almost all states (20 in North Carolina).[7]

Many of the unemployed are long termers: 4.9 million for more than six months as of October 2012, averaging 41 weeks, and 30 percent more than a year.

In the 2008-10 period, the heaviest job losses were among mid-wage workers earning $13.84 - $21.13 an hour (4 million jobs lost), while lower wage workers ($7.69 - $13.83 an hour) lost 1.2 million jobs, and higher-wage workers ($21.14 - $54-55 an hour) lost 700,000 jobs. Each of these cohorts had a third of all jobs.

But in 2011-12, there were job gains: in the lower-wage sector, 2 million (the largest gainers); the mid-wage, 800,000; and the high-wage, 500,000. These statistics indicate that mid-wage workers suffered most because their jobs were automated or sent abroad. High wage jobs have also not recovered previous employment levels again because of business consolidation, automation, and offshoring. Overall, for the first seven months of 2013, low-paid, part-time work (working less than 35 hours a week) was 77 percent of employment growth, mostly in retail and fast food and restaurants, earnings averaging $20,000 annually.[8]

With regard to re-employment after being unemployed, older workers, age 55-64, have a more difficult time procuring full-time employment and when they do, it is usually at a much lower wage. Regarding average weeks of unemployment: in the 1960-2000 period, 10 to 20; after 2000 steeply up, 40 in 2012.

In February 2014, 10.1 million workers were unemployed, 6.6 percent of the workforce, 36 percent (3.6 million) long term unemployed for more than 27 weeks, facing economic catastrophe.[9]

The current unemployment crisis, especially from 2008 to 2010, saw 55 percent of the workforce experiencing either unemployment or a reduction in pay, or change of job status from full-time to part-time.[10]

Unemployment itself causes not only economic hardship and intense psychological pain, equal to the death of a spouse, strained family interpersonal relations, and even higher death rates among men in their forties and fifties. Also, unemployment is a leading cause of mental depression, anxiety, alcoholism, and suicidal thinking, forcing employed workers to be more docile, fearful of losing their jobs.[11]

According to Jacob Hacker, a political scientist at Yale University, with declining wages as backdrop, when unemployment and/or major illness occur, leading to at least a 25 percent drop in income, a family is deemed economically insecure, in crisis; 12 percent were so in 1985, 20 percent in the recession year of 2009.[12]

Concerning job creation, from Jan. 2009 when Obama took office to Feb. 2010, four million jobs were lost, but from Feb. 2010 to Aug. 2012, four million jobs were created.[13]

According to the Economic Policy Institute (a leftist think tank), Republican obstruction of Obama's Jobs Act of 2011 and Republican state governors laying off public sector workers resulted in the loss of one million jobs which, in turn, led to the further loss of 750,000 jobs in the private sector related to reduced government contracts and lower consumer demand. Another 400,000 jobs were lost in the private sector because of state social-welfare cuts, resulting in further lower consumer demand by the poor and unemployed. Total job loss because of the preceding figures is 2.8 million who, if working, would have dropped unemployment to the 6 percent range instead of the high 7 percent one in October 2012.

To be sure, economic downturn and sluggish economic growth along with increasing business concentration from 1996 to 2011 have seen a 25 percent decline in new business starts, with a third loss of their projected employees adding to unemployment.

Unemployment itself and resultant lower wages are exacerbated by generous immigration policies. There are now about 21 million foreign workers (12 million undocumented), 15 percent of the workforce; annually, 1.2 million green cards to work are issued to immigrants, three-fourths of whom are employed.

Regarding undocumented workers, most are Mexican, mercilessly exploited, resulting in up to 7 percent lower wages for unskilled workers. Also, 85,000 skilled foreign workers annually arrive in the U.S. to perform work unable to be done by U.S. workers in the H-1B visa programs.

Also temporary visas are granted to foreign workers that are trained by American ones before being displaced by the same companies who trained them.

In the recessions of the 1980s and 90s, job losses recovered within two-three years; in the 2001 recession, four years. As of May 2013, employment was still 2.1 percent below the 2007 level.

To be sure, the Great Recession and subsequent slow economic growth has resulted in a lower quit rate for dissatisfied workers (60 percent lower, for instance, in November – December 2013). Then, too, work pace increases and wages continue to stagnate or decline because of weak unionism, technological innovation and job offshoring.

Furthermore, to make matters worse for unemployed workers, retraining programs for them have been cut, from $17 billion in 1980 to $5 billion recently. Republicans in the House in 2012 voted to further cut workers' retraining programs by $2.5 billion, but were prevented to do so by a Democratic Senate.

Even college graduates today, who traditionally have low unemployment rates, have difficulty in finding work (40 percent of recent college graduates are unemployed) and 48 percent of the 2010 class in 2013 work at jobs of lesser skill – what a waste!

Higher unemployment benefits favored by Democrats allow the unemployed to have more time and resources to search for the best job, contrary to the Republican stance of less time and fewer resources, forcing workers to be employed in worse hobs, lower wages, increasing capitalist profit. Finally, in a weak social welfare system, an unemployed worker with no dependent children can scarcely receive any welfare payments and without family and friends, shelter and food are at best provided by private charity, like the Salvation Army.

By the end of 2014, the unemployment rate dropped to 5.6 percent, but if we add millions of part-time workers, many wishing for full time employment, the U.S. unemployment rate is still 11-12 percent. Nevertheless, 7 million jobs were created since 2008-09, fewer than previously.

The present job market is still bleak despite unemployment being just under 6 percent in 2014. In pre-recession of 2007-09, 63 percent of adults were working; in 2010-13, 58 percent. Adult male's employment has dropped precipitously, from 96 percent in 1954 to 80 percent in 2011.

To be sure, there are more women in the paid work force: 35 percent in 1950, 70 percent in 2014. Why? Greater gender equality and to supplement stagnant male wages. Generally, unemployment is related to education and race; in September 2013, for instance, for adults over age 25: 10.3 percent for high school drops; 7.6 percent for high school graduates; 6 percent for some college; 3.7 percent for a bachelor's degree or more. Nevertheless, unemployment for college graduates under age 25 percent was 8.0 percent in 2013 and the rate of underemployment for college graduates in 2012 ages 22-27 was 44 percent, compared to 33 percent in the last two decades. Teenage unemployment (ages 16-19) in 2012-13 is 21.4 percent, black youth 40 percent. For blacks in the same period, 12.6 percent; whites, 6.6 percent.

Projections by the CBO for the entire 2010-20 period are for slow job growth, as compared to the past, which promises increasing socioeconomic/political instability: from ages 16-24, down 10 percent because more people attend school; from age 25-34, up 7.2 percent for men, 9.8 percent for women; from age 35-44, up 6.5 percent for men and 3.9 percent for women; from ages 45 to 54, down 7.6 percent for men and 8.6 percent for women; this cohort is replaced by younger lower-paid workers. But over age 55, up 33.2 percent for men and 43.3 percent for women. Why? Because defined pension benefits have declined, and of lower wages when younger. Most of this employment will be part time.

I should note that European social democracy has not solved the unemployment problem; in fact, in many of its nations it is higher than in the U.S. Unemployment in selective EU nations, in percentages in 2015: Greece, 27; Spain, 25; Portugal, 15; Ireland, 13; Poland, 13; Italy, 13; France, 11. This economic catastrophe has resulted in lower living standards/wages and social benefits.

In mid-2015, U.S. unemployment was at 5.5 percent, but job growth increased at about 225,000 jobs monthly. But two-thirds of jobs pay relatively low wages and are part-time. Furthermore in the first half of 2015, according to the Economic Policy institute, youth unemployment ages 17-20 is 30 percent among whites, 51 percent among blacks – information cited by Bernie Sanders on Free Speech TV in June 2015.[14]

In a capitalist-controlled profit driven schema, workers are only hired if profit can be made from their labor, thus chronic unemployment and resulting workers misery. In a worker-controlled socialist economy where the proceeds of technology and labor are equally shared by all, there is a general equilibrium between production and consumption, any imbalance resulting in longer vacations with pay.

Possible solutions with increased social democracy to lower employment: 1) much retraining; 2) subsidize corporations to hire workers; 3) federal jobs programs for the unemployed as during the

New Deal in the 1930s; 4) reducing the workday via progressive/ union action.

Ultimately, only socialism can solve the unemployment problem and its train of ills: by guaranteeing full employment as a right, along with job retraining in a milieu of great socioeconomic welfare, including an income whether you work or not, this is an era of increasing automation/computerization and robotics. Another possible solution would be drastically reducing the workday with higher wages.

The loss of American manufacturing jobs to abroad is part of an overall pattern of neoliberalism also occurring in Europe and Japan to cut costs and increase profits by replacing higher-paid domestic workers with inexpensive foreign labor in poor Third World nations. Share of the manufactured goods sent by developing nations to developed ones: 1955, U.S., 10; Japan, 10; 2012, U.S. 50, Japan, 60, EU, 40.

Snapshot regarding employment, unemployment, wages and other pertinent facts for June 2015: the employed are 59.3 percent of the population. Type of work in millions: nonfarm, 141.8; services, 122.3; goods, 19.6; agriculture 2.5. Average weekly earnings of rank-and-file workers, $861. The unemployment rate is 5.3 percent: white, 4.6 percent; black, 9.5 percent; Hispanic, 6.6 percent; Asian, 4.1 percent; teenagers (16-19), 18.1 percent. Hidden unemployment in millions: working part time but wishing full time work, 6.6 million; 6.6 million unemployed; or unemployment, 9 percent. There are also many millions of discouraged workers, adding at least another 2-3 percent to unemployment. Duration of unemployment in weeks, 28.1; median, 11.3. Unemployment by education level in percentages: less than high school, 8.2; high school, 5.4; some college, 4.2; Bachelor's or higher, 2.6. Unemployment under President Trump in 2018, under 4 percent.

Chapter 7: Taxes, Budget, Politics

This chapter observes the low taxes paid by the richest 1 percent of Americans through their basic control of the political process and mass media.

Budget deficits in the 2000-13 period have been large for the federal government because of the costs incurred by the Iraq and Afghanistan wars, the Great Recession and subsequent weak economic growth, as well as rescuing Wall Street and the auto industry, aiding the states and the unemployed and further reducing already low taxes to spur investment and consumer demand. According to the CBO, federal taxes in the 2009-12 period fell by a fourth because of the Great Recession and its aftermath; nevertheless, budget deficits have been declining lately.[1]

The following are federal taxes in 2009: 45 percent from individual/household income; 45 percent from Social Security/ Medicare jointly called from Federal Insurance Contributions ACT (FICA), fully funded by taxpayers; 6.8 percent from corporations; 2.4 percent from excise (sales) taxes, and 1.2 percent from estates upon death.[2]

How much did the various income groups contribute to federal taxes in percentages in 2011 as an example? To be sure, the wealthy because of steep income inequality and scarcely progressive taxes paid about a third (the richest 1.8 percent earning over $250,000, with 23 percent of all income, paid 35 percent); those earning between $30,000 and $250,000, 52 percent of taxpayers, paid 65 percent; those earning under $30,000 generally, 46 percent of households because of the earned income tax credit for children and home mortgages, paid no federal income. But low income taxpayers paid FICA and other taxes (gasoline and so forth), consuming up to a fifth of their income in some states.[3]

We now observe annual taxes paid in 2011 by discrete income groups in the following order: 1) local/states taxes; 2) payroll/other miscellaneous federal taxes; 3) federal income taxes; 4) total taxes paid: $33,000 - $53,000, 11.3 percent, 10.6 percent, 3.3 percent, totaling 25.2 percent; $53,000 - $88,000, 11.2 percent, 10.7 percent, 6.4 percent, totaling 28.3 percent; $88,000 - $127,000, 11 percent, 10.6 percent, 7.9 percent, totaling 29.5 percent; $127,000 - $176,000, 10.7 percent, 9.8 percent, 9.9 percent, totaling 30.3 percent; $176,000 - $452,000, 9.9 percent, 7.4 percent, 13.1 percent, totaling 30.4 percent; above $452,000, 7.9 percent, 5.2 percent, 15.8 percent, totaling 29 percent. These taxes are scarcely progressive but often regressive.[4]

Why do the rich pay low income taxes? Because a large part of their income is taxed at a 15 percent rate (20 percent beginning in 2013) on capital gains, dividends and interest. Capital gains taxes for the richest 5 percent account for 32.1 percent of income; for the richest 1 percent, 43.4 percent. Indeed, 75 percent of capital gains income goes to the richest 0.1 percent. Furthermore, under Reagan, CEOs of corporations were allowed to buy stock at a low price and sell it at a high price, paying only a capital gains tax.[5]

The Forbes richest 400, for example, paid on average of 18.1 percent in federal income taxes in 2008 and 19.9 percent in 2009, the latest reported year. Some paid nothing. As for actual total federal income taxes paid by the rich, when the highest marginal tax rate was 80-90 percent, they were in the mid-40 percent range; when the highest marginal tax rate was 35 percent, it was about 20 percent.

Historical background on the highest individual federal marginal income taxes: 77 percent by the end of World War I under President Woodrow Wilson; 25 percent in the early 1920s under President Warren G. Harding; 94 percent by 1942 under President Franklin Delano Roosevelt; 91 percent under President Dwight D. Eisenhower in the 1950s; 71 percent under President John Fitzgerald Kennedy in the early 1960s; 29 percent (28 percent in capital gains) under President Ronald Reagan in the 1980s; 39.6 percent (20 percent on capital gains) under President William Jefferson Clinton in the 1990s; 35 percent (15 percent on capital gains) under President George W. Bush in the 2000s; 39.6 percent (20 percent on capital gains) under President Barack Obama (2009 – 2017).[6]

From 1961 to 2006, the wealthy saw a 60 percent drop in federal income taxes, while the average taxpayer paid 20 percent less. But for the bottom 80 percent of taxpayers, total taxes have increased because of higher FICA, local and state taxes and fees.[7] Why? Because of the rise of political conservatism, especially after the Reagan Revolution in the 1980s.

But the Obama and Democratic 2008 electoral victory resulted in higher taxes on the rich: individuals annually earning about $400,000 and couples above $500,000 had taxes raised from 35 percent to 39.6 percent and capital gains/dividends taxes were lifted from 15 percent to a maximum of 23.8 percent. An estate tax of 40 percent was levied on individuals worth more than $5.43 million, on couples worth $10.86 million. It will generate $246 billion in revenues in the next 10 years. Only 0.2 percent of estates qualify.

The Democratic increases on the richest 1 percent overall rose by 6 percent and on the richest 0.1 percent by 9 percent. Also, in 2013, the temporary Social Security cuts were restored, a worker earning $50,000 a year paying $1,000 more. And an $83 billion tax cut was imposed, half from military expenditures and half from mostly social programs.[7]

The highest marginal income tax rates are much higher in Western Europe and Japan than in the U.S. because even if some have conservative governments, social democrats have much popular support. Francois Hollande, the new socialist president of France, will tax earners above $1.2 million at 75 percent. Top income tax rates today in other selective nations (in percentages) include: Sweden, 57; Japan, 50; Britain, 45; Germany, 45; Italy, 43; Russia, governed by a crony-capitalist kleptocratic elite, 13.[8]

The wealthy include private equity and hedge fund managers/ partners who by a carried-interest tax provision are taxed at a maximum 20 percent capital gains tax on investment profits, paying half the tax rate, for example, of other managers, as in retail. Another tax provision allows them to value their investments in such a way as to permit them to place much more money in their individual retirement accounts, whereas ordinary tax payers are limited in this respect. These tax loopholes are made by their PACS and lobbyists.

Mitt Romney, a capitalist buccaneer and once-head of Bain Capital (a private equity corporation), became the 2012 Republican candidate for president. He earned $33.9 million in 2010 and 2011 combined, paying 14 percent in federal income taxes. As for his IRA in 2012, it was worth between $20 million and $101 million; he also has had a Swiss bank account, $30 million invested in the Cayman Islands, and also monies in Bermuda, all well-known legal tax havens. Thus it is that much of Romney's estimated wealth in 2011, from $190 million to $250 million, comes from paying low taxes and parking his money in tax havens.

Romney made most of his fortune as the CEO of Bain Capital, which buys companies with weak sales but large cash reserves. Romney and his partners would put down a small amount of their own money and with it borrow much more from banks to purchase majority ownership of the acquired company, a maneuver called a leveraged buyout made possible under President Reagan.[9]

To be sure, when foreign, local and state taxes are added to the federal one, large American corporations pay more: in 2012, 12.6 percent in federal and 4.3 percent in foreign, local, and state, totaling 16.9 percent. The official tax rate, 35 percent.

Other selected central government tax rates on large corporations in percentages, circa 2013: France. 43; Japan, 28; Italy, 27.5; Britain, 24; Germany, 16.

American TNCs employ many strategies in tax avoidance, including transferring profits to subsidiaries located in tax havens with little to low taxes and shifting money among various jurisdictions to avoid being accurately taxed.

Tax havens, as in the Cayman Islands, Luxembourg and Bermuda, used by the wealthy and TNCs, deprive the federal government of a fourth of the $400 billion it loses to tax avoiders. A case in point: Bank of America has many subsidiaries in the Cayman Islands, paying no U.S. taxes. Consequently, it received a $1.9 billion federal tax rebate in 2012. Generally tax havens offer their clients very low or zero taxes.

The economic scope of tax havens is so great that half of the world's banking assets, half the stock, and a third of its foreign direct investment are routed through them. For instance, in 2008, eighty-three of the largest hundred American companies have foreign subsidiaries. More than $12 trillion by U.S. wealthy/TNCs are in such tax havens in 2012, depriving huge tax revenue for the federal government. Also, William Mulholland, the CEO of the Bank of Montreal, informed a Canadian parliamentary committee that "I can hide money in the twinkling of an eye from all the bloodhounds that could be put on the case." If these capitalists were properly taxed, the U.S. budget deficit would be greatly reduced.

Then, too, American TNCs have accumulated $1.4 trillion in profits abroad by 2012, not paying taxes on them. TNCs wish to return this amount to the U.S. to be taxed again at 5 percent, as in 2004; it will likely happen, which is another tax giveaway.

To lower federal tax rates, American corporations are purchasing foreign companies in lower tax nations (Britain, Ireland, and Netherlands) and incorporating there, at the same time keeping headquarters at home; this "inversion" is facilitated by Wall Street banks earning a billion dollars by August 2014. Two of these companies are Activis and Eaton. President Obama, even without Congressional approval, can stop this tax dodging, but as of early August 2014, he has not done so. Republicans in Congress generally oppose legislation to correct the problem. From 2011 to 2014, 22 inversions have occurred and in 2014 alone, 25 companies are considering them. In the next decade, tax revenue loss by inversions is estimated at $20 billion. Corporate tax loopholes are so pervasive that a fourth of U.S. corporations pay no federal taxes in any given year. For instance, in 2010, General Electric earned $14.2 billion worldwide, $5.2 billion of which in the U.S. – all the while paying no U.S. taxes.

To be sure, corporations also receive subsidies from local and state governments to locate in their jurisdictions at $80 billion annually in 2012. Indeed, if corporations would have continued to pay 25 percent of the federal tax burden as in the early 1950s, federal budget deficits would be largely eliminated.

Also, U.S. corporations in the 2003-12 period have received $65 billion in bonds from local and state governments, exempt from federal taxes, again resulting in the loss of billions of dollars in federal tax revenue. Furthermore, in 2012, banks received $83 billion gratis from the Federal Insurance Deposit Corporation as insurance for financial losses. TNCs are also allowed tax write-offs to shut down plants in the U.S. and move them abroad. Democrats in the House of Representatives voted in 2011 to end this egregious tax loophole, but Republicans in the Senate successfully filibustered it.

Carbon involved (petroleum, natural gas and coal) corporations also received $49 billion from the IRS annually in generous depleted allowances and paid no taxes on negative externalities, costs related to illness like lung cancer and to the natural environment.

Overall, one estimate had the U.S. tax rate recently as the fifth lowest among OECD nations. Also, according to Steve Rattner, a Wall Street executive, according to the OECD, U.S. tax revenues for 2014 will be smaller on a relative basis than those of any other member nation.[10]

From September 2011 to September 2012, the federal government collected $2.3 trillion (15.5 percent of an approximately $15 trillion GDP), but spent $3.6 trillion or 24 percent of it, leaving a $1.3 trillion deficit or 8.7 percent of GDP. State and local governments spent $1.42 trillion, or about 10 percent of GDP, and collected 10.3 percent of it in taxes, about the same amount. Total government spending was $5.02 trillion, about a third of GDP, while total government taxes collected were 26 percent of GDP, leaving a total budget deficit of 7 percent, almost all of it by the federal government.[11]

But if FICA payments, fully funded by the workforce/employers at $800 billion, are excluded from the federal budget, only $1.5 trillion was collected by the federal government, 10 percent of GDP (President Johnson in the 1960s included social security and Medicare in the federal budget to allow for a lower official deficit).

Federal deficit spending to counter the Great Recession's anemic economic growth, resulting in lower tax receipts, continued. Large military costs in Afghanistan and Iraq and further tax cuts in 2009-12 of $1.3 trillion to FICA and business by President Obama added another $6 trillion to the federal debt. Under Bush II and Obama, 2001-13, the federal debt almost tripled - $17 trillion by 2015, 100 percent of GDP.

In 2007, the richest 0.1 percent of taxpayers with 12.3 percent of national income earned more than $1 trillion; their effective federal income tax rate was in the 16-20 percent range. Thus, at most, they were paying $200 billion in federal taxes.[12] (The federal budget deficit in 2009-12 averaged $1.5 trillion, falling to $642 billion in 2012-13, or 6.2 percent of the federal budget (from 1973 to 2012, average percentage interest paid on it was 10.6 percent).

If the federal government raised the top marginal tax rate to 80 percent on the richest 0.1 percent, they would pay another $200 billion more in taxes, their total now being $400 billion. Doubling the effective tax rates on corporations to 20 percent would add another $160 - $180 billion. Adding a small tax of 0.5 percent on stock and bond sales would add another $50 – 100 million. A special wealth tax of 5 percent on about 400 U.S. billionaires would also raise another $75 billion; ending the huge annual tax depreciation giveaway on corporations would add another $30 billion, a small tax on tax havens, $100 billion more.[13] Also, universal health care would cut federal/ state expenses (Medicare, Veterans Administration, Medicaid) by the many hundreds of billions of dollars (Of healthcare GDP percentage 2014: U.S., 18; France Germany, Britain, 9-11).[14]

Military spending is another important reason for the huge federal government deficit. Under the official federal budget, military expenditures in 2011 of $711 billion are 20 percent (the U.S. spends 40 percent of the world's military budget). But if we exclude fully funded by taxpayer Social Security and Medicare from the budget and include Veterans Affairs, endless war, and nuclear war programs, and so forth, the military portion of the budget in 2009 is $965 billion or between 54 and 60 percent of it. The military budget itself doubled from 2001 to 2012 because of the Afghanistan and Iraq wars. For starters, the military budget should be cut in half; military Keynesianism generates less jobs than education and other public sectors – see "Great Recession" chapter (China, 2015, is second in military spending, $145-48 billion versus the U.S. of $525 billion).

The awe-inspiring U.S. arsenal includes approximately 2,000 strategic nuclear forces in a triad of 440 intercontinental ballistic missiles, many Lear bombers and submarines and as many as 2,000 cruise missiles. Warplanes number 5,500 (4,700 Air Force, 770 Naval Air Force). There is the Pacific Fleet of 5 aircraft carrier strike groups (each carrier sustaining 70 warplanes) and an Atlantic Fleet of 8 aircraft carrier strike groups and 40 attack submarines. Also, the U.S. operates 700 military bases abroad (174 in Germany, 113 in Japan, etc.). In 2012, their operating cost was $175 billion; in 2014, $156 billion. Furthermore, eventual costs of the ill-fated Afghanistan and Iraq wars (both invasions were uncalled for, the second of which was a definite breach of international law) are in the $5 trillion range with over 6,000 U.S. military killed and many tens of thousands injured, hundreds; hundreds of thousands of Iraqis, for instance, were also killed. Add to this arsenal of death, in 2015 a trillion dollar upgrade of its nuclear forces, part of the second Cold War between the U.S. and the Russian Federation.

Also, there is approximately $25 billion of bureaucratic waste annually at the Pentagon, according to a study by The Nation, June 16/23, 2018, p. 25.

In 2013, the U.S. also spend $52.6 billion on intelligence gathering and drone operations ($23 billion is spent by military intelligence). Of this amount, the Central Intelligence Agency (CIA) received $14.7 billion (21,000 employees); the National Security Agency (NSA), $10.8 billion; and the National Reconnaissance Office (NRO), $10.3 billion – these are the top three of 16 governmental spy agencies employing 500,000 private contractors who hold top secret clearances.

Indeed, when the Republican's scream against big government, they should begin to shrink its largest single expense: the Military Industrial Complex. For starters, the war machine budget should be reduced by at least half, which in turn would save hundreds of billions of dollars.[15]

Also, if workers' wages kept up with productivity, workers would at once pay higher taxes and consume more, lowering the possibility of economic downturn with its higher budget deficits, while social welfare payments to the poor would decline because more of the poor would be gainfully employed. Such suggestions would more than likely almost erase federal budget deficits.

The proposed higher marginal tax rates for the rich at 80 percent might lead them to invest their capital elsewhere (many are doing so already in tax havens), but laws could prevent this. In any case, many investments of the wealthy do not lead to jobs and income growth but to destructive Wall Street casino gambling.

Indeed, according to Eduardo Porter of The New York Times, many economists assert that raising the top marginal income tax rate to 80 percent would still allow for enough capital accumulation to fuel the economy.[16] The current annual investment rate in the U.S. is 16 percent of the GDP, or approximately $2.25 trillion.

As for the rich working less if their taxes are significantly raised, this will not happen according to Peter Lindert, Distinguished Professor of Economics, University of California, Davis.[17] Indeed, this is a silly argument.

The following information shows contrasting Republican and Democratic views on taxes and social welfare costs affecting the federal budget in the 2012 elections: Republicans: Romney, a former Republican candidate for presidency, was a liberal Republican governor of Massachusetts who approved of its comprehensive health care insurance program covering all of its citizens. In the Republican primaries, he posed as a conservative Republican, but to win votes when running against the Democratic Obama for the presidency, he became once again a liberal Republican. His vice-presidential choice, Paul Ryan, a Wisconsin congressman, is a conservative Tea Party favorite. But he voted for the unfunded Iraq and Afghanistan wars and the federal government prescription drug program, Medicare Part D, which prohibits the federal government from negotiating with drug companies over price.

The following is a composite basically of the Romney/Ryan and Republican-dominated House of Representatives position unless otherwise noted. The top federal income tax rate for individuals and corporations would be reduced almost a third, from 35 percent to 25 percent, resulting in an average tax reduction for the richest 1 percent of $237,000 to $250,000; for the richest 0.01 percent, $1.2 million. The only other tax bracket would be 10 percent, which includes even poor workers, eliminating their income tax credit, tax deductions for dependent children and so forth. Since Reagan, Social Security payments are taxed, but are offset for the poor by the income tax credit. The federal estate tax on the rich and of U.S corporate profits made abroad would be eliminated, as well as taxes on capital gains, allowing rich individuals like Romney to pay much less in federal income taxes. Romney himself in the next decade would increase military expenditures by $2 trillion (to keep up with inflation), adding to the federal budget deficit, but Ryan would only increase them by $400 billion in the next decade. These measures would have the wealthy and corporations pay $4.3 trillion less in taxes in the next decade.

To compensate for these revenue losses, the Romney-Ryan axis in the next decade would reduce federal social-welfare programs by $3.3 trillion, slashing Medicaid by $800 billion and transferring it to the states in block grants and cutting 27 million individuals from its rolls, with costs to increase 1 percent annually, although medical costs generally increase at least double this rate or at times even triple. This constitutes a 20 percent reduction for these programs.

Also, Republicans would repeal the Affordable Care Act (ACA), which would remove another 20 million individuals from Medicaid. Those on Medicare would receive health insurance vouchers at $8,000 annually to purchase from government-subsidized health insurance companies. After a public outcry, this plan was dropped. Then, Medicare eligibility would be raised from age 65 to 67. But Romney, contrary to Ryan and House Republicans, would leave Medicare as it is.

The Ryan/House Republican proposals would increase individual annual health care costs by $6,400 by 2022, according to the nonpartisan Congressional Budget Office.

Regarding the poor without Medicaid or any insurance, Republicans would have them go to the hospital emergency room if ill; the poor, invariably in debt, are reluctant to go because of high hospital bills, which in turn has led to higher mortality rates.

The ACA, with its health care savings of $716 billion over the next 10 years, extracted from insurance companies and hospitals, but promising them up to 30 million more patients, extends economic viability of Medicare from 2016 to 2022. The unequal American class system itself decrees that the richest 30 percent of people consume 89 percent of health care costs.

The Republicans also favor a regressive value added tax (VAT) on sales, the losers being the working class. They would weaken public school education and the pro-Democratic teachers' unions by favoring for-profit privately-owned charter schools. Then, too, they would reduce college Pell Grants for low-income students.

Regarding Republican propaganda that the Democratic proposal of raising top federal income tax rates from 35 percent to 39.6 percent would hurt "small business," it is pure nonsense. They include in this category of "small businesses" law and accounting firms, as well as corporate executives serving on the boards of directors of corporations employing thousands. Even if "small business" includes corporations whose annual income is under $19 million, the Treasury Department claims that only 2.5 percent would face higher taxes but that their tax deductions are sufficient enough not to hinder their employment practices.

Ryan himself would dismantle present Social Security arrangements, but then relented after encountering stiff public opposition: seniors under age 55 could then stay on Social Security as now constituted or place a portion of their benefits into private pension accounts, enriching Wall Street. But in the event of economic downturn, they would suffer severe economic losses. But then Ryan/Romney backtracked on this plan to keep Social Security as it is – an election tactic (two-thirds of the budget cuts proposed by the Republican-controlled House in 2013 were at the expense of the poor).

The Ryan-Tea Party crowd closely follows the dictates of

Friedrich August Von Hayek who in <u>The Road to Serfdom</u> (1944) was a proponent of much social welfarism for workers – health insurance, disability and old-age pensions, a basic minimum of food, housing and clothing, regulating hours of work and so forth. But in his late 1950s book, <u>The Constitution of Liberty,</u> he railed against progressive income taxation, labor unions, and the welfare state in general.

The Republican electoral program would economically savage the poor, cutting them from federal assistance, to rely on aid from the states, which would vary widely, and private charity. These proposals would return us to a pre-New Deal America of unmitigated social Darwinism. Its main appeal is to political conservatives who believe that they "earned" their economic success, forgetting that wealth is also accumulated within a socioeconomic and political context. They subscribe to the shibboleth of "personal responsibility," inevitably blaming the poor/disabled for their poverty.

The Democratic plan would protect Social Security, Medicare, Medicaid, the ACA, food stamps and other social-welfare programs. The Bush II tax cuts for individuals earning over $200,000 and families over $250,000 annually (the richest 2-3 percent) would be raised to 39.6 percent, adding $80 billion yearly to federal revenues. Dividends would be taxed as ordinary income instead of the current 20 percent rate. Top corporate taxes would be cut from the present 35 percent to 28 percent with fewer loopholes. Furthermore, the depreciation allowances for business in 2011 allowing corporations to write off the cost of investment in the initial year would continue, saving business up to $53 billion annually. Then, a "Buffett Rule" would require those earning more than a million dollars annually to pay a tax of at least 30 percent over that amount. These modest tax proposals would cut the annual federal budget by approximately $130 billion. Military spending in the next decade would also fall by $487 billion.

Overall, if one includes Republican spending in the next decade on social welfare programs and others, like infrastructure, Romney would spend $6.9 trillion, Ryan $9.3 trillion, and Obama $12 trillion, itself a 9 percent reduction from present levels.

The Democratic electoral plan, of a moderate center-right party, is to slightly increase taxes in the rich and slightly reduce social welfare programs, a proposal that at least has a modicum of social solidarity and community.[18]

According to CBO May 2013 projections for the 2012-13 fiscal year ending September 30, the federal deficit will decline to $642 billion or 4 percent of GDP and slightly rise in the next five years, peaking at $750 billion in the last. In 2015, the nation witnessed higher tax collections from households and business, increased revenues from Freddie Mac and Fannie Mae now profitable, and lower federal spending on health care and military.[19]

In January 2015, Obama proposed a 2016 federal budget of almost $4 trillion ($3.5 trillion from taxes) that would increase revenues $1 trillion by 2025 and increase the federal budget from 20 to 22 percent of GDP. But it would also decrease the federal budget deficit from $583 billion in 2015 to $474 billion in 2016, 2.5 percent of GDP. The capital gains tax in dividends/interest would also be raised to 25 percent.

Regarding taxes, Obama proposed a one-time federal tax of 14 percent on overseas U.S. corporate profits held there ($2 trillion in 2014), then a 19 minimum percent tax. But he would then reduce the overall corporate tax rate from 35 percent to 28 percent, 25 percent for manufacturers; then raise capital gains taxes from 20 percent to 28 percent. These taxes would only slightly hurt the wealthy.

These tax increases would allow the funding for free two-year tuition in public colleges, universities; allow earned-income tax credits for childless individuals, increased tax credits for child care increased funds for job training, a 4.5 percent military budget increase and allow for an infrastructure fund increase of $478 billion in the next six years.

Chapter 8: Left vs. Right in the United States

This chapter delves into the relative strength in the U.S. between the left and right division in various areas: in the media, political spectrums, social psychology, including wasteful dysfunctions of American capitalism, and their negative affects – especially on the working class.

In the mass media – television, newspapers, periodicals, radio, internet – capitalist control is overwhelming. They are important in influencing the mindset of the general public. In following the oligopolistic pattern of American capitalism, 95 percent of them are owned by a half dozen or so corporations. They include, among others, Comcast, CBS, Walt Disney, Rupert Murdoch's News Corporations, Verizon, The New York Times, Viacom, and Clear Channel Communications.

A brief description of a selected few are as follows: Time Warner, the world's largest media company, owns 150 magazines, including Fortune and large movie companies like Warner Brothers Pictures, New Line Cinema, Castle and Rock Cinema. Murdoch's News Corporation owns Fox TV, The Wall Street Journal; Comcast, with 30 percent of the cable market, acquired NBC Universal, but its bid to purchase Time Warner Cable in 2014 was rejected by the federal government; if the acquisition had been successful, it would have had 57 percent of the cable market.

This drive to oligopoly was accelerated when the Reagan Administration and succeeding ones did not basically enforce the anti-monopoly Sherman and Clayton Anti-Trust acts. Furthermore, from the 1930s to the 1970s, commercial radio and television were bound by the Federal Communications' Fairness Doctrine of the 1940s to report news objectively which meant that it was presented in a middle of the road manner, i.e. neither favoring Republican nor Democrats. Conservative business, which dominates the media, was not sympathetic to this view and in the 1980s under President Reagan, the Federal Trade Commission overturned the

Fairness Doctrine. Soon afterward, right-wing Republicans like Rush Limbaugh dominated radio, followed by the Fox News Channel. With the demise of the Fairness Doctrine, mainline television news departments were downgraded to "infotainment news." I also add that the 1996 Communications Act under President Clinton accelerated the drive to corporate consolidation.

Corporate news programs, especially local, mostly feature petty crime, murder, accidents, fires, weather, and sports personalities. There is scant serious muckraking or in-depth political commentary. National television news is presented by millionaire anchors who internalize the conservative views of television owners/commercial sponsors.

Evening television news on the principal four corporate capitalist stations – CBS, NBC, ABC, Fox – also cover political news superficially; it is "infotainment." Fox is now right-wing Republican, while the other three outlets supposedly are more balanced between Republicans and Democrats. PBS, semi-public, covers the news in a more in-depth manner. MSNBC is about evenly balanced between Republican and Democratic positions. CNN is supposedly neutral.

Up to half of TV time is devoted to commercials of capitalist corporations, which keep TV and other media economically viable and which obviously influence the contents of news and other programming. The Project Censored at Sonoma State University in California has done outstanding reporting on how TV corporate news distorts political, social, and economic reality to favor the rich/corporations complex by generally neglecting to mention such vital topics as ravages of poverty, unemployment, increasing socioeconomic inequality and so on. Since television is the main source of news for most Americans, they are politically ill-informed. The usual fare includes: weather, accidents, fires, and human interest.

Concerning the 2015-16 presidential primaries, the TV corporate networks devote much attention to the Republican frontrunner Donald Trump while scarcely any to the Democratic Hillary Clinton and Bernie Sanders. As for vital issues dividing the parties – silence.

Corporate television is also the principal source of mass

entertainment, mainly of the working/lower middle classes, overworked, plagued by economic uncertainty and dominated in the workplace, the most alienated classes. It thus panders to them to gain as much commercial revenue/popularity as possible in inane programs featuring police and violence, romance, comedy, entertainment, personalities, old movies, sports and so on. The aim is distraction from the pressing daily problems, and not to question the status quo. This fare does not enlighten or dwell into the depths/ problems facing the audience; instead it titillates and numbs their senses, constantly interrupted by commercials. The verdict? TV entertainment is a wasteland, with PBS as the exception.

In radio, Clear Channels Communications, with 840 stations, dominates. Politically, it is reactionary, starring Rush Limbaugh, with up to 15 million listeners, among others; Limbaugh constantly attacks the Democratic Party, the poor, social welfare programs, undocumented immigrants, gays and so forth.

In fact, 95 percent of talk radio commentary is reactionary, capturing 14 percent of voters, important for Republicans, 40 percent of whom believe that President Obama was not born in the U.S., 50 percent that he wishes to impose Moslem Sharia law on the U.S.

Movies are also of great importance in popular entertainment, featuring sexual attraction, violence, comedy, science fiction and so forth.

For the upper-middle class and wealthy, entertainment consists of expensive entertainment home systems, plays, concerts, the opera and frequent costly vacations.

The leading capitalist newspapers include <u>The New York Times</u>, <u>The Wall Street Journal</u>, <u>USA Today</u> and <u>The Washington Post</u>. Some favor social welfare/reform, especially <u>The New York Times</u>, a clearly liberal publication. But "liberal" in the U.S. is generally to the right of European conservatism which accepts much more social-welfare programs than their American counterparts. In the 2012 elections, outside the South, Obama was endorsed by many "liberal" newspapers in New York City, Boston, Denver, Washington D.C., Philadelphia, Chicago, and Los Angeles, among others.

For the more affluent/educated/liberal cohort, The New York Times is preferred reading; for their conservative counterpart, The Wall Street Journal.

The leading national periodicals, like Time, Bloomberg Businessweek, Forbes, US News and World Report, among others, are obviously pro-capitalist, as is The Economist (widely read), a British periodically. To their right is The National Review, the leading conservative journal.

The left (left liberals and socialists) also have their periodicals, including Mother Jones, Rolling Stone, Harpers, The Atlantic Monthly, The Nation, The Progressive, In These Times, Monthly Review (Marxist), Z Magazine (anarchist orientation), The New Yorker (mainly literary), The New York Review of Books, and Dissent (democratic socialist).

As for leftist television stations, there are three: Free Speech, Link and Russia Today (RT). The first features, for instance, such sterling commentators as Thom Hartmann (he is also on RT), Amy Goodman, Bill Press. Their content on socioeconomic and political issues is in-depth and incisive. RT is sponsored by the kleptocratic Russian government. Its leftist muckraking bent, of course, criticizes the ills of American life, which increases social discontent.

The left is also well represented on the internet by the Huffington Post, Politico, Moveon.org, and Wikileaks.org and so forth.

Regarding think-tanks, important policy centers, wealthy capitalist richly fund the conservative Manhattan Institute, Cato Institute, and American Legislative Council (ALC) of the reactionary Kock Brothers, the last spending millions of dollars annually influencing politicians. Left think-tanks include the labor-funded Economic Policy Institute, Demos, The Center for American Progress, Public Citizen, and Common Cause.

On the whole, media exposure by the left is not significant, but is nevertheless important among the intelligentsia.[1]

In political contributions to candidates, some background: In 1907, prompted by President Theodore Roosevelt, Congress passed the Tillman Act which prohibited corporations (not individuals) to contribute money to political candidates for all offices. In 2010, the Supreme Court in a 5-4 decision in <u>Citizens United v. Federal Election Commission</u> decisively reversed the act on the basis that it violated First Amendment free speech rights; this opened the floodgates for corporations, unions, and the wealthy to contribute unlimited amounts of money to political action committees (PACs), including 501 (C)(4) or "dark money" Super-PACs, social welfare organizations where the wealthy/corporations can spend unlimited and undisclosed amounts of money in electoral campaigns. Recently candidates can meet with these Super-PACs to plan strategy.

Big Money once again prevails.

This "dark money" spent 85 percent on Republicans and 15 percent on Democrats. Leading billionaire contributors for Republicans include the Koch brothers (Charles and David) and Sheldon Adelson who have largely captured the agenda of the Republican Party.

In 2014, in <u>McCutcheon v. Federal Election Commission</u>, the Supreme Court in a 5-4 decision also allowed wealthy individuals to contribute directly up to $5,200 to every federal candidate/PAC and political party committee in a 2-year electoral cycle, a single donor thus able to contribute millions of dollars. These two court cases were predated by <u>Southern Pacific Railroad v. Santa Clara County</u> (1886) where corporations had the same rights as people and in <u>Buckley v. Valeo</u> (1976), equating money with free speech.

In the 2012 election cycle, for instance, the Kochs' alone spent $417 million; richest 0.01 percent, 28 percent; richest 0.1 percent, 44 percent; richest 1 percent, 80 percent. PACs themselves have proliferated: 600 in 1974, 4,500 in 2009. PACs of business include the U.S. Chamber of Commerce, The National Association of Manufacturers, Business Roundtable of the CEOs of the 200 largest American corporations, and of specific industries and discrete corporations.

PACs representatives in Congress are the lobbyists, in Washington D.C., approximately 12,000 registered, 100,000 unregistered. There are also many lobbyists in state legislatures. In this area, capital outspends labor by a 15 to 1 margin.

Examples of special-interest lobbyists and money spent by them to influence Congress: healthcare, 1998-2012, 6 for every congress member at $5.36 billion; Wall Street, 1998-2008, 3,000 at $5.00 billion; pharmaceuticals, 2012, $250 million; Wall Street to repeal Glass-Steagall, $300 million. Lobbyists often write legislation proposals for Congress members.

The importance of special interest PACs is illustrated by the salient fact that they contribute about 10 times more to candidates than political parties do. Money spend on Congressional races: for the Senate, $743,000 in 1974, and $8 million in 2006; for the House, $56,000 in 1974, and $1.3 million in 2006.

The richest 0.01 percent alone in the 2012 elections contributed $410 million directly to candidates and $500 million to Super PACs, a quarter from Wall Street. Among other donations: 60 percent to Republicans, 40 percent to Democrats. In fact, to protect their economic interests, these PACs gave money to every elected member of Congress.

Selected PAC money by industries to Democrats in 2008 and 2014 in percentages, the remainder to Republicans: commercial banks, 48, 28; Securities and Investments, 58, 38; hospitals and nursing homes, 62, 48; much of manufacturing, 40, 28; retail sales, 52, 38; agricultural services and products, 40, 25; health services/HMOs, 61, 45. Corporate contributions to Democrats are substantial and far exceed those of labor unions.

The influence of the Koch Brothers on the 2016 elections in indicated by their January 2015 seminar, where approximately 300 wealthy Republicans pledged $889 million for campaign contributions. Among Republican presidential hopefuls attending: Wisconsin Governor Scott Walker, Florida Senator Marco Rubio, Texas Senator Ted Cruz, and Kentucky Senator Rand Paul. New Jersey Governor Chris Christie is also close to the Koch family.

Another metric of PAC strength is that House members spend up to half of their working time soliciting money from them.

To be sure, elections are becoming ever more expensive. The 2012 elections cost $10 billion, when money spent by PACs, on local/

state elections, is included, not the $6 billion regularly reported by the media. Of this amount, supporters of Obama spent $1.1 billion; of Romney, $1.2 billion. In fact, between 2000 and 2012, expenditures on federal elections doubled.

The large sums of money spent on TV political advertising are basically directed at low-information voters who are the critical component for electoral success, according to Ralph Nadar, America's most notable advocate for reform.

In 2007, Congress passed legislation forbidding members from accepting gifts from corporate lobbyists, but it was bypassed thus: Corporate lobbyists/executives and Congressional members would meet at resorts to enjoy themselves and discuss matters of mutual interest – PAC money for corporate favors. The corporate lobbyists/executives' pay their own expenses as do the lawmakers from a personal leadership PAC, replenished after the festivities. The cost, often involving 50-100 persons, in the many tens of thousands of dollars.

Lobbying should only be allowed for information, impossible now because of corporate power.

Reform itself is also stifled by the personal economic ambitions of Congressional members in both major parties. When they lose office or retire, half become lobbyists and many enter in lucrative positions in corporations, thus becoming more receptive to corporate lobbyists when in office. Corporate lobbyists offer Congressional members future jobs while serving in office. Furthermore, it is perfectly legal for Congressional members to receive stock market tips from Wall Street.

American conservatism is also reinforced by the fact that virtually all U.S. senators and half of House members are members of the top 1 percent and know that if they serve the top 1 percent, they will be rewarded well when they leave office.

Amount of money spent in elections is very important in winning. In 2010, most money won 95 percent of House and 75 percent of Senate races. Incumbents, already having ample corporate money, in 2012 won 90 percent of House and Senate races.

To be sure, many wealthy Congress members are liberals, especially in left-leaning House districts, but their liberalism does not threaten their wealth too much. Altruism is a factor here.

Examples of Congress members graduating to the Elysian fields of Big Money include: House member Billy Tauzin, instrumental in negotiating Medicare Part D (drugs) and who prevented the federal government from negotiating their prices, was rewarded the presidency of the pharmaceutical association at a salary of $2 million annually. Senators Trent Lott (Republican) and John Breaux (Democrat) established a lobbying firm together, earning $11 million in 2009.

Several well-known cases of political corruption by Republicans include: In 2005, Randy Cunningham, an eight-term House member, received an eight-year prison sentence for bribery and tax evasion. Jack Abramoff, a lobbyists, received a 10-year prison sentence for bribing House members with free gifts, expensive trips, and jobs for spouses; Robert Ney, a House member from Ohio, was also imprisoned. To be sure, several Democratic House members in scandals were guilty of corruption and also received prison sentences.

On the state level, political corruption usually intersects with capital. In New York, where political corruption is endemic, in the autumn of 2015, Sheldon Silver, a Democrat, former Assembly speaker, and Dean G. Skelos, a Republican, and former majority leader, are being tried in federal courts in Manhattan for nepotism, extortion, and bribery for enrichment and so forth. In New York, state legislators can work part-time outside of their elected office, opening opportunities to combine politics and business. On Nov. 30, 2015, a jury found Silver guilty: he loses his Assembly seat and will face years of imprisonment.

Political corruption also exists in cities, specifically in Cleveland, Ohio. My friend Irving Chudner, a reformer intimately tied to its politics from the 1960s to the early 2000s as president of the West Side Neighborhood Association, confided in me about many political kickbacks and other skullduggery from business to politicians. In capitalism, politics is a business – often corrupt.

A study by two political scientists, Mark Gilens of Princeton and Benjamin Page of Northwestern, conducted over a 22-year period covering 1,779 political policy decisions, found that the interests of the wealthy and corporations were overwhelmingly favored at the expense of average citizens.

The preceding facts indicate an incestuous relationship among federal lawmakers of both major parties who enrich themselves with ties to corporations. These are delved into by Mark Leibovich, chief correspondent of <u>The New York Times Magazine</u> in <u>This Town</u>.[2]

The U.S., politically, is now run by a corrupt plutocratic oligarchy. Economic inequality invariably leads to political inequality; in this vein, Joseph E. Stiglitz quotes Warren Buffett: "There's been class warfare going on for the last 20 years and my class has won." Also in a recent Thom Hartmann program in the summer of 2015 (July 28), President Jimmy Carter stated that corporate money to politicians has transformed the nation into an oligarchy.

A description of the Democratic and Republican voters is as follows.

For Democrats: In 2012, a 2-to-1 advantage among the poorer 40 percent, disproportionally African-Americans, Hispanics, single mothers, youth; the majority of women, unionized blue- and white-collar workers. In the 2014 elections, Democrats captured the minorities vote: 63 percent Latino, 66 percent Asian, and over 90 percent Blacks (percentage of the population in 2015: Whites, 64, Latinos, 18, Blacks 12, Asians, 6). This is largely due to racism and poverty among blacks and Latinos. The lower-middle class is contested with Republicans. Among the affluent mainly white elite earning annually over $200,000, the Democrats at times prevail.

For Republicans: A majority among the richest fourth of Americans; of white voters with a high school education, 60 percent Republican in 2008 and 64 percent in 2012. These largely working-class voters, many unskilled and semi-skilled, especially blame blacks, who compete with them for jobs, for being "lazy and on welfare," while they are working and paying taxes, all the while allowing Republican wealthy to pay lower taxes and to rob them of needed reforms like strengthening Social Security/Medicare, Medicaid and federally mandated laws for paid sick and maternity leaves, vacations, free public college tuition and so on.

To be sure, there is also a sharp social cleavage between these white workers and blacks, the legacy of slavery and Jim Crow, one which has caste-like features.

Importantly, most Americans falsely believe that social welfare programs are the principal cause for higher taxes. As already indicated, means-tested social welfare is a miniscule part of taxes. It is the military-industrial-intelligence sector that is the chief culprit of higher taxes. The mass media misinform the public relative to taxation. Furthermore, government jobs programs for the unemployed and poor would be profitable. But private business is against this model because it would compete with them, lowering their profit margin.

To be sure, these white Republican voters as yet because of caste-like social relations maintain a socioeconomic advantage over blacks in un- and semi-skilled jobs. Thus it is that in the Deep South, for instance, 90 percent of whites vote Republican. Caste ideologies and racism prevails.

Thomas Frank's <u>What's the Matter With Kansas?</u> And others have examined this social phenomenon. But also these whites know that the capitalist elite cannot now be fought successfully: they are too strong, so they scapegoat the blacks to maintain their advantage in the jobs market.

Among college educated white voters, in 2008, the majority voted for the Democrat Obama, but in 2012 they tilted to Romney. Why? The Democrats offered Pell Grants to poor students but scant aid to largely middle-class whites. Also, the Republican mantra of lower taxes was appealing. Also of note, Republicans would privatize all public services – a literal nirvana for the wealthy.

Regarding religion and Republicans: Forty percent of their voters are white Fundamentalist Protestants, mainly racist working class Southerners wishing to protect their socioeconomic superiority over blacks. The Civil/Voting Rights Revolution in the 1960s turned most of these Democrats into Republicans, who supposedly follow the Bible by condemning abortions and gays, lesbians, all the while neglecting the teachings of the Hebrew prophets, including Jesus of Nazareth, to aid the poor and fight the injustices of the rich and powerful.

From a religious denomination perspective, 69 percent of white Protestants and the majority of white Catholics in the 2010 elections voted Republican. Another large Republican cohort is the Tea Party – 14 million strong, comprising small business owners, mostly self-employed, who in the 2012 elections elected many House Republicans. They oppose the Wall Street/large corporate combination favoring free trade and their special tax breaks, especially for hedge fund billionaires and Wall Street bankers causing the Great Recession, and what they consider to be generous social welfare to the poor. Many in this cohort are economically marginal, not reporting half their income to the IRS. As Republicans, they objectively aid the wealthy. The majority of whites vote Republican, 61 percent in 2012. Socioeconomically they are superior to blacks and Hispanics.

A poll of 2,400 respondents in 2013 on the 2012 elections by NBC/*Esquire* observed voting patterns of eight distinct political cohorts: two in the democratic left, two on the Republican right and four in the center. On the left: (1) 10 percent of "Bleeding Hearts," reformers, mostly white and well-educated, for social-welfare legislation, abortion, and gay rights, 96 percent voting for Obama in 2012; (2) 11 percent of fundamentalist Protestant blacks, against abortion and gay rights, but favoring more social welfare legislation – raising the minimum wage, paid sick and maternity leaves, and so on – 99 percent for Obama.

Their antithesis is the Republican right composed of two parts: (1) 14 percent, of mostly Southern white Protestant racist "God" Fundamentalists, against abortion and gay rights (their key issues), 87 percent for Romney; (2) the "talk radio heads," 14 percent, primarily older white racists, the Rush Limbaugh crowd, against gays, abortion ("God" issues), government welfare favoring Blacks and other minorities at the expense of employed white workers, thus splitting the working class vote. Also, they fetishize the gun as a protection against "big government," a silly notion: 99 percent Republican. These two groups are mostly "creationists," who interpret the Bible literally, as do many Southern blacks who vote for Democrats (37 percent of Americans are "creationists.").

The center of four cohorts, with 52 percent of the electorate, have views falling between left and right, but lean towards the Democrats (36 percent Democratic, 36 percent Independents, 28 percent Republican). Importantly, the center wishes higher taxes on the rich and polluters, which Democrats also favor.

With regard to voter participation, 75 percent of the top income quintile vote while only 25 percent of the bottom one percent do. Voter turnout in recent elections is near 60 percent – 62.3 percent in 2008, 57.5 percent in 2012, but 36 percent in 2014; in the last, Republicans extended their lead in the House, recaptured the Senate and won the majority of governorships.

To increase voting participation, procuring a driver's license results in automatic voter registration for citizens: Oregon and California, as of now, have it; Republicans oppose it because more voters results in fewer Republican electoral victories.

A decided Republican advantage over Democrats in voting is the persistence of the Protestant Calvinistic frontier/capitalist ethic which views the poor and those on welfare as morally deficient, in contrast to the virtuous employed (economically viable whites, but falling to the margins as of late).

This mindset is reflected in a recent poll of Republicans, Independents, and Democrats of "Why Are People Rich or Poor?" (1) Rich work harder: Republicans, 57 percent; Independents, 37 percent; Democrats, 27 percent. (2) Circumstance beyond an individual's control: Republicans, 32 percent; Independents, 51 percent; Democrats, 63 percent. (3) Socioeconomic differences involved: Republicans, 32 percent; Independents, 51 percent; Democrats, 63 percent. This poll indicates that the Calvinist/Capitalist mindset is stronger with Republicans, weaker with Independents and Democrats.

Related to frontier Calvinism is the fact that three-quarters of conservatives according to a recent Pew Research Center poll, believe that the welfare poor have an easy time of it.

This conservatism and low-voter turnout in non-presidential elections have allowed Republicans in 2015-16 to control both the governorships and legislatures in more than 20 states, including every Senate and governorship seat in the Deep South.

I add that if Americans voted at the same rates as most Europeans, the political climate would be further to the left because of large Democratic majorities among poorer voters.

Voting restrictions/low voter turnout is a national disgrace, the U.S. ranking 138 out of 172 worldwide democracies. The Republican Party is primarily responsible for this conditions, by discriminating against the infirm, poor, minorities and college students with restrictive voting impediments: 34 states have introduced official photo identification laws, 17 of proof of citizenship, 16 to limit registration periods, 9 to reduce early-voting time.

Gerrymandering, delineating electoral districts to favor a particular party, is also anti-democratic. In the 2014 general elections, Democrats, for instance, garnered 5 million more votes than Republicans, but the latter won more than a 40 seat majority in the House.

We now observe a state under Republicans – North Carolina – in 2013-16, in which they launched a savage class war against workers, women and the poor. They cut public education by $200 million, lowered taxes on the richest 5 percent, while raising them on the bottom 80 percent, refused to extend ACA Medicaid coverage to 500,000 poor, imposed strict voting identification, ended public financing for judicial races, eliminated state earned-income credit for 900,000, terminated federal unemployment benefits for 170,000 and imposed greater restrictions for abortions.

These severe cuts to education, social welfare, with lower taxes on the rich but higher sales taxes, reducing workers' income, were also enacted under Republicans in Kansas and Wisconsin, following the conservative theories of Laffer already observed in Chapter 5.

The Republican 5-4 majority on the Supreme Court has also

favored conservatism (At the time of this writing, Justice Antonin Scalia died in mid-February 2016, leaving Obama nearly a year to appoint another and setting off a fierce political debate). It has weakened the Voting Rights Act of 1965 that prohibited conservative/ White-dominated states from discriminating basically against blacks, now also Hispanics, relating to voter restrictions and gerrymandering electoral districts. They also in a series of 5-4 recent cases (<u>Ledbetter v. Goodyear Tire and Rubber</u>, <u>Walmart v. Duke</u>, <u>AT&T v. Conception</u> invariably favored large corporations regarding gender discrimination of women and class-action suits in consumer injury, and so on. In recent decisions, large corporations won 93 percent of them.[3]

The U.S. left: Its largest bloc is the left-wing of the Democratic Party, the 72 members of the House Congressional Progressive caucus who are in a social democratic mode. Their program: increase taxes on the wealthy/corporations, universal healthcare, paid sick and maternity leaves, free college tuition in public colleges, clean energy, pro-union card check, government jobs program/rebuild the infrastructure, end the Iraq and Afghanistan wars. The Progressive Democrats of America, a Democratic interest group, primarily activates this Democratic left. [4]

The Democratic Socialists of America platform envisions an expansive social welfare complex, including universal healthcare, paid sick/maternity leaves, state child care for working parents, lowering the workweek, free tuition from kindergarten to college, early retirement, and conversion to clean energy.

These reforms would be progressively enacted as the socialist public-sector gradually displaces capitalist socioeconomic and political hegemony over the working class. In this progression, participatory democracy at work/society increases. To be sure, small privately owned enterprise exists. Regarding taxes, until socialism arrives, they are steep on high income individuals/corporations.[5]

The program of the miniscule American Communist Party is very similar to the Socialist one. Its political activity is primarily directed to blue-collar workers and minorities.

The Green Party is a rather important social-democratic party which has elected many local and even state candidates and even does quite well in presidential races with Jill Stein in 2012, 2016. The Green platform emphasizes "grassroots democracy," i.e. "participatory democracy" of citizens in economic, political and social matters, and is for decentralization as much as possible: a concrete example would be cooperative local and state banks to obviate the credit control of large capitalist ones.

To be sure, Greens would also encourage a technology of miniaturization/computerization to allow various localities to cooperate regionally, nationally, and even internationally, in which there is a mixture of "socially responsible" privately-owned companies, worker-owned cooperatives, and public enterprises. This framework would encourage gender equality and respect for "cultural, ethnic, racial, sexual, religious and spiritual diversity."

To preserve humanity in the face of global warming, the Greens urge for a government crash program in clean energy (solar, wind, etc.) by 2030 and to rebuild a crumbling infrastructure generating 25 million jobs, part of a "living wage" proposal to grant a decent standard of life for all workers, including a job guarantee. Greens are for free public college tuition, end of military adventurism in Iraq and Afghanistan and military aid to anti-democratic governments. Also, Greens are for extensive social welfare, like universal healthcare and so forth and high taxes on the wealthy and large corporations.

Anarchism is to the left of socialists and Greens in that it does not believe that the plutocracy will democratically allow for a socialist-anarchist society.

Thus, anarchists are invariably revolutionary, envisioning that economic/ecological crises ultimately will compel the majority of the people to revolt, joined also by the police and military. According to anarchist-communism, society would be constructed on community ownership of the means of production and exchange, to be run through participatory democracy and the guiding principle of mutual aid to ensure a society of general economic, social, political, and cultural equality. Localism, of course, is encouraged as is technological miniaturization, the aim being to foster integrated labor, combining the manual and mental, ending mindless, boring stressful/alienating labor. To be sure, anarchist solidarity encompasses the extensive social welfarism of other socialists. Anarchists politically have local communes federate nationally in which decision-making involves participatory democracy in all major planning decisions. To be sure, anarchists support the importance of rapid conversion to clean energy, which is essential to preserve life. Let's add this about anarchism: voting at times is permissible, as in Spain during the 1930s Civil War between the Republic and Fascists; also, anarchists support specific reforms as reported by Jean Grave, a well-known French anarchist.

Anarchism, which has many active groups, has another important current, that of revolutionary syndicalism, which stresses worker-owned cooperatives working together in one big union. Like the anarchist-communists, they envision a society based on participatory democracy and mutual aid to override capitalist market principles.

Also of interest, the U.S. left opposes the American imperialism/ MIC complex and is for world peace.[6]

Despite the rule of capital in the U.S., about 35 percent of GDP is public/socialist. It includes the military sector (used as a cash cow by corporations), which consumes half the federal budget; the semi-public U.S. Postal Service; most K-12 schools and colleges. The Tennessee Valley Authority (TVA), a public corporation with $11 billion in sales revenues, 11,000 employees, and nine million customers furnishing electricity. A fourth of electricity output is owned by government; there are many municipally-owned waterworks; a fifth of hospitals are publically owned; there are 5,000 neighborhood corporations; North Dakota has a successful state-owned bank. The Alaska Permanent Fund established in 1976 by a Republican governor collects royalties from oil companies distributed to citizens. Texas has a permanent School Fund financed by land and mineral rights in the public domain; in 2014 it gave $838.7 million to public schools. Texas' Permanent University fund owns more than two million acres of land, proceeds of which support state universities. Wyoming has a mineral trust fund of more than $7 billion replenishing its budget. Also approximately 450 communities have built partial or full Internet systems. Overall,

10 percent of the workforce outside government is in non-profit cooperatively owned enterprises. Consumer-owned credit unions have 130 million members with assets of $1 trillion. Social Security and Medicare are publically-owned corporations with huge assets. Also factor in public welfare agencies like Medicaid, HUD and so forth, as already examined.

Regarding economic efficiency, Gar Alperovitz and Thomas A. Hannah, referring to a recent study in The Harvard International Review, assert that public enterprises are as efficient as privately-owned ones. My example – Medicare administrative costs are 2.2 percent, capitalist healthcare corporations at 25 percent on average, but after the ACA, costs fell to the 15 percent range. Also, the cost to administer Social Security is in the 1-2 percent range, much less expensive than private insurance plans whose expenses in high CEO pay and so forth are in the 20 percent range.

Also of importance regarding public enterprises which produce profit: they negate depending on taxes to raise public revenue. This feature of socialism was commented by Joseph Schumpeter, a well-known conservative 20th-century economist.[7]

A troubling development: the K-12 public schools are now under assault by large capitalist foundations (of Bill and Melinda Gates and Michael and Susan Dell, both of whom made their fortunes in computers). Republicans and Democrats like President Obama who wish to privatize many of them into Charter Schools, most of which are for-profit. Their excuse for this is to improve student achievement (test scores), scapegoating teachers for this. To be sure, some teachers are incompetent. Their ultimate aim? Destroy public education and teachers' unions for private profit.[8]

Probable socialist constituencies, many economically marginalized: 1) African Americans enduring a caste-like existence; (2) Hispanics, many of whom are poor undocumented workers; (3) the poor and disabled (4) many unionized blue-and white collar workers; (5) divorced working- class women homemakers thrown late into the job market, and divorced working-class men with heavy child payments (half of first marriages end in divorce, 75 percent of second marriages end); women are generally the low paid workers; (6) other low-wage workers; (7) nurses and K-12 teachers, mostly women and underpaid, thus highly politicized; (8) a sizeable element of the intelligentsia and artists, highly politicized; (9) the youth in general, mired in low-wage jobs and heavily indebted if attending college; (10) capitalist patriarchy and its ills to women should also induce women towards socialism, related to (5) and (7).

Thus it is that in a Wall Street Journal/NBC poll in August 2014, 76 percent of respondents age 18 and older believed that the next generation would be worse off than they are and 71 percent opined that the nation was on "the wrong track." In the long run, the left should benefit politically from this state of economic affairs, and by much lower upward social mobility.

The economic malaise, especially the advent of the Great Recession, has led to increasing class-conflict. In the Pew Center's two polls of 2009 and 2011 question of if there are "strong conflicts between rich and poor." In the former, the affirmative overall, 47percent; 18-34 age group, 57 percent; among Democrats, 55 percent; among Republicans, 37 percent. In the latter, overall, 66 percent; 18 -34 age group, 71 percent; among Democrats, 73 percent; among. Republicans, 55 percent.

Also, a 2011 Pew Center poll in the 18-29 age group found 49 percent favoring Socialism; African Americans, 55 percent; Latinos 44 percent. Also two Rasmussen polls saw American youth equally divided on the merits of capitalism and socialism.

Youth disenchantment is also observed in a June 26, 2014 Pew Research center survey's question of U.S. "stands above all other countries," where in the 18-29 age group only 15 percent said yes. Discontent was also amply manifested in a December 4-7, 2014 New York Times Poll in which 45 percent claimed that the U.S. economy was unfair. An October 2015 Your Gov.poll found that Democrats favored socialism over capitalism by a 47 to 37 percent margin (The Nation, Jan.4, 2016, p.18).[9]

To be sure, the recent movement launched mainly by youth, many being college students, with their cry "We are the 99 percent" indicated a deep revulsion against a predatory capitalism which is increasingly impoverishing workers. This one hundred city movement, which resonated deeply into the national consciousness, had many tens of thousands participants, one of which was estimated at 350,000 (*Z*, Feb 27, 2016).

This author was privileged to interview one of its participants in Cleveland, Ohio, an electrician who felt appalled by being exploited by capital via his bosses. His alternative: to live in a socialist society in which workers are in command – a socialism which is neither the state capitalism embodied by the Communist Party of the Soviet Union, nor the Capitalism embraced by the Chinese Communist Party. Instead, it is one of worker-controlled cooperatives working together in a spirit of general socio-economic equality.

To be sure, as already observed, the left has to contend with capitalist socio-economic and political hegemony in a society riven by class and status divisions which normally favor the status quo. Also as already observed, blacks and undocumented Hispanics are locked into caste-like positions relative to whites, including their workers, fearful of job competition from them. Thus for instance, the majority of white blue-collar workers vote Republican. In the preceding scenario for blacks, there is the legacy of slavery and Jim Crow.

As a Socialist, I accuse the plutocratic oligarchy of the following: misdeeds and waste. An addition to the chapter on Taxes, is the waste perpetuated by the military-industrial complex of having 47,000 troops in Japan, 38,000 in Germany, 28,000 in South Korea, and 12,000 in Italy. The annual cost of overseas bases: $250 billion. The Cold War with the Soviet Union ended when Gorbachev withdrew Soviet troops from Eastern Europe. China itself is also not a military threat; it is a relatively poor nation, with one small aircraft carrier. In fact, China is closely related to the U.S. through trade and capital investment.

This military industrial complex is intimately related to a pervasive nationalist jingoism in which military service is a form of social-welfarism, including medical care and free education once in civilian life, which comes at a steep price if wounded or killed in war combat. To be sure, this induces many poor working class youth to join. Thus personal economic security, including upward social mobility is tied to military services aiding conservatism.

Tragically, the 65 million beneficiaries of Social Security from 2001 to 2015 have lost almost a fourth of their real benefits to price inflation: About half of these retirees rely on them for half their income, a quarter for at least 90 percent of it and half have an annual income of less than $28,000. Also, Seniors on Part B Medicare but not on Social Security (17 million), will in 2016 pay much more in health care premiums.

The wasteful healthcare system should include hospitals as dangerous places for patients. A 2001 report in Health affairs had medical errors and negligence causing approximately 450,000 annual deaths and many hundreds of thousands more of serious injury.

The high cost of healthcare for those age 65 and older is a national disgrace. For instance, a typical 65-year-old couple in 2015 will spend $245,000 on healthcare, not including dental or long term care. This includes their being on Medicare with parts B and D. This $245,000 is 11 percent higher than in 2014, although general inflation is under 2 percent annually in the same period. Also healthcare costs for people age 60-65, is greater than the net worth of 44 percent of women and 41 percent of men. These statistics were compiled by Scott Burns, a well-known financial analyst. His concluding remarks: "People live in fear of healthcare. It's time for change. Big change. My solution: universal healthcare."

I accuse drug companies view of charging outrageous drug prices that have nothing to do with the cost of research and development. To be sure, there are no federal laws to prevent the gouging. Examples per pill of recent drug price increases: Albuterol Sulfate (asthma treatment) from 11cents to $4.34, up 4,014 percent; digoxin from 11 cents to $1.10 up 884 percent; a drug to slow down lung cancer, $300,000 annually. Ten recently approved cancer drugs cost $190,000 annually. Daraprim, a drug treating parasite infections, increased from $13.50 a pill to $750.00. Even with discounts and insurance coverage, 20 percent of patients report not filling prescriptions due to financial reasons.

The rape of patients should be corrected by Universal Healthcare and Government ownership of all its aspects, hospitals, drug companies and so forth as in Britain.

Another current drug scandal in the U.S. includes a severe shortage of 150 medications requiring rationing: pain killers, anesthetic antibiotics, and cancer treatments. Why? Because drug companies are supposedly having problems manufacturing them and not making enough money in selling them. The federal government response: nothing to compel them to end the shortages. In this scenario, drug PACS /lobbyists and those in the /private corporate sector deem it so.

I accuse mainly the poverty and joblessness in black neighborhoods for their high gun death rate: black men are 15 times more likely than white men to die. Thus U.S. lives lost annually by guns – 33,000 – is more than automobile deaths. Annual gun deaths in selected developed nations recently per 100,000 people: U.S., 3; Switzerland (nearest to U.S.), 0.7; Canada, 0.5; Germany, 0.2; Britain and France less than 0.1. Two thirds of black children live in poor neighborhoods. Worse still is this tragic fact: 70 percent of black children raised in the middle fifth of income families will experience lower social mobility. What should be done to correct this socioeconomic tragedy? A massive federal government program to guarantee full employment and providing for part-time work for black and other youth. Two thirds of black children live in poor neighborhoods.

I accuse real estate agents of still perpetuating much segregated housing. A September 2015 report by the National Fair Housing Alliance indicates extensive steering of blacks, including affluent ones, to black neighborhoods despite Congress' outlawing housing discrimination almost 50 years ago. To be sure, this adversely affects a better education for back children and parents' wealth from rising house prices.

I mainly accuse Republicans for capitalist corporations running part of the prison system for profit with 6 percent of state and16 percent of federal prisoners; they lobby for tougher correction laws. The U.S. imprisons 2.3 million people (almost half are black), a quarter of the world's total; the system's annual cost is approximately $80 billion. Also, solitary prison confinement in the U.S. is widespread, often lasting for decades. This cruel punishment affects 80,000 inmates, and is seldom used elsewhere. Fortunately, some prison reform is now occurring, like early release for nonviolent crimes, including drug offenders, and less solitary confinement.

I accuse the tobacco industry of delaying to warn the public of the dangers of smoking cigarettes; of petroleum companies delaying to remove lead from gasoline; of paint companies delaying to remove lead from paint; of automobile companies failing to manufacture safer automobiles (Ralph Nader's Unsafe at Any Speed (1965) saved many lives). Nader also exposed the dangers of diseased meat, harmful chemicals, lack of workplace safety, and capitalist corporate influence in Congress. In Who Runs Congress? (1972), he also founded Public Citizen, an important public interest organization. Nader, along with I.F. Stone in his Weekly and Bill Moyers in his Journal at PBS are three outstanding American muckrakers after World War II to the present.

Furthermore, the capitalist elite has allowed corporate power to underfund federal regulatory agencies. For instance, the National Highway Traffic Administration (NHTA) claimed lacking information for many years to force General Motors to replace a defective ignition switch of 10 years standing, which cost less than a dollar. Consequently, 174 individuals have lost their lives by October 2015 with hundreds more injured. Ultimately the defective ignition switch was replaced. GM paid a $900 million fine and with settlements for deaths and injuries, the total cost came to about $5.5 billion. No GM employee was jailed.

Automobile recalls to correct problems by June 2014 were in the 20 million range. In May 2015, a massive recall of 34 million defective automobile air bags was announced; costly fines and law suit followed. Again in 2015, Volkswagen was caught purposely engineering software to evade emissions regulations on its automobiles. Its CEO resigned, costly law suits and fines to follow.

I accuse President Obama of promoting, with labor and environmental representatives excluded, the Trans Pacific Partnership, an agreement that will expand free trade in 12 Pacific bordered nations, including the U.S., Canada, Mexico and so forth) – China excluded. According to a Tufts University study, the TPP will result in 500,000 jobs lost, with labor income falling 1.3 percent and raised drug prices; it will gut banking and environmental regulations, which is a bonanza for big business. As of November 2015, it is opposed by Democratic presidential candidates, Bernie Sanders and Hillary Clinton, and most Democratic Congresspersons. For it to become accepted, Obama must rely on Republicans.

In following NAFTA and WTO, the TPP would allow TNCs to sue governments for safety regulations and impinge on profits. They could appeal for arbitration to an international trade court staffed by corporate lawyers for compensation. A case in point: The tobacco company Philip Morris is now suing Australia and Uruguay for compensation for their bold labelling of cigarettes as dangerous to health, resulting in falling sales.

I accuse House Republicans of passing legislation weakening oversight testing of medical devices by the Food and Drug Administration (FDA), including heart defibrillator, among others. I accuse Congress for not amending the 1872 mining law which allowed mining companies to purchase federal land cheaply without paying royalties and providing minimal environmental protection. According to the Environmental Protection Agency (EPA), drainage from mines has contaminated 40 percent of Western watersheds. There are 500,000 abandoned mines in the US, many emitting toxic material in the environment.

Another egregious proposal by Obama was to privatize TVA. It failed because of intense opposition, including that of Republican officeholders, because it would have raised electricity rates

It is axiomatic that government Keynesian intervention to correct economic downturns is widely practiced. But government activity to foster research and development is also an important element to spur technological innovation and economic progress, the thesis of a timely work by Marian Mazzucato, The Entrepreneurial State. This is the case because private enterprise is deficient in promoting basic R&D because it is very expensive and uncertain, with a long time horizon, thus lessening profit.

In nuclear energy, aviation, green technology, the internet, touch screens, batteries, pharmaceuticals, it is government, in the military (Defense Department), the Department of Energy, National Institutes of Health, and public universities which have taken the lead in their development, not the private capitalist sector which reaps the economic rewards with scarcely any compensation to government.

Some specific examples: The underlying research in Apple's technology of the iPod, iphone, and iPad was funded by the Defense Department. The NIH develops drugs given to pharmaceutical companies almost gratis, which then charge the public exorbitant prices for them. Thus it is that I accuse the plutocratic oligarchy of using government funds/innovations to enrich themselves. The government should at least have had part ownership in these capitalist corporations profiting from its contributions. Better yet, the socialist solution is government ownership of them.

To be sure, economic concentration in the U.S. and worldwide is great. In 2015, U.S. mergers and acquisition set a record, $4.7 trillion, surpassing the 2007 one of $4.3 trillion. In 2014, worldwide, the largest 2000 companies had revenue which accounted for about half of the world's GDP ($38.4 trillion), $2.9 trillion profits.

A prime example of economic concentration in U.S. industry today is in the consumer technology field where five corporations dominate: Amazon, Apple, Facebook, Google, and Microsoft. Uber in transportation is a new arrival but the big five dominate.

Furthermore, as already observed, American TNC's are responsible for investing in manufacturing and other investments abroad for cheap labor – China, Mexico, Vietnam and other nations – in the trillions of dollars resulting in the partial deindustrialization of the nation, and loss of millions of jobs and many billions of dollars in tax revenues. Foreign manufacturing investment in the U.S. is of a lesser extent than of the U.S. abroad.

In 2014 alone, S&P 500 corporate stock buybacks to increase their stock value totaled $1 trillion, especially enriching their CEOs, most of whose compensation is related to stock options value. Only 2 percent of the $1 trillion was devoted to R&D; more capitalist greed injuring the general economy. Instead of buybacks increase workers' wages. Completing the triad of increasing socioeconomic inequality is the salient fact that half of government and corporate leaders graduate from 12 elite Ivy League schools, Stanford and so forth.

It is welcome news that a few corporate big wigs will now be jailed. In September 2015, Stewart Parnell, former owner of the Peanut Corporation, was sentenced to 28 years in prison for knowingly shipping salmonella-contaminated peanut butter; it led to nine deaths and hundreds of serious illnesses. Also, in December 2015 Don Blankenship, former CEO of Massey Energy was found guilty for conspiring to violate mine laws concerning the 2009 Upper Big Branch mine collapse in West Virginia that killed 29 miners. He faces a year in prison, but not for the death of the miners.

I accuse the plutocratic oligarchy of continuing inversions which will result in $20 billion in tax losses in the next decade. Democratic presidential candidates, Hillary Clinton and Bernie Sanders, oppose these inversions.

I accuse the Republicans of following the dictates of Wall Street bankers, corporate CEOs of large insurance and healthcare companies to privatize the $5.7 trillion home loan market dominated by Fannie Mae and Freddie Mac. This significantly increases consumer costs for services in the many hundreds of billions of dollars annually, thus correspondingly increasing capitalist corporate profits by many tens of billions of dollars. Another addition to the Tax Chapter 2012 indicates the low federal taxes paid by the richest 400 billionaires: 26.4 percent in 2015; 16.7 percent in 2012; 20.9 percent in 2013 (the latest). Their armies of tax lawyers and congressional lobbyists keep their taxes low. For comparison: An average family earning $100,000 annually pays 17 percent in federal taxes.

To add to the fraud involved in the Great Recession already

observed: In July 2016, Goldman Sachs will pay a $5 billion civil settlement for selling faulty mortgage securities to investors.

Food safety in the U.S. is lax. In April 2015, for instance, the FDA proposed that meat and poultry producers stop excessive use of antibiotics to control and prevent disease, voluntary for three years. Why so long? Industry muscle by PACS/Lobbyists. Also in 2015, the FDA will ban trans-fats in three years, which are in many processed foods to extend shelf life; these fats cause coronary heart disease. But it will allow the food industry to petition retaining them! Why wait so long? Guess. Healthcare costs and other savings from this reform: $7 billion annually.

Annually, two million Americans become ill by eating infected animal food that often cannot be successfully treated with antibiotics, resulting in 23,000 deaths, $20 billion in medical costs, and 35 billion in lost productivity. Of course, the food corporate PACS/Lobbyists cry "big government" to ending their use. Furthermore, the 8,600 meat inspectors of the U.S. Department of Agriculture (USDA) are understaffed in inspecting 6,300 packing/processing plants. Of course if more meat inspectors were employed, the Republicans would again scream "big government."

In the 2002-07 period there were 47.8 million annual food poisonings on average (a sixth of the population), with 128,000 hospitalizations and 3,037 deaths, 70 percent originating in the kitchen, related to harmful germ – infested food. In addition, 5.5 million Americans are infected by a Norovirus, a gastrointestinal germ, primarily spread by workers in the food industry by cooks and waiters in restaurants. Then, there is the salmonella germ from processing poultry, cattle, pigs, which annually results in one million becoming ill and upward of 350 deaths, costing $3 3 billion.

To correct food illness, there should be federal legislation to protect workers in all phases of food processing and delivery, i.e. slower food processing assembly lines, to protect whistle blowers and provide sick leave to all workers in the food chain. After the 2014 elections, for instance, only 3 states and 16 cities provided sick leave for restaurant workers, poorly paid and non – unionized, who invariably work if ill, often fired if absent from work. Of course, any reforms in these areas are opposed by the Republican mantra of "big government".

Regarding genetically modified organisms (GMOs) in food which employ dangerous herbicides like Monsanto's glysophate in growing corn and soy, the FDA has still allowed their use. The European Union, Russia and China, among other nations, prohibit growing GMO foods. Many Republican complaints against "big government" are directed at the EPA which aims to reduce fossil fuel emissions and regulate chemicals to improve human health. In these endeavors, corporate profits may be slightly reduced. Republican controlled congress in 2011 – 16 have slashed the EPA budget by 30 percent. There are 80,000 chemicals used in consumer products, many injurious to human health, like carcinogens. The EPA annually tests from 5 to 20, but California 100. Europe and Canada have prohibited hundreds of toxic chemicals used in the US with its lax standards. The chemical industry in 2012 – 14, spent $190 million lobbying Congress; their money was well spent in fighting "big government".

To protect the public against shoddy goods, the Sunshine in Litigation Act proposed in 2014 would prevent secret court agreements between injured parties and corporations and allow federal consumer protection to act more swiftly to protect the public. Other public protection laws should increase corporate liabilities for defective consumer products. Federal regulatory agencies (SEC, FCC, EPA, FDA etc.) are weakened by appointing their top officers from corporations which they regulate. Well paid civil servants should staff these agencies. Two examples of this revolving door: After leaving Citigroup, Jack Lew and Stanley Fischer received million dollar exit packages, the former becoming Treasury Dept. Secretary; the latter Vice Chair of the Federal Reserve.

A disturbing recent development: white Americans, with high school education or less, died at a 22 percent higher death rate in the1999-2013 period than previously. This cohort from poor families, performing un- and semi-skilled labor saw real income drop 19 percent during this period; free trade, rapid technological change are contributing factors. To cope with economic disaster, like low wages and high unemployment, they use legal tobacco and alcohol and illegal (heroin, etc.) drugs in excess, leading to lung and liver diseases. Suicide rates are significantly higher. The economic outlook for these poor whites and blacks (their death rate is higher than that of whites) is grim because of the political power of America's plutocratic oligarchy is to stifle reform.

The general weakness of the U.S. labor-left compared to the Western European one is vividly catalogued in the South Progress Index, authorized by Michael E. Porter, a Harvard business school professor (a Republican) and a team of collaborators, in a two–year study of 132 nations measuring "livability," or quality of life. This Index measured progress in education, healthcare, ecology, access to water and sanitation, freedoms like speech, press, religion, personal safety, women's rights, vacations, maternity leave, and so forth. It placed the U.S. at no. 10, behind European social democracies as Switzerland, Norway, Sweden, Denmark, Finland, Germany, France, and Britain. Specifically, for instance, no. 39 in basic education, 70 in health, 69 in ecology, and 31 in personal safety.

A final tragedy: According to HUD, there are 564,708 homeless people in the U.S. in 2015. Many of these people work infrequently at low wage jobs and cannot afford to rent, many with severe psychological problems, many without family support. They include those living in shelters, transitional quarters, cars, streets, and so forth. That they are not adequately supported is a national disgrace.

To summarize: Capitalist fraud and socioeconomic and political inequality led to the Great Recession, to great riches for the few and great poverty and higher death rates for the poor, meager social welfare, lower upward social mobility, wasteful imperialistic adventures, high federal budget deficits owed to the U.S. rich and foreign governments, a wasteful non-comprehensive welfare system.[10]

The political system is dominated by a wealthy oligarchy. Unsatisfactory response to global warming is discussed later. The waste/dysfunction sketched of American Capitalism are of a selective nature, by no means exhaustive. To understand this claim, follow the path of the Communist Karl Marx in <u>Capital I</u>, of the socialist Thorstein Veblen in <u>The Theory of the Leisure Class,</u> and of the Communist Anarchist Jean Grave in The <u>Dying Society and Anarchy.</u>

Chapter 9: American Labor's Historical Odyssey

In examining the struggle of American labor against capital, I note the importance of "race"/ethnicity/religion in impeding its unity, as related to successive immigrant waves and slavery.

To begin, as a British Colony, America in the late 18th century had a large African-American slave population, up to a third of it, freed as a result of the Civil War, but also enduring Jim Crow in the South and severe discrimination in the North. This rigid racial division among blacks and whites continues to this day.

The overwhelming majority of immigrants to America were poor Europeans who became part of the working class, including farmers. In this mixture, earlier Protestant immigrants from northwestern Europe (English, Germany, Scots, Scots-Irish, and Welsh) were higher on the status class scale than largely latter Catholic arrivals from eastern and southern Europe who also included Eastern Orthodox and Jews, the last being the most educated and wealthiest of Americans today. The Catholic Irish who came in the 1840s were the first large Catholic contingent.

Principally, the 1965 Immigration Act and later others considerably liberalized immigration because now there are many Arab Moslem, Taiwanese, Indian and Hispanics, among others, in America. In this mélange are many undocumented workers among them; Hispanics number a sixth of the population today.

Europeans now constitute 70 percent of the American people, the most numerous being Italians, Germans, English, and Irish.

Generally, immigration tended to divide the white immigrant groups from the poorer blacks and Hispanics, thus the importance of "racial" divisions as an important factor in dividing the working class and impeding social reform and socialist consciousness.

Despite the preceding difficulties, American unions and socialism in its various manifestations have played an important role in American history, which this chapter recounts.

America has always had a large working class – invariably poor and much of it, in the early stages being African American slaves in the South. Alongside them were free farmers and workers in the north laboring in small farms/enterprises, as in breweries, shipyards, candle works, construction, and so forth. To be sure, large enterprise first existed in the South in large slave plantations, but then also sprang up in the North in the textile industry by the 1820s-1830s.

The following unions and their strike actions greatly involved American workers in bitter class warfare – the world's most violent – in the 19th and 20th centuries.

The first significant strike waged by U.S. workers was by the "Yankee Girls" in the textile mills of Lowell, MA. in 1834 over wage cuts. It lasted a day and was unsuccessful. In the mid-1830s, workers in various northeastern cities founded the National Trades Union, composed of journeyman, carpenters, printers, tailors, weavers, plasterers, and so forth. With 300,000 members between 1834 and 1836, it conducted 168 strikes for higher wages and less hours of work, many successful. The Panic of 1837 and following depression with high unemployment destroyed it.

With the rise of rapid industrialization begun by the Civil War in the 1860s, a large urban working class appeared, igniting union activity/strikes.

In 1866, craft workers in the north established the National Labor Union, which by the early 1870s had 300,000 members. It fought for the 8-hour work day, higher wages, workers' cooperatives, and women's rights. The 1873 depression terminated it. The Knights of Labor, founded in 1869, grew rapidly under Terence V. Powderly's leadership in 1879. It was composed of skilled and unskilled workers, welcomed African-Americans and women, was involved in political activity, fought for the 8-hour-day, favored worker-owned cooperatives, and engaged in strikes. Peak membership reached 700,000 in 1886, spurred by the 1886 Haymarket Riot in Chicago whose leading labor spokespersons were anarchists. It expired in the 1890s because of failed strikes and working class divisions and racism.

The principal union, which has endured to the present, was the

American Federation of Labor (AFL), founded in 1886 and led for many years by Samuel Gompers. It was composed of skilled craft workers in separate unions, somewhat similar to medieval guilds, with long apprenticeships, allowing workers to control their numbers and pace of work, leading to good wages. In this progression, workers had considerable power in the production process. This union favored strikes for higher wages, less hours of work and job safety. It also accepted capitalism. By 1904, it had 2 million members, three-fourths of union members.

The Western Federation of Minders founded in 1892 was involved in many violent strikes, about half of which were successful; it was later destroyed by the mine owners and their lackey's in law enforcement.

The American Railway Union (ARU, now the United Transportation Union) was founded in the early 1890s by Eugene V. Debs, an outstanding socialist. This militant union was engaged in many strikes, notably the Pullman one of 1894, defeated by federal troops.

The United Mine Workers of America (UMWA), also founded in the early 1890s, was a militant miners' union conducting many successful strikes. It was composed of white and black workers, with blacks prominent in a leadership role.

The International Ladies Garment Workers Union (ILGWU), founded in 1900, was basically composed of immigrant women garment workers, mostly Jewish and Italian, centered in the garment sweatshops of New York City. This was a militant union, involved in many strikes for higher wages and better working conditions. Its leadership was socialist.

The Industrial Workers of the World (IWW), founded in 1905, included in its leadership "Big Bill" Haywood and Mary Harris Jones, also known as "Mother Jones" – Mother Jones magazine named after her. This was a revolutionary anarcho-syndicalist union opposed to capitalism, favoring a cooperative worker-controlled society of one big union. Its members were unskilled workers, like miners, farm and textile workers. In 1912-13, it led notable strikes in

Akron, Ohio, Lawrence, MA, and Patterson, NJ. Employers and their police stooges destroyed it, but it has recently resurfaced in many college and other chapters.

The Congress of Industrial Organizations (CIO), founded in 1936, represented un- and semi-skilled workers in mass industries like auto, steel and rubber on an industrywide basis. It is a major union today.

The Molly Maguire's, a clandestine organization of Irish immigrant workers of coal miners in eastern Pennsylvania in the 1860s and 70s, killed scores of company men before the forces of order crushed it, hanging 10 and jailing 14 of its members.

We now proceed to describe important strikes.

In 1877, railroad workers staged a nationwide strike against railroad companies when wages were reduced. Pitched battles occurred between workers and federal troops in which more than a hundred were killed and much railroad property was destroyed. This failed strike was the most violent in U.S. labor history.

On May 3 and 4, 1886, in Chicago, in the Haymarket Riot, striking workers, many of whom were anarchists, fought police; approximately 30 were killed, including seven police. Eight anarchist spokespersons were tried for the police deaths without any proof; four were hanged, one committed suicide, and the remaining were pardoned by Illinois Governor Peter Altgeld.

To be sure, anarchism had many workers' adherents in the late 19th and early 20th centuries, among Russian, Jewish and Italian immigrants.

The 1892 Homestead Steel Strike (near Pittsburgh) by the Amalgamated Association of Iron, Steel, and Tin Workers was precipitated by wage cuts, lockouts, and "scab" replacements. Armed workers defeated 300 armed Pinkertons (a private army of capitalist thugs). Then, the PA governor sent 8,000 federal troops who crushed the union, killing several workers.

The 1894 strike by American Railway Union against the Pullman Palace Car Company, in what is now Chicago, was precipitated by sharp wage cuts, speedups, layoffs of workers laboring in a company town in the midst of depression. The Pullman Company and other railway companies pitted private strikebreakers and federal troops against the strikers who fought back, scores of workers killed and much railroad property destroyed. The workers and ARU were crushed. Debs was jailed and became a socialist after reading Marx.

In 1911, the Triangle Shirtwaist Company fire in New York City killed 146 young immigrant workers, mostly Jewish and Italian. This industrial tragedy highlighted the commonplace and horrific working conditions in which workers labored during the 19th and well into the 20th centuries. It spurred reform to ameliorate working conditions.

In fact, even today, working conditions for workers in construction and other industries are horrendous. In the pitched battles between workers and capitalists, there occurred the Ludlow Massacre in Colorado, where in bitter fighting, the state militia set fire and machine-gunned workers' tents, killing 14 – 13 of whom were children and a woman on Easter 1914.

After World War I, 1919-20, a series of 4,000 strikes erupted across the nation by 4 million workers to catch up with the war's price inflation. Notable strikes included the Seattle General Strike of 1919, started by 35,000 shipyard workers who shut down the city. It ultimately failed.

The U.S. Steel and Bethlehem Steel Strikes of 1919-20 involved almost 400,000 workers who worked 69 hours a week at low wages. Capitalist owners brought in strikebreakers and employed police and soldiers to prevent syndicalist William Z. Foster (he later led the American Communist Party) to organize a steel workers' union. In early 1920s, the strike was crushed with 18 strikers killed.

The 1919 Boston Police Strike also failed. But during that same year, the 400,000 coal miners of the UMWA were successful in their strike, receiving a substantial wage increase. The capitalist press blamed Communists for these strikes.

The Great Depression of the 1930s witnessed increased labor militancy and a labor-friendly president in Democratic President Franklin Delano Roosevelt (FDR) and his New Deal.

Parenthetically, unionism occurred at first in a largely rural

America in which farmers, many of whom were tenants and share croppers, were 50 percent of the workforce in 1880, 40 percent in 1900, 22 percent in 1930s, and now under 2 percent. The rural exodus of poor farmers and immigration helped to depress wages and made union organizing more difficult.

Strike activity was aided by the Norris-La Guardia Anti-Injunction Act of 1932, which prohibited court injunctions to prevent strikers from picketing unless employers could prove union violence and a reasonable effort to negotiate a settlement. This act negated an 1895 Supreme Court decision allowing judges to employ injunctions against strike activity as "a conspiracy in restraint of trade." This phrase in the Sherman Anti-Trust Act of 1890 was mainly employed against labor, not corporations. Although the Clayton Act of 1914 exempted labor from this phrase, declaring it not a commodity, the conservative courts continued to follow their interpretation of the Sherman Act until the early 1930s. Furthermore, Norris-La Guardia struck down yellow-dog contracts, approved earlier, which forced workers when hired to pledge that they would not join unions.

The green light for mass union organizing was the National Labor Relations Act (NLRA), (Wagner Act) of 1935, allowing labor to engage in collective bargaining with capital after gaining a plant majority. Also, a company could not hire anti-union workers by establishing the "closed shop," workers initially to be hired by unions; made it illegal for companies to dismiss workers fighting for collective bargaining. But penalties for employers to fire union organizers were weak, allowing for many appeals and if found guilty, paying only small penalties, thus often hampering unionization. It prohibited financing of company unions or use of company spies to report on union activity and outlawed blacklisting, of not hiring militant workers who had been fired by employers. It also established the National Labor Relations (NLRB) Board, to investigate complaints by workers against employers.

With the rise of the CIO, mass unionism and strike activity in the 1930s became widespread. It was led by John L. Lewis (UMW), the socialist David Dubinsky (LGWA), socialist Sidney Hillman of the

Amalgamated Clothing Workers, and Philip Murray of the United Steel Workers (USW).

Let it be said that the AFL labor aristocrats of craft workers were not too interested in organizing the CIOs un/semiskilled workers – an example of status divisions weakening labor unity.

Sit down (plant occupations) strikes in the 1930s were labor's most effective weapon against capital. They basically began in Akron, Ohio, spreading to Cleveland, Toledo, Flint, Minneapolis, Atlanta, and San Francisco. They were initiated by the United Rubber Workers (URW) in Akron, rapidly unionizing Goodyear, Firestone, and other rubber companies there. Then these strikes spread to General Motors plants in Cleveland, Flint and other cities, led by the United Auto Workers (UAW) which rapidly unionized General Motors and Chrysler, Ford in 1941. In steel, the USW quickly won at U.S. Steel; "Little Steel," Bethlehem, Republic and Youngstown Steel and Tube were unionized in 1941. Communists were important in much of union organizing in basic industries.

The 1930s also tragically witnessed the Memorial Day Massacre in 1937 in Chicago when 10 peaceful union pickets were killed by police who without any provocation shot at a crowd of workers and their families. Workers made further gains with the enactment of The Fair Labor Standards Act (FLSA) of 1938 which established a minimum wage in industry, including the few women working there. It outlawed child labor (under age sixteen), and mandated a 44-hour week as the norm in industry; amendments to it in 1941 decreed the 8-hour day, 5-day week, with overtime pay after that for industry, not covering agricultural, domestic, and maritime workers insisted by Southern racists. For the sake of comparison, industrial workers in 1900 generally labored a 10-hour and 6-day week.

To obviate the FLSA, capital shifted many employees' jobs to administrative/professional categories of salaried workers, allowing for their greater economic exploitation by not having to pay for overtime work and a minimum wage. Also, workers could be hired as independent contractors, who scarcely had any rights at work. Furthermore, college graduates often had internships with a company before permanent employment, not bound by minimum wage/ maximum hour laws. These gaps to the FLSA should be remedied.

World War II, with very low unemployment, spurred unionism: percentage of the workforce when unions were strong; in 1945, 37 percent; 1950, 25 percent; 1960, 26 percent; 1970, 23 percent; 1980; 23 percent. Then in dipped to 16 percent in 1990 and progressively became less to the present. The heyday of American labor was in the 1940-80 period when real wages during the 1940-60 period in industry increased by a third.

After World War II, 1945-46, there was another post-war strike wave (in 1942-45, wages rose 15 percent, prices 45 percent), of 8 million workers, resulting in large wage increases.

The Taft-Hartley Act of 1947, passed by a Republican Congress over President Harry Truman's veto, weakened labor considerably. Its following provisions included the abolishment of the closed shop, but allowed union shop union plant majority representing all workers in collective bargaining. It also permitted the U.S. president to call an 80-day cooling off period if a strike affected national security; forbade unions to contribute to political campaigns; granted employers the right to influence workers to not join a union; outlawed secondary boycotts and mass picketing during a strike (the secondary boycott allowed strikers to be joined by other workers, striking in other companies to support them). It also weakened union democracy by requiring union officials to take an oath that they were not Communists; and restored court injunctions against unfair labor practices like wildcat (or spontaneous) strikes to reinforce grievances.

An example of a favorable union contract negotiated in the 1950s when unions were still strong: in 1955, the UAW forced General Motors to continue a 1950 contract for a cost-of-living annual wage increase, now reinforced by a guaranteed annual wage.

Another example of union power in the 1950s was the UAW strike against the Kohler Company manufacturing plumbing fixtures in Wisconsin. It lasted from 1954 to 1961, this despite company use of scab strikebreakers. The strike succeeded because of UAW Aid to the strikers and a culture of strong union solidarity.

The rise of conservatism, with the advent of the Reagan presidency in 1981 was inimical to labor. He crushed the 1981 strike of the Professional Air Traffic Controllers Organization (PATCO) by decertifying this union of government workers and dismissing the strikers. Reagan's action against this strike was warning to government workers. Ironically, PATCO supported Reagan in the 1980 elections.[1]

Union workers since the early 1980s experienced steep job losses and lower wages because of the following reasons: (1) Taft-Hartley, which weakened unions; (2) government deregulation of railroads, trucking, airlines, energy and communications, leading to more competition and fewer jobs; (3) plants moving to the non-union/lower wage South; (4) WTO and NAFTA free trade allowing plants to go to low wage nations like Mexico and China; (5) technological changes including computerization, automation, robotics, leading to great job losses; (6) foreign competition: by 1980 Japanese carmakers had a quarter of the domestic market, since then joined by South Korean, German and others. Up to 2015, foreign car plants in the U.S. have not been unionized; (7) shift from an industrial to a service economy now employing 80 percent of the workforce (service workers are difficult to organize because may are situated in small and scattered work sites, as in the fast food industry).

As a result of these developments, an average male worker in real wages earned $33,880 in 1968, $32,986 in 2011. Since the successful capital offensive against labor of the 1980s, workers have been more exploited with a two-tiered labor market (new hires with lower wages than others) and with an increasing amount of part-time and temporary workers with scant or no benefits. These cohorts now number approximately 50 million or about a third of the workforce, whose wages are approximately up to a half lower than comparable full-time workers.

Unions are also needed more so than ever to ensure safe working conditions. In 2010, for instance, 4,547 workers were killed and 60,000 were injured on the job. To spur unionism, card check would be most helpful. It would allow union organizers outside a work site to persuade workers to join a union without capital's awareness, and then, with a majority, ask the NLRB to conduct an election. Also, legislation should be passed to disallow strike breakers (scabs) to work at striking plants.

Unions have been especially weakened by right-to-work laws (an Orwellian term used by corporate apologists) in half the states in which a certified union cannot force individual workers to pay full union dues and in some instances none at all, although receiving union benefits, like higher pay, protection from arbitrary firing, and so forth. A fifth or more of union members in these states do not pay full or no union dues. These laws aim to destroy unions, lower workers' wages and allow for arbitrary firings. The ultimate aim? A docile workforce.

The conditions already observed make workers' strikes more problematic. Another example: workers are warned by capital that a strike would lead to plan relocation – the South, Mexico, China, etc., or employment of "scabs."

One unlikely remedy, mostly due to present political circumstances, to protect union organizers is to extend the 1964 Civil Rights Act which prohibits discrimination based on race, sex, religion and national origin, to union organizers to spur unionization. Because of labor's weakness, strikes have dramatically decreased: for instance, 381 strikes were held in 1970; 39 in 2000; 5 in 2009. Indeed, strikes today involve a high probability of usually workers being replaced by scabs, who are typically unemployed or undocumented workers.

Traditionally, full-time union workers have higher annual wages/benefits than non-union ones: in 2012, in earnings, $49,000 for the former, $38,000 for the latter. Even so, union workers have been forced to accept wage/benefit cuts because of free-trade competition, automation and the Great Recession.[2]

From the 1980s to the present, because of the reasons enumerated, labor has been on the defensive. Here are examples: in 1983, shipyard workers in Groton, MA, lost a 15-month strike for higher wages/job protection, 43 percent of strikers losing their jobs. A 1984 strike by the UAW against General Motors resulted in lower cost-of-living and wage increases. In Austin, Minnesota, the Hormel packing house workers' union, the United Food and Commercial Workers waged a long strike in 1985-86, gaining wide labor support. But poor/ unemployed workers from this economically depressed area (scabs) replaced strikers and with the assistance of the state National Guard broke the strike.

The corporate assault on unions was best exemplified by Frank Lorenzo, the CEO of Continental Airlines. In 1983, he bankrupted the company to destroy union contracts, then offered workers new ones at half pay, precipitating a strike. He then hired scabs from the many unemployed pilots and machinists who lost their jobs in the recession of the early 1980s. The strikers lost.

Another significant strike occurred in the mid-1990s in Decatur, Illinois, by the Allied Industrial Workers Local 837. The workers, locked out by the company, fought for two and a half years, but lost because workers in the building crafts refused to join them.

In 2012, in Joliet, Illinois, the machinist union settled a long strike against Caterpillar ($4.8 billion profits in 2011) with major concessions: a six-year wage freeze, pension cuts, doubling of healthcare contributions.

A classic example of a corporation successfully extracting concessions in 2013-14 from labor and government in pursuit of higher profits is Boeing, a giant and profitable aerospace company in Seattle whose profits alone in 2012 were $3.9 billion. When it threatened to leave the state of Washington for South Carolina (a low-wage state), workers, fearful of losing their jobs, decided not to strike and were forced to surrender their defined pension plan for a volatile and less generous 401(K), as well as allow the company to outsource work to non-union plants; the state also capitulated with an $8.7 billion subsidy for the company.

Unions have been losing membership significantly, especially since 1980. In 1983, 17.7 million or 20.1 percent of workers were unionized; in 2013, 14.5 million, or 14.3 percent, 35.3 percent in the public sector, 6.7 percent in the private one, and about 7 million in each.

The relatively strong union presence in the public sector is because jobs there cannot be easily outsourced, but Republicans in many states are passing right-to-work laws to vitiate or end collective bargaining.

Let's add that federal public employee unionization was established by the Johnson Administration in the mid-1960s, a great boost to unionism, and then extended to various states by state laws.

In 2011-12, unionized public sector workers fought back against austerity wage cuts, benefits and attempts to end the union shop. In Wisconsin, these unions launched a recall of Republican governor Scott Walker who won in a subsequent election, but Republican control of state government led to a right-to-work law ending collective bargaining of teachers and other public employees.

In Ohio, John Kasich, the Republican governor, and his Republican cohorts in the legislature ended union collective bargaining for public sector workers. But the unions went to the ballot box with State Issue 5 and defeated the Republican law.

In 1995, the AFL and CIO merged, forming the AFL-CIO; in 2009, it had 8.4 million members. In 2005, the Teamsters and other unions left the AFL-CIO to form the Change to Win coalition which now has more than 6 million members. There are also unaffiliated unions.

The largest unions in 2013 in descending order in millions of members: The National Education Association (NEA), mostly of K-12 teachers, 3.2; the Service Employees International Union (SEIU), 2.1; American Federation of State County and Municipal Employees (AFSCME), 1.6; American Federation of Teachers (AFT), 1.5; International Brotherhood of Teamsters (IBT), 1.4; the United Food and Commercial Workers International Union (UFCWIU), 1.3. Other large unions in the thousands include: UAW, 400 (in 1979, it was 1.5 million); the American Postal Worker (APW), 330. Other unions with sizeable numbers include the International Association of Machinists (IAM); the American Association of University Professors (AAUP), and nurses' and pilots' unions.

The typical union worker today is more likely to be a teacher, nurse, office and service worker than a blue-collar one in auto, rubber, and steel, more of females than males.

Despite the anti-labor laws/court decisions, there was a flurry of strike activity in 2012, resulting in victories by the 25,000-strong Chicago Teachers Union, and port workers in Los Angeles and Long Beach.

In 2012-15, spontaneous one-day worker walkouts for higher wages/benefits in the low-paid, non-union fast food industry and Walmart have involved unions and progressive community groups cooperating with 200 workers' centers nationwide.

Two examples of this coordinated strike action in 2012 includes: On August 29, workers in 60 cities were involved; on December 5, strikes and protests were waged in 100 cities, mostly in larger ones – New York City, Chicago, Los Angeles, Detroit, Washington D.C., Minneapolis, and so on.

On May 15, 2014, again workers in 150 American cities joined others abroad in 80 cities in about 30 nations, staging one day strikes in the fast food industry, and aided by the SEIU, demanding $15 an hour wage. Again, on April 15, 2015, in the largest demonstration ever, tens of thousands of fast food and retail workers marched in over 200 cities in the U.S. and abroad, demanding $15 an hour wage plus union recognition to win sick leave, job protection and other rights. Again the SEIU was in the forefront in organizing.[3]

These strikes, walkouts, and initiatives among low-wage workers earning under $20,000 annually follow the Occupy Wall Street movement of late 2011 and early 2012 when tens of thousands of students, workers, and others, many unemployed, marched and established ad hoc camps in more than a hundred towns and cities.

Without unions, workers are exposed to many inequities. A case in point are the 5 million low wage and part time fast food and other restaurant workers who are forced to quit work when sales are slow, work split shifts or to be on-call to work anytime, changing weekly work schedules (two-fifths of workers in their twenties and early thirties know of their work schedules a week or less in advance). Other statistics from federal data have 66 percent of food servers,

52 percent of retail workers, and 40 percent of janitors and house cleaners having a week's notice of work schedules. In addition to low pay (minimum wage or just above), they have neither sick pay nor paid vacations.

Low pay and more years of education required to be employed have 45 percent of younger workers (2012) under age 30 living with older family members, usually parent(s). These poverty-stricken individuals are likely candidates of those over age 25 who will never marry: in 1962, 9 percent of blacks, 8 percent of whites; in 2012, 36 percent of blacks, 16 percent of whites. I add that men of primary ages to marry, 25 to 34, earn 20 percent less in 2015 than in 1980, adjusted for inflation; women age 65-plus, especially hit hard, 1 in 6 of whites, 1 in 3 of blacks, 1 in 2 of Hispanics live in poverty.

Many low paid fast food, retail, and other poor enough to qualify for Medicaid, food stamps, HUD assistance and so forth – federal aid to them mostly with some state assistance, ca. 2015 is $150 billion annually, $6.2 billion for Walmart employees alone. By contrast, fast food workers in social democratic Denmark earn $25 an hour and enjoy these nationwide benefits: universal healthcare, 4-5 weeks paid vacations, paid sick and maternity leaves, and free college tuition.

In 2015, the federal minimum wage is still $7.25 an hour, but Democrats are for $10.10 an hour, and Bernie Sanders, a Democratic primary candidate, has called for $15 an hour. In July, 2015, Krugman in The New York Times and other economists opined that raising the minimum wage would not lead to higher unemployment; in fact, an increase has positive results like lower worker job turnover rates, improved worker morale, in turn leading to higher productivity. Thus, government action can aid workers' economic lot.

Relative to government action aiding workers: A novel tactic by workers to redress workplace wrongs, falling short of unionizing, is to form workers' committees which are recognized by the NLRB. The success of one in Santa Fe, NM, forced an employer to compensate immigrant workers and to rehire them after firing them. This action will embolden 230 immigrant centers to undertake similar actions.

Relative to low wages and poverty, 51 percent of immigrants

(15 percent of the people in 2015) are on some government welfare, as opposed to 30 percent of natives; with children, it increases to 76 percent, as opposed to 52 percent for native-born. This is not surprising because most immigrants are poor and uneducated, comprising a large part of the lower-paid workforce.

The AFL-CIO is now also expanding its Working America Affiliate of 3 million members of sympathetic non-union workers in trying to organize daycare and homecare workers, and is allying itself with the NAACP, Hispanic organizations, and the ecological Sierra Club to increase union membership.

In a boost for fast food unionization, the NLRB in August 2015 ruled that the McDonald Corporation exercised sufficient control over its private-owner franchises to be sued for unfair labor practices, like firing union organizers. This ruling opens the way for unionizing the fast food industry.

To be sure, employers are well-armed against unionization, spending $2 billion annually in this effort. Although low wage workers now receive $65 billion annually in income tax credits, conservatives oppose the $15 an hour minimum wage and the income-tax credit but favor a $150 billion annual government subsidy to these workers. This scheme would be more favorable to businesses than to workers because it would result in partly lower workers' wages, thus increasing profits.[4]

To reduce workplace violations, like paying workers under minimum wage, extending daily/weekly work hours, neglecting safety regulations, and so forth, in July 2014, President Obama by executive order decreed that federal contracts ($81 billion in 2012) be denied to construction and other companies if their repeated workplace violations were not corrected by 2016. In 2007-12, 49 leading contractors were penalized 1,776 times for $196 million.

To be sure, the Associated Builders and Contractors (building trades hiring many undocumented workers and generally non-union) promised to fight the Obama executive order in courts and in Congress. In fact, if a Republican president is elected in 2016, the Obama order will most surely be rescinded. The lack of unions in construction and other work venues condemns their workers to a life that is short and brutal. In this vein, government workplace inspections to ensure safety are few and far between.[5]

Immigrant labor, especially the many undocumented Hispanic workers, presents a major problem for American unions because they have played a significant role as Scabs in destroying packinghouse workers' unions and many unions in construction like carpentry. With that said, I must state I do not blame undocumented Hispanic workers from coming to America from poor nations to live better lives.

A 1986 law under President Reagan and afterward providing stiff penalties for hiring undocumented workers was lifted, thereby ushering in significant tides of workers. In the autumn of 2014, Obama issued an executive order for 5 million undocumented workers (4 million residing in the U.S. for 5 years and 1 million "dreamers," who came to the U.S. when younger) that allowed them to gain legal status to remain in the U.S., to work and to enroll in Social Security; however, they did not acquire government healthcare benefits (though hospital emergency rooms will admit them, to significant cost). Republicans hypocritically have denounced this amnesty.

In 2018 alone, 700,000, or two-thirds, of undocumented workers came to the U.S. with visas (legally), the largest contingent being Canadian and Mexican, followed by Venezuelans, Colombians, and Brits (Anne Applebaum, Washington Post, columnist, and ABJ, Dec. 30, 2018, p. A 14.)

I accuse the U.S. capitalist class of abetting the arrival of undocumented workers. An example includes American corporations in Mexican border towns advertising for their employment in the U.S., prompting them to search for better and more prosperous lives. Obama's action will allow these people to at least earn a federal minimum wage of $7.25 an hour (many working while undocumented at half of that amount because employers would threaten to report them to immigration authorities). Also, these workers potentially might be added to the unionized workforce.

Recently, 64,000 skilled workers at Apple, Google and other

high tech companies successfully sued them to end collusion of not hiring each other's' workers to lower salary increases. Each worker received $3,750 in compensation. Aren't such practices within these companies reminiscent of serfdom?[6]

Examples of recent anti-labor activity by legislative bodies and courts: In 2014, the Supreme Court ruled that home care workers servicing Medicaid patients were not required to pay service costs to a union representing them in collective bargaining because private Medicaid Individuals are not employers and because workers have First Amendment rights to disagree with a union.

Also, in 2014, a California court held that state teachers' tenure, dismissal, and layoff contracts were unconstitutional. The ruling is not final because of union court appeal.

When Florida counties passed anti-wage theft laws, the Republican legislature failed to overturn them. A multicity study indicated that employers often do not pay the minimum wage or reimburse low wage workers for all their work hours, two-thirds of them on average losing 15 percent of their wages. Workers thus lost many millions of dollars of pay.

In 2015, the Supreme Court will decide if workers not belonging to a union but represented by it do not have to pay agency fees to it for protecting their union rights like arbitrary dismissal and securing higher wages and benefits. Of course, these non-union members are also exempt from contributing to labor PACs.

A recent Tennessee law dictates that unemployed workers after 13 weeks will have to accept a job paying 75 percent of previous wages; after 25 weeks, 70 percent; and after 38 weeks, 65 percent. This law forces workers to more readily accept lower wage jobs, further impoverishing them.

Republicans in Idaho, Maine, Minnesota, Ohio, and Wisconsin have unsuccessfully tried to relax teenage work-hour laws. In Maine, the Republican legislature passed a law against restaurant employees, holding that "service charges" were not tips, employers allowed to keep them.[7]

In a new ultra-modern Volkswagen auto factory in Chattanooga,

Tennessee, in which the average hourly worker's wage is $19.50, the UAW in February 2014 lost certification by a narrow 712 to 626 vote. Republican state politicians and the business community waged a scare campaign against unionization there, arguing that it would discourage companies to locate in a union-strong area. These recent Republican/Conservative actions against unions are part of a perpetual drive to weaken and, ultimately, destroy them.[8]

In the U.S. today, a welcome development is workers' partly/wholly owned cooperatives, 11,000 of them employing 13.6 million workers (145 million U.S. workforce), some under the aegis of participatory democracy.

An economically successful group of cooperating worker-owned co-ops under the nonprofit "Evergreen" label in Cleveland, Ohio, have a commercial laundry, a solar-panel installation company, and a large greenhouse. Also, there are 130 million members of consumer cooperatives, and 92.5 million member-owners of credit unions having more than $1 trillion in assets.[9]

For unions and Democrats, the main issue in the 2014 elections was to raise the minimum federal hourly wage from $7.25 to $10.10 an hour by 2016. This would benefit 24 million wage workers earning $7.25 to $10.10 an hour. About 90 percent of these workers are over age 20; educationally, a fourth have less than high school, a third finishing it, a third some college, a tenth finishing it. Incidentally, in 2014, Germany, France, Britain, among other nations, have a higher minimum wage than the U.S. By 2015, 29 states have a higher minimum wage than the federal one. Also, a plethora of cities will raise the minimum wage: Seattle, San Francisco, Los Angeles to $15 an hour by 2020; New York City, and Washington D.C., proposed $15 an hour by 2020; Chicago, $13 an hour by 2020. Others by 2020 include San Diego, $11.50; Oakland $12.25; Louisville, KY, $9. In September 2015, Democratic Governor Andrew Cuomo has also endorsed the $15 an hour bandwagon.[10]

The decline of unions, in essence the principal organized force for progressive socioeconomic reform in the Democratic Party, has led to their decreasing role in contributing money and campaign workers to it. Thus it is that the Democrats now rely more on Wall Street and other corporations for funds. This shift occurred during the Clinton Presidency which supported free trade legislation via NAFTA and WTO. As the Democrats became more conservative, so did the Republicans regarding organized labor and social welfare.

Nevertheless, unions today are still the main progressive political force in American society, the most important single backers of the Democratic Party, providing it with much money and foot soldiers. Their political program includes universal healthcare, higher Social Security and SSI benefits; free state college tuition, higher taxes on the rich and corporations, end of sexual, ethnic, religious discrimination, endless wars, and for a government jobs programs for the unemployed.

The weakness of American labor relative to capital is also expressed in its longer work week. American workers now work more hours than in previous decades: in the 1970s, 16 percent worked more than 49 hours weekly; in the 1990s, more do so. Actual average weekly working hours for them increased from 40.6 in 1973 to 50.8 in 1997. Thus, weekly free time for workers fell from 26 hours in 1973 to 19.5 hours in the 1990s. In fact, in the 1990s, U.S. workers worked a month longer than in the previous generation. According to the OECD, hours worked per year by workers ca. 2007 in the following selected nations: U.S., 1804; Britain, 1669; France, 1564; Germany, 1434. Even Japanese workers invariably overworked, who, in 1970, worked 2.200 annual hours as opposed to the 1900 hours of U.S. workers, in 2012 worked 1750 hours to the U.S. workers 1800 hours. A 2014 Gallup poll of U.S. full time workers found an average work week of 47 hours – 42 percent, 42 hours; 39 percent, 50 hours; 18 percent, 60 hours; salaried employees, 49 hours; hourly employees, 44 hours.

In addition to a longer workweek American workers face speedups in hospital, retail, fast foods and in industry to increase profits, leading to more accidents. Highways now are less safe because truck drivers are subjected to longer driving hours. Furthermore, because of the Great Recession, most workers labor additional hours with no pay.[11]

Sadly, a sizeable part of U.S. workers is conservatives under the impression of Fox News and right-wing talk radio – two-thirds of white male workers voted for the Republican John McCain in 2008. Why? In an economy of average lower wages, and high unemployment, these white workers are fearful of losing their status advantage over African-American and Hispanic workers who are becoming more assertive in demanding equal justice, including more jobs.

Recently the HB program allows 85,000 visas annually for highly skilled foreign workers to work for American companies in need of scarce skilled labor. Lately this program has been abused by companies including Walt Disney World in Orlando and Southern California and Edison, laying off workers for these foreigners who work at lower wages/benefits. Many displaced workers had to train these newcomers! As yet, this abuse has not been rectified. This injustice is an example of American corporations wanting cheap, exploitable, disposable labor to increase profits.

Specificity for the "cheap" element: The decline of unions alone accounts for about one-third of income inequality among men in the last 35 years. Among construction workers, for instance, unionization has fallen from 40 percent to 14 percent from 1973 to now, resulting in a $10,000 annual decrease in pay adjusted for inflation. As already observed, many undocumented workers toil in this area. When unions were strong wages and productivity rose in tandem, but after 1980, although productivity increased, wages stagnated. Recent statistics by the National Employment Law Project have real wages in 2009-14 declining: 5.7 percent for the lowest paid, a fifth of workers; 4.7 percent for the second lowest; 4 percent for the middle fifth; 3 percent for the second highest; and 2.6 percent for the highest fifth.[12]

For wages to match productivity, not only do unions have to regain their former strength, but the horrendous income inequality between workers and the wealthier classes, especially the richest 1 percent, should be rectified. How? Legislation should be passed to tax the wealthy at much higher rates and transfer the proceeds to workers according to their wages in sliding percentages, lower wage workers receiving more than higher wage ones. These steps would obviously increase consumption and spur economic growth. Under present political circumstances, however, this is utopian.

For labor to regain the initiative over capital, I recommend supporting the fast-food, retail and other workers' demonstrations and increased strike activity, including sit-ins and even general strikes as in Europe, the two illegal in the U.S. To be sure, as living standards in the U.S. decline, the working class as already observed, will become more active in its pursuit of equality and improved living standards.

According to Center for American Progress researcher's, high union density, with its high wages, is a significant factor in upward social mobility for people ages 29-32 of poor parents: nationally parents in the 25th income percentile had children progressing to the 41st one. Thus, unionization is a positive good for the nation as a whole.[13]

American labor now confronts two major problems: global warming and increasing automation.

To solve global warming, a consumerist/profit-based capitalist society will be forced to curtail the plethora of goods and produced for profit. Will this development steer workers towards a socialist society which will ensure high living standards by more communal sharing? Or will labor be quiescent and allow with others global warming to continue, possibly leading to humanity's extinction?

Technological progress/innovation in developed nations – today, computerization/automation/robotics are progressively making human labor ever more superfluous. It may be not be too far in the future when robots may assume the leading role in production and services, with automated assembly lines and so on. In fact, it is not in the realm of science fiction for intelligent robots to product other robots to perform much or most of the work, including mental labor.

Aristotle envisioned this possible state of affairs in his <u>Politics</u>:

> If every tool, when summoned, or even of its own
> accord, could do the work that befitted it, just as the

creations of Daedalus moved of themselves, or the tripods of Hephaestus went of their own accord to their sacred work, if the weaver's shuttles were to weave of themselves, then there would be no need of apprentices for the master, workers or of slaves for the lords.[14]

A possible scenario in this complex of events is for human labor to be non-existent serving only the few remaining human capitalists. Another one is for labor to assume political lower in a socialist society to allow technology to present labor with more leisure time and high living standards despite global warming.

In any event, the class struggle between workers and capitalists can only intensify, given the preceding scenario: I do hope that the former will prevail

A rare labor victory was the April-May 2016 strike by the 39,000 Communications Workers of America against Verizon. The workers won an 11 percent wage increase over four years, profit sharing, better medical benefits, and the limiting of outsourcing jobs. The strikes were supported by the union movement and the Obama administration.

## Postscript

As already noted, since about 1980 to now, 90 percent of U.S. workers have had lower wages, adjusted for inflation, including K-12 public school teachers.

The Great Recession of 2008-09 and its aftermath of slow economic growth, along with the political rise of the Republican Tea Party movement with its program of sharp cut tax cuts for the rich/corporations via their PACs/lobbyists has shrunk public revenues, resulting in no real wage increases for K-12 public school teachers and other local/state government workers. The result: many of these teachers during the school year moonlight to supplement income.

As already observed, the capitalist juggernaut economically savaged manual labor and is now doing so with college-educated mental labor.

In response to their dire economic position, K-12 public school teachers in February-May 2015 launched a series of wildcat (illegal) strikes in Republican-controlled state of economic austerity, first in West Virginia, then in Kentucky, Oklahoma, Arizona and Colorado. The strikes featured mass teachers' demonstrations of up to 50,000 participants marching to their respective state capitols for higher wages/benefits for themselves, other school staff and school funding.

Teachers in West Virginia and Oklahoma have succeeded to achieve their economic demands, but in the remaining states as if this writing their economic outcomes are uncertain.

Some context for public workers: It is illegal for them to strike, but states allow them to unionize, but these unions are hampered economically by right-to-work laws which prohibit democratically-elected unions from collecting dues from workers not wishing to do so, hampering union political activity via PACs/lobbyists. But unions protect teacher seniority, personal disputes with school administratons and also are involved in collective bargaining with school boards on economic and other matters.

To be sure, public education employs more than half of local/state workers. K-12 public teachers themselves have wide public support beccause of education's importance in preparing youth for higher education/jobs.

There are 19.5 million local/state workers; the federal government has 2.8 million, including postal ones [15]

In 2018, U.S. unions only represent about 10 percent of American labor, as it was before the FDR New Deal; their peak was about 1960, with 35 percent of it. Now, half of union workers are in the public sector. Before the 1980s, there were several hundred strikes annually. In 2017, there were seven.

The "open shop" is now the rule in the majority of states, allowing individuals to refuse to pay dues to democratically elected unions. Janus v. AECME now extends the "open shop" to public workers.

Also, a U.S. Supreme Court decision prohibits workers in many companies from initiating class action suits for individual arbitration. NYT, May 22, 2018, pp. 131 and B4 (Also, see various articles in the DSA periodical Democratic Left, Fall 2018 (24 pp.).

A rough gauge of capitalist economic exploitation of workers is the Karl Marx (an outstanding socialist thinker) ratio, of annual corporate profit per median-wage worker. It does not include high executive pay bonuses and other factors.

Four elements for 2017 are presented: 1) profit per workers; 2) median workers pay; 3) Marx ratio; (4) number of workers: Walmart: 1) $4,288, 2) $19,177, 3) 0.22, 4) 2.3 million; McDonald's: 1) $22,095, 2) $7,017, 3) 3.15, 4) 235,000; IBM: 1) $15,693, 2) $54,491, 3) 0.29, 4) 366,000; Ford Motor Company, 1) $37,762, 2) $87,783, 3) 0.43, 4) 147,202; JP Morgan Chase: 1) $76,781, 2) $77,799, 3) 1.24, 4) 252,000; Macy's, 1) $10,357, 2) $13,810, 3) 0.75, 4) 142,000; AT&T: $116,865, 2) $78,437, 3) 1.49, 4) 252,000; Verizon: 1), $196,589, 2) $136,623, 3) 1.55, 4) 155,000; Berkins Hathaway: 1) $119,204, 2) $53,510, 3) 2.23, 4) 377,000; Boeing: 1), $58,217, 2) $111,2014, 3) 0.52, 4) 140,800. Neil Irwin, "Capital vs. Labor...and Who's Winning," NYT, May 22, 2015, pp. B1 and B5.

# Chapter 10: Alienation in Class Society and its Costs

The philosophical concept of alienation is important in socialist theory because of its centrality in its Marxist stream to explain the consequences of social misery/oppression; its lineage will be briefly discussed before examining the views of Marx and others, usually socialists/near socialists, on its devastating social effects under capitalism.

Alienation holds that although human beings are social animals, individuality divides them in varying degree. For instance, while others may empathize with one, only he/she experiences first hand joy and sorrow, futility and rage, life and death. In a general sense, then, alienation is concerned with the estrangement of human beings from one another, of individual dread and despair, of inner loneliness.

Alienation, however, is largely magnified in class-exploitative societies, with their inordinate competitive features, pitting, in varying degree, individuals, status groups, classes, nations, and religions against one another: since the dawn of civilization the individual has been psychologically and ethically deformed by these antagonistic/ exploitative socioeconomic and other relations. To be sure, although there was less alienation in primitive cultures than in civilization because of intense mutual aid and equality, its potential to increase based on economic scarcity and labor division was omnipresent.[1]

Allusions to alienation are of old vintage, as in the Old Testament describing early humanity's living in the innocence of equality, peace, and relative abundance in the Garden of Eden, which were destroyed when Eve, deceived by Satan who personified evil, tempted Adam to eat the apple of knowledge. Anthropologically, this myth described the consequences resulting from the Agricultural Revolution and civilization, of woman's subordination to man, of the lot of most of humanity to be brutally exploited by governing elites while the arts and sciences flourished. The not knowing right from wrong would refer to the absence of private property, which allowed for broad sexual intimacy within early communities, of group solidarity, as against its more restrictive forms with the rise of the nuclear family and its relative exclusivity from others.[2]

In the modern period, alienation was well explored by Marx; it was greatly influenced by thinkers like Rousseau, but especially Hegel, who employed the term to describe the troubled individual under civilization. In *Discourse on the Origins of Inequality*, Rousseau contrasted the tormented, yet civilized, individual at war with others, with the happy and noble savage. In *The Phenomenology of the Spirit*, Hegel observed that normally, despite alienation, human beings desired not only to fulfill themselves, but also to aid and respect others (the mutual-aid aspect). But since human existence was confronted by the perennial problem of economic scarcity, there not being enough to fully satisfy material and social human needs, conflict arose, in the course of which the winners became the masters while the losers became slaves, part of whose labor was appropriated by the former, the two fearing and hating one another. Furthermore, the masters were not creative, but parasitical, while the slaves, the productive and creative classes through their understanding of the technology, would ultimately win independence.

The importance of the concept of alienation in modern thought may also be measured by Existentialism, basically a bourgeois philosophy whose leitmotif was concerned with the essentially alienated or lonely individual engulfed in anguish and dread, whose life was essentially absurd and meaningless, without hope. Its founder is the conservative religious Danish philosopher Soren A. Kierkegaard who flourished in the first half of the 19th century. To be sure, Sartre incorporated existentialism within a Marxist framework, an exception to the rule.[3]

Marx and Engels saw instances of at least some alienation in which individuals were separated from one another in primitive cultures, marked by the first inescapable labor division or the "sexual act," with others following "naturally by virtue of natural disposition (e.g., physical strength), needs, accidents." In the early family itself, there was a form of "latent slavery," in which "wife and children are the slaves of the husband." Then, "labor division and private property are moreover identical expressions: in the one the same thing is affirmed with reference to activity as affirmed in the other with reference to the product of the activity." It is this early division of labor, for them, which "implies the contradiction between the interest of the separate individual or the individual family and the communal interest of all individuals who have intercourse with one another." And, they contended, once a society reached a sufficiently high level of technological development with accompanying labor division, "each man has a particular sphere of activity which is forced upon him and from which he cannot escape." Thus:

> A cleavage exists between the particular and the common interest – as long, therefore, as activity is not voluntarily but naturally divided, man's own deed becomes an alien power opposed to him, which enslaves him instead of being controlled by him.

This condition itself was related to the dichotomy between manual and mental labor.

Marx suggested that alienated labor, along with technological advances and greater economic surplus, led to the emergence of private property, and ultimately to class society and the state, both of which become involved in an intricate clockwork of socioeconomic, political, and cultural inequalities with their concomitant elements of conflict.

To be sure, this alienation at times was of unbearable proportion, especially when some individuals were bereft of property, while others had an overabundance of it, like under capitalism, thus "my means of life belong to someone else that my desires are the unattainable possession of someone else...that an inhuman power [capital] rules over everything."[4]

For Marx, workers were the most unfree and thus the most alienated group in capitalist society because they must sell their labor-power to capital, thus becoming commodities in which exchange value, as opposed to use value, affected almost all human activities and institutions in the competition for wealth and power among individuals, status groups, and classes. In this progression, workers had the choice either to accede to becoming commodities to make other commodities, or starve.

To be sure, as observed in *The Holy Family*, capitalists were also alienated to some degree by the capitalist market place/property, but less so than workers:

> The propertied class and the class of the proletariat present the same human self-alienation. But the former class finds in this self-alienation its confirmation and its good, its own power: it has in it a semblance of human existence; the class of the proletariat falls annihilated in its self-alienation; it sees in it its own powerlessness and the reality of an inhuman existence. In the words of Hegel the class of the proletariat is in abasement...and indignation to which it is necessarily driven by the contradiction between its human nature and its condition of life which is the outright decisive and comprehensive negation of that nature.[5]

For instance, bourgeois occupations, like physician and lawyer, were rather creative and satisfying, but the worker, being a mere commodity for the capitalist, was "exposed to all the vicissitudes of competition, to all the fluctuations of the market."

In his *Economic and Philosophical Manuscripts*, Marx stated:

> First, that the work is external to the worker that it is not part of his nature; and that consequently he does not fulfill himself in his work but denies himself, has a feeling of misery rather than well-being, does not develop freely his mental and physical energies but is physically exhausted and mentally debased.

Thus, the worker felt fully human only when performing animal functions or at home. How could it be otherwise as "the worker sinks to the level of a commodity?" For Marx, this alienation was part and parcel of a long historical process that began with the advent of "private property acquisitiveness, the separation of labor, capital and land, exchange and competition, value and the devaluation of man, monopoly and competition – and the system of *money*."[6]

In *Capital*, capitalism, with its almost infinite labor divisions, inexorably made "the laborer into a crippled monstrosity, by forcing his detail dexterity at the expense of a world of productive capabilities and instincts." And as the labor power of labor produces more capital, the greater the domination of labor by capital:

> All means for the development of production transform themselves into means of domination over, and exploitation of the producers: they mutilate the laborer into a fragment of a man, degrade him to the level of an appendage of a machine, destroy every remnant of charm in his work and turn it into a hated toil; they estrange from him the intellectual potentialities of the labor-process in the same proportion as science is incorporated in it as independent power; they distort the conditions under which he works, subject him during the labor process to a despotism the more hateful for its meanness; they transform his lifetime into working time, and drag his wife and child beneath the wheels of the Juggernaut of capital.[7]

And:

> The special skill of each individual factory operative vanishes as an infinitesimal quantity before the science, the gigantic physical forces, and the mass of labor that are embodied in the factory mechanism and, together with that mechanism, constitute the power of the "master." Not surprisingly, for Marx, workers could not but

be the "slaves of the bourgeois class," as they were "enslaved by the machine, by the over-looker, and above all by the individual bourgeois manufacturer himself," and once paid "set upon by the other portions of the bourgeoisie, the landlord, the shopkeeper, the pawnbroker, etc."[8]

Marx also employed three specific terms in examining alienation – "commodity fetishism," "objectification," and "reification."

The first posited: "There...is a definite social relation between men, that assumes, in their eyes, the fantastic relation between things." In a capitalist society, the fetishism of money, itself related to exchange value commoditization, representing universal capital, "conceals, instead of disclosing the social character of private labor, and the social relations between individual producers," thus leading to mystifying socioeconomic relations, denigrating labor by making it simply one of a myriad of commodities.

The second term (Marx borrowed it from Hegel) postulated that human activity expressed itself in products made, not only everyday-common ones, but also art itself. This was related to the truism that individuals invariably wished to realize themselves positively, but because of a capitalist world of exploitation/oppression: "The performance of work appears in the sphere of political economy as a vitiation of the worker, objectification as a loss and as servitude to the object, and appropriation as alienation." Thus: "So much does objectification appear as loss of the object that the worker is deprived of the most essential things not only of life but also of work."

This manifestation included the difficulty of workers procuring jobs and "that the more objects the worker produces the fewer he can possess and the more he falls under the domination of his product, of capital."

The third, intertwined with the other two, insisted that labor division under capitalism again distorted social relations, viewing individuals from the perspective of work performed, making them into things, obviously diminishing their humanity. (Althusser, a French Marxist philosopher, in *For Marx*, disagreed that reification was a Marxist concept; for him, in *Capital*, "the only social relation that is presented in the form of a thing...is *money.*" Ollman, in *Alienation,* believed otherwise.) [9]

Do the antagonistic-alienating socioeconomic relations of capitalism encourage technological innovation? Yes. But this is only part of the truth of invention/discovery: first, curiosity itself in any technological construct promotes it; second, it is the result of cooperative effort, built upon the experiences of past and present generations, increasingly more so today than before as scientific complexity constantly increases, undermining any supposed unique genius. Furthermore, socialism itself has just as much or even a greater desire to foster technological breakthroughs to raise living standards than capitalism because with the lessening of scarcity, admittedly a problem posing some relativity, human-socialist solidarity should increase. Furthermore, socialism uses inventions as much as possible to lessen routine-deadening labor while disdaining useless-alienating consumerist junk; but capitalism is unconcerned with alienation and is condemned by an archaic profit motive to promote conspicuous waste.

Non-alienating work itself is situated in a society marked by a high level of technology, especially of automation, of integrated labor, in which use value overwhelms market relations of exchange value for exploitation/profit and where participatory democracy at work/society among general equals prevails.

That the work place should make workers into simple automatons was central in the writings of Frederick W. Taylor, the father of scientific management, and practices of Henry Ford, the auto magnate who initiated the moving assembly line of the meatpacking industry, calling for a continuous synchronization between the mobile human body and the material handled, reducing work to a few bodily movements. Taylor, the principal father of work-time studies, had no less an object in mind than to reduce manual labor to a series of mindless motions, specifically removing any mental element on the factory floor, the end being a de-skilled and inexpensive blue-collar work force. Before Taylorism became widespread in the early 1900s, skilled blue-collar workers had much autonomy in the work place.

Taylorism itself was symptomatic of the fact that the power of capital led to a technology and organization which in the end reduced blue-collar workers to a generalized mass of poor and dependent retainers in an increasing labor division, itself spawning more bureaucracy, signifying the growing socioeconomic distance between capital and labor.[10] Smith himself in *Wealth of Nations* praised the increase of labor division in the Lombe Brothers factory employing children, but admitted that labor division in the main makes workers "as stupid and ignorant as it is possible for a human creature to become." [11]

Taylorism was further refined after World War II in Japan by "Toyotism," named after the labor organization pioneered by the Toyota automobile company, instituted after the crushing of Japanese unions in the Red Scare prompted by the Cold War in the late 1940s and early 50s. Its basic element was the utilization of the team approach in an assembly line, each member being able to perform the work of others, all interdependent on one another. The skills involved here were not complex, the work itself being utterly repetitive, although the simple rotation of tasks somewhat relieved the monotony. In this setting, workers occupied the bottom rung of a hierarchical structure, their immediate superior being the team leader, with no input as to how rapidly they worked or other matters, but expected to discuss among themselves as to how they should better work or exploit themselves and monitor one another. But there was more, for workers were herded to hear inspirational sermons about the glories of their company and to sing its praises.[12] This team concept was tied to lean production with its just-in-time arrival/delivery of goods and flexibility for efficient production, made possible by the electronics revolution in computers and increasing automation, including greater use of robotics.

We should also add that lifetime-employment (to age 55) policies in Japan applied only to the larger companies, employing about a fifth of the workforce. The workers of the smaller independent companies doing contract work for the leading ones, like supplying them with parts for final products (these companies in turn have smaller contractors working for them – there are up to four tiers involved here), were not promised lifetime employment and received lower wages. Even within the companies themselves, janitorial and other work was again done by outside firms. This model of capital/ labor organization resulted in further fracturing and dividing the Japanese working class.[13]

Up to now, there is only one major instance of the assembly line ever being discarded in the automobile industry. In the Volvo plant in Uddevalla, Sweden, in 1985, teams of workers, usually from 10 to 12 each, would assemble a car in its entirety. This model, which proved to be efficient enough, was inaugurated because of an acute labor shortage, but terminated with the rise of unemployment.

The moral of the story is that no one voluntarily likes to do boring/repetitive work.[14]

The delineation between work and alienation/oppression continues in many recent studies. A key one by the Marxist Braverman, *Labor and Monopoly Capital*, held that the wondrous technological advances since the 1950s only intensified worker dissatisfaction in the work place. This condition was because the technology was designed to magnify workers' powerlessness, condemning most workers to doing work requiring little or no intellectual challenge, as well as chaining them to a "round of servile duties." Indeed, as the technology advanced most workers became ever more inconsequential because they did not "own the machine and the labor power." [15] Another by the Marxist Bertall Ollman, *Alienation: Marx's Concept of Man in Capitalist Society*, saw that Marx's theory of alienation represented "the devastating effect of capitalist production on human beings, on their physical and mental states and on the social processes of which they are a part." [16]

These views were similar to those of two socialist academics who labored in factories as workers: Simone Weil, the noted French anarchist (*La Condition ouvière*), in 1930s Paris; and Richard M. Pfeffer, a Harvard Ph.D. in government and member of the John Hopkins faculty (*Working for Capitalism*), in the 1970s in greater Baltimore. Both unsparingly accused the capitalist factory system of viewing workers as things or objects to be used, caging them in a social milieu of strict bureaucracy and inhumanity, with almost endless job gradations, rules, and regulations whose aim was to exploit, divide and disempower them as much as possible. But workers might also at any moment be subject to dismissal, either singly or in groups, thrown into the whirlwind of more helplessness and despair. Furthermore, foremen treated workers like children, using harsh language and other devices to discipline them, further eroding their human dignity. The work itself was abominable with long workdays and low wages, repetitive and utterly boring, at maximum speed in hellish working environments, making a mockery of their human existence, further confirming their belonging to the inferior and humiliated class. This was not surprising since workers themselves neither owned the work place nor were consulted in the organization of work, and with their limited education, the mechanical and other principles of science remained a mystery to them, further increasing their alienation.[17]

That work basically defines a person's life, associated with status and class divisions and all they entail, was poignantly described by Studs Terkel (an icon in Left journalism) in *Working*, a magnificent tome of oral history in which more than a hundred Americans recounted how work affected their lives in general. In the continuum of work/class, this study affirmed the obvious of more losers than winners in the race for success; for most workers, jobs were usually physically exhausting and psychologically stressful, as they were caught in a hierarchic cage of humdrum work routines. But for the fortunate ones, the happy few, work was creative and often accompanied with great financial rewards. To be sure, there were a few socialists questioning the status quo. [18]

Terkel's observations were confirmed by Barbara Garson, a well-known social activist, in two works: in *All the Livelong Day*, a brilliant reportage of the work lives of blue- and white-collar workers who were stripped of all dignity and autonomy as labor division increasingly multiplied, ever more fragmenting work and accelerating its pace. In *The Electronic Sweatshop*, she indicted the new and spreading computer technology for subjecting white-collar workers to a new work slavery, the aim being to de-skill them, "restrict their autonomy," and "to make people cheap and disposable." She also observed the deleterious effects of electronic surveillance at work, recording/evaluating every second in the office assembly line, white collars being effectively proletarianized, with "Big Brother" watching them. In this critique, she followed Braverman's objections to Taylorism. [19]

Another major study on capitalist work relations in America, *The Hidden Injuries of Class*, was by two well-known Left writers, Richard Sennett and Jonathan Cobb. In addition to recounting the wasteland of work for most workers, they described the underlying social psychology of a ferociously competitive society dividing people between the successful and failures, the latter usually blaming themselves for their shortcomings.[20]

Yet another well-regarded study on the workplace is by Chris Argyris, Beach Professor of Administrative Sciences, Yale University. *Personality and Organization* relied on a number of detailed studies on work to demonstrate that workers at the lower end of the work/class progression experienced infinitely more feelings of powerlessness and frustration than those performing mental labor. Thus, assembly-line workers faced with the rapid pace and repetitive nature of their work, along with long work hours, more often succumbed to psychosomatic and related illnesses, like high blood pressure and heart disease, and were more prone to accidents than others.[21]

The problems caused by unremittingly boring/repetitive work at high speed, now often electronically monitored, have been recently examined by three studies: A report on the United States by the International Labor Organization, "Job Stress: The 20th Century Disease" (1993); Mitchell Marks' *From Turmoil to Triumph* (1994); and Jeremy Rifkin's *The End of Work* (1995). The first insisted that the annual economic costs of alienation at work on the American economy in the form of illness, absenteeism, lower productivity, and job turnover was in the $200 billion range, while in Britain, as much as 10 percent of its GDP. It also found that as many as 40 percent of Japanese workers feared death by overwork, or "karoshi."[22] The second, by a psychologist on organization and consultant to business, lamented the damage done to workers' morale and disenchantment with management in the wake of recent mergers and downsizing, increasing unemployment and work time (the latter resulting in "burnout"), and decreasing real median wages. The third, by a labor economist, reiterated in great detail the problems posed by the first and second and recommended a 30-hour work week.[23]

Before proceeding to present in some detail the annual human and material costs of an alienating class society in the U.S., usually for the 1990s, these approximate annual statistics on it are in order. There are about 2.25 million deaths from all causes, a 100 million work full-time, and the GDP is as much as $9 trillion.

The American workplace itself has been traditionally driven by violence, reflecting the classist, sexist, and racist (including ethnic and religious divisions) nature of American society. For instance, a 1996 report by the National Institute for Occupational Safety and Health revealed about 1 million crimes annually in the workplace (11 percent of the total), including 1,100 murders (4 percent of the total), and 8 million robberies. A survey conducted by the Northwestern National Life Insurance Co. of 600 workers in 1993 obtained similar results to those of the Justice Department, a sixth claiming to be physically attacked and a fifth threatened by physical harm. The "workplace avenger" who kills fellow workers and supervisors in a fit of rage is not unknown. Then, there is the specter of "covert," "passive" or "hidden aggression," directed against workplace competitors, including malicious gossip, dirty looks, rudeness, and hostile criticism, impinging on efficiency/profits, whose high costs are difficult to quantify. In a recent study of 452 anonymous employees surveyed in six states in a period of a month or less, three university professors – Robert A. Baron, Joel H. Neuman, and Deanna Geddes – more than a quarter reported experiencing such aggressions, while a sixth saw themselves at times as recipients of discourtesies, as not being informed of meetings.

Workplace aggression is undoubtedly related to the earlier

bullying of children by parents, which in turn manifests itself in children bullying one another on the street and in school, including for ethnic and religious differences, especially virulent in a racist and multi-ethnic and religious U.S. where "strong (usually the majority or the stronger) prey on the "weak" or minority by speech (teasing and name calling), shunning or physical attack. At times, those picked on may resort to indiscriminate murder as in the Columbine High School case in Colorado in 2001. A recent study of bullying in school, for instance, reveals that a third of children from the sixth to tenth grades indicate verbal or physical bullying concerning race/ethnicity, religion, and disabilities, like speech.

There are also high human costs related to an unhealthy and hazardous workplace environment, including toxic air, dangerous machinery, unsafe work procedures, and speedups. According to the National Safety Council, 250,000 workers died on the job from 1970 to 1995, many from employer negligence; in this time, only four people, according to the Occupational Safety and Health Administration (OSHA) – a federal agency monitoring the workplace – served a prison sentence for subjecting workers to an unsafe work environment. But the average number of annual deaths by accidents in the 1990s has dropped by 40 percent, or to 6,000. Nevertheless, there are still from 50,000 to 70,000 annual deaths from occupationally related illnesses, like lung cancer, and 6 million are injured, of whom 1.4 million leave the workplace for varying periods of time, 50,000 permanently. OSHA itself in 1987 had less than 800 inspectors to cover 6 million work sites.

These workplace disasters are related to an increasingly helpless work force, with ever less union protection and job security, which is constantly driven to perform ever more in less time. A 2001 report issued by the Families and Work Institute, "Overworked: When Work Becomes Too Much," claims that almost a third of the American work force believes that it is chronically overworked (the "karoshi" syndrome), up to half at times. Not surprisingly, the study concludes that this alienation results in "physical and emotional health problems," like "loss of sleep" and resentment towards bosses.

Now, to high worker mortality rates: In Indiana, for instance, construction workers, most of whom are males, live 10 years less than the national average for men, and in a study of two Lordstown automobile plants near Youngstown, Ohio, the respective mortality rates from cancer are 40 to 50 percent higher than the average. From an overarching perspective on life longevity, an article in the New York Times, "For Good Health, It Pays to be Rich and Important," reports that wealthy white men live 6.6 longer than their poorer counterparts, while whites live longer than blacks, at age 65, 7.4 years for men, and 3.7 years for women.

Tensions and conflicts at work are now exacerbated by downsizing as permanent lifetime jobs are becoming ever scarcer. Since most workers identify themselves closely with their work, intimately related as it is with socioeconomic self-worth, unemployment often results in feelings of shame and worthlessness. When debts cannot be repaid and family possessions dwindle, the psychological health of all family members is imperiled. Not surprisingly, the long-term unemployed have a 30 percent higher rate of divorce than average and abuse their children and spouses more often and more severely than others. From a general perspective, a 1 percent increase in unemployment in America results in a rise of 4 percent for suicide, almost 6 percent for murder, and 4 percent for men and 2 percent for women in admittance to state psychiatric hospitals.[24]

Middle and upper management also cannot completely escape alienation at work, especially its competitive part. Although workers in unionized corporations have some job protection from arbitrary dismissal, this is less so for middle and upper management. Furthermore, the rewards of money and power are so great for managers that they spend not only much of their lives working, but equally spend their social lives networking and politicking for promotion. In this labyrinth, uncertainty reigns. Middle management is now also being savaged by recent trends in corporate downsizing and introduction of new technologies, leading not only to mass layoffs and corresponding lower salaries, but also to increased workloads, inexorably to greater job stress and burnout. This group is also losing its favored status in the workforce because mass higher education has increased its numbers.

In the contemporary Darwinian jungle of middle and upper management, the supposed rationality and efficiency of merit in the business world is largely mythical. For instance, in promotions, more than half of middle managers readily admit that they are made on a "largely subjective evaluation or arbitrary decision."

Even top executives have been concerned with recent downsizings and increased workloads accompanying them. In a 1991 survey of senior executives in the largest thousand American companies, 54 percent feared losing their jobs and 26 percent experienced "burnout," the two leading anxieties. (Of course, senior executives usually have clauses in their contracts protecting them for a number of years in case of dismissal, but workers do not.)

Along with the irrationalities in promotion, there is the specter of inherent economic waste in the American corporation because of its conflict/alienating model in the workplace, which David Gordon, an economist, in *Fat and Mean*, contrasted with the more cooperative German and Japanese ones, necessitating that American corporations have three times as many managers and supervisors as their Japanese and German counterparts, despite recent downsizings also involving management. Whereas Germany and Japan had 4 percent of their work force as managers and supervisors, the U.S. had 13 percent in the early 90s.[25] The task is now to relate the alienation of capitalist work/technology and socioeconomic inequality to the socialization of the individual within the alienated family. It is within the family that most children first become socialized in the primary human patterns, trust and love, fear and hate. In Erik Erickson's eight stages of human psychological development, five critical ones (three to age five, like "trust versus mistrust," "autonomy versus shame and doubt," and "initiative versus guilt" – and two from ages six to eighteen) transpired when the individual was closely associated with the immediate family.

Thus it is that for the neo-Marxists Eric Fromm, as in *Escape from Freedom* and *The Sane Society*, and Theodore W. Adorno and others in *The Authoritarian Personality*, children socialized in an "exploitative child-parent relationship," itself reflecting a society deeply driven by inequality and conflict, as adults became sadomasochistic and obsessive compulsive, attempting to mitigate their insecurities through incessant work and submission to the prevailing religious, socioeconomic, and political authorities, basically intolerant of different ethnic and religious groups and those lower on the socioeconomic scale, more prone to follow Nazism and other authoritarianisms.[26]

Manifestations of the consequences of alienation/oppression in the American family include the following: Shepard, in *Sociology*, presented a series of surveys in the 1970s with these results:

> Almost seven of ten parents had used some form of violence on their children....Nearly 8 percent admitted to kicking, biting, or punching their children; 4 percent had beaten up their children; and 3 percent had threatened their children with weapons.

But there is more; statistics here encompass the 1980s and 90s: perhaps as many as a fifth of men and a third of women have been sexually abused in childhood, usually by either father, or mother, or near relative who has an essentially compulsive personality, addicted in varying degrees/combinations to work, religion, power, and sex, according to the American Psychological Association and others. The pattern of the Adornian male abuser may also be applied to females.

Is it any wonder that one of ten teenagers attempts suicide, as research from the Centers for Disease Control and Prevention states in a survey conducted in 1997. This child abuse is related to violence between spouses in a third of marriages. To be sure, there is also sibling rivalry/violence, and abuse of the elderly, especially the "weak, disabled or female." It is estimated that from half million to 2.5 million elderly parents are annually battered by their children.

The consequences of alienation also extend to the bedroom. The harried, insecure, competitive existence of modern life obviously contributes to sexual dysfunction. A recent and extensive study, conducted by Sociology Professor Edward O. Laumann and Dr. Raymond C. Rosen of the Center for Sexual and Marital Health at the Robert Wood Johnson Medical School in New Jersey, found that, of 1,750 women and 1,410 men studied (the most thorough study since the discredited Kinsey Report of the 1940s), a fourth of women fail to achieve orgasm and a third between age eighteen and 39 lack any interest in sex; for men, 30 percent have problems with premature ejaculation, and 15 percent lack sexual interest. Not surprisingly, the study concludes that poverty, various family stresses, and early and later traumatic sexual experiences like molestation and/or rape lead to the greater possibility of sexual dysfunction. Economic problems also play an important role here as women, whose incomes declined by more than 20 percent in the last three years, have a 60 percent greater likelihood of lower sexual desire than those whose incomes increased. Furthermore, more education and wealth translate into a healthier sexual life, the truism being that the bourgeoisie are less alienated than the working class.

In conjunction with these statistics, there are high divorce rates in the U.S. and in the rest of the world. In the first alone, half of first marriages, three-fourths of second, and nine-tenths of third end in divorce. To be sure, these numbers indicate a weaker nuclear family as an all-encompassing economic unit, although it is still of decisive importance in status/class relations, including social mobility.

Early emotional and physical abuses (the two are related), in addition to various socioeconomic stresses like poverty and insecurity, lead to later neurotic/psychotic behavior. According to Dr. Judith Lewis Herman in *Trauma and Recovery*, from 50 to 60 percent of psychiatric patients requiring hospitalization and from 40 to 60 percent of outpatient ones, were physically and mentally abused in childhood. To be sure, genetic predisposition may be present in mental illness, especially in psychosis, but it is certainly exacerbated by environmental factors. More than a fifth of the population today suffers annually from diagnostically recognizable neurotic symptoms like excessive anxiety and depression, pronounced phobias, obsessive- compulsive disorders, manic depression, and a little more than 1 percent are psychotic or paranoid schizophrenic. Indeed, over a lifetime, perhaps as many as 70 percent of the people have some form of mental illness.[27]

The elite of alienated societies are also composed of deeply alienated individuals, hungering for wealth and power in varying combinations, who routinely lie to defraud, and use others. These are the able sociopaths or psychopaths, the "aggressive egocentrics" and those exhibiting "paranoid, hysterical and obsessional patterns," obviously well-endowed to survive in the Machiavellian labyrinths of the higher economic and political complexes. In this respect, Hitler and Stalin come readily to mind, both psychopaths able to function and succeed in their political ambitions, undoubtedly terrifying those about them to further consolidate and maintain their power. Furthermore, as Dr. Alex Comfort, a neo-anarchist critic of culture, points out in *Authority and Delinquency in the Modern State*, paranoiacs in difficult times have a powerful hold over people as they are able through projection to identify their common hatreds, thus able to find scapegoats, like ethnic/religious minorities. Harold Greenwald, a well-known psychologist, reinforces his views:

> The reasons why we generally do not discuss the successful psychopath is because we would then have to discuss many of the rulers of the world....Many of the symptoms...as lack of morals and apparent lack of guilt, exist widely among people of power and influence.

Of course, through the services of the sensationalist tabloids, the general public now knows the "sins" of their "betters" or "rulers." An earlier commentary on elite psychopathology was the well-regarded work by the political scientist Harold D. Laswell in *Psychopathology and Politics* (1930), presenting detailed descriptions of personages caught in the web of neurosis and power.[28]

In observing alienation under capitalism, in which the focus is generally on the United States, there is also the awareness of the intense alienation in former socialist societies like the former Soviet Union, whose top layers rejected civil liberties and workers' control of the work place and participation in economic planning, decisive elements indicating intensely antagonistic socioeconomic and political relations. In fact, it was within this deformed socialism (it did have some socialist tendencies, like a rather high degree of socioeconomic equality and extensive social welfarism) that private capitalism developed, existing socialist tendencies obviously overwhelmed by non-socialist ones.

There are many other consequences of alienation/oppression, which in its more extreme forms manifests itself in illness, including anorexia nervosa, obesity, compulsive gambling and buying, extensive use of both legal and illegal injurious drugs, and in criminal activity. The psychic costs of these manifestations are incalculable, but the annual ones (human and economic in the 90s) are largely measurable: the first two phenomena, involving eating disorders, cause the deaths of 300,000 and economic costs in illness, work missed, and early death is certainly more than $200 billion. The third, or compulsive gambling, heavily engages 5 percent of the population, who bet much of the more than $500 billion legally wagered, and many tens of billions illegally, profits being $50 billion. Although legal gambling (most gamblers are men) pays taxes, the social costs of gambling (robbery to pay debts, child and spousal abuse, divorce, and job loss) are $90 billion in 1988. Its twin, compulsive buying (90 percent are women) wastes tens of billions of dollars.

In the realm of psychoactive drugs, legal or illegal, human and material losses are indeed very high. The two most harmful legal drugs are smoking tobacco and alcoholic drinks. Now annually, tobacco, with 50 to 60 million users, has an economic cost of $150 billion and results in more than 440,000 deaths; alcohol, with 100 million habitual users, results in the deaths of 65,000 and costs $185 billion, including treatment of 14 million alcoholics and 30 percent of 37,000 automobile deaths from accidents involving alcohol. In the area of illegal drugs, like marijuana, cocaine, and heroin, they inflict 16,000 annual deaths among 12 to 15 million addicts, 3 million being hard-core, with $200 billion in costs for purchasing the drugs, treatment, property stolen, and incarceration.[29]

Crime itself in its various manifestations denotes the lack of human solidarity in a society stricken by deep individual and social antagonisms, in which economic insecurity and competition drive individuals to be endlessly acquisitive. Crime may be divided into three parts – within the family (already examined), street, and business. The second, or street crime, of burglary and robbery (motor vehicles, jewelry, currency, and household goods) annually consumes $16 billion.

A detailed Justice Department report released in 1996, "Victim Cost and Consequences: A New Look," asserts that the total annual cost for family and street crimes – including rape, injury and murder, factoring in physical injury and psychological trauma and attendant hospitalization, time lost from work, and police and legal costs – is $450 billion. This cost neither includes the $40 billion expended for prisons and related parole and probation systems, nor does it include the $210 billion spent for business and individual security, including anti-theft devices and 1.5 million private security guards.

The third, or business crime, is all pervasive, its annual burden to the public now at $300 billion, with corporations employing kickbacks, bribery, fraud, extortion, violating federal regulations, and tax evasion, while employee embezzlement is merely in the 20 to 40 billion range. In any given decade, about a fifth of the largest 500 corporations are fined by the federal government. Among the more costly frauds/wastes annually in billions of dollars in the last decade include the Savings and Loan debacle (20), and in healthcare (100).

Some of the more egregious examples of this in fines and restitution in dollars for the 1999-2000 period are Marc Rich's corporations (Rich is an international trader living in Switzerland who often shaves legality, pardoned in 2001 by President Clinton before leaving office), which paid $200 million. Prudential agreed to pay $1.7 billion to policyholders because of deceptive practices. SmithKline Beecham paid $325 million in fines for false billings to

Medicare. Archer Daniels Midland, paid a $100 million fine for price fixing. Michael Milken, the "junk-bond king," paid a $1.1 billion (he will still be worth $125 million) for financial fraud. One of his cohorts, Ivan Boesky, was only fined 100 million. Martin A. Frankel, another financial wizard who fled the country to Germany, will return in 2001 to face financial fraud charges of $208 million. Blue Cross and Blue Shield of Illinois paid $144 million in civil and criminal fines. Columbia/HCFA Healthcare and Quorum Health Group paid a $1.1 billion fine for fraudulent expense claims. In 2001, Walter A. Forbes, former chairperson of Cedant is charged for causing its investors a loss of $19 billion by declaring "phony profits." Cedant itself has compensated shareholders at $2.8 billion. Furthermore, employers illegally withhold from workers $20 billion annually, according to an employer-sponsored think-tank. Lawyers and their ancillaries, of course, cannot be done away with under these circumstances; their cost, $125 billion annually.

To be sure, under the rubric of crime, these elements of it should not be neglected. Half the repairmen overcharge their clients. Furthermore, according to the Internal Revenue Service (IRS), underreporting of income is 20 percent for professionals, 30 percent for farmers, and 50 percent for small business. In any given year many of the S&P 500 corporations and individuals in the Forbes 400 do not pay any income taxes, and in cases involving more than $10 million owed between them and the IRS, its recovery rate is 17 percent, as it is faced by a multitude of lawyers, all part of a pattern (it includes $3 trillion in illegal offshore tax-free bank accounts and various domestic phony trusts) that siphons $300 billion annually from the IRS. The IRS itself has lost 19,000 employees (a third of its staff) to "streamline" the government, allowing rich tax cheaters to further flourish.

A recent United States Judiciary Committee report bewails that America is the "most violent and destructive nation on earth," with the highest homicide and robbery per capita rate among the economically advanced nations. This is reflected in statistics for 2000: prisoners number two million (a third in city and county jails, two thirds in state and federal prisons, a fifth incarcerated for drug-related offenses) of whom 46 percent are black, 34 percent white, 17 percent Hispanic, and 3 percent other, four-fifths having illegal drug and alcohol problems suggesting high stress levels and mental illness. Black males especially are in involved in this social catastrophe: almost a third of them will know prison under present incarceration rates (7 percent of them are in prison at any given time, many as repeat offenders), and of 17,000 murders per year, over half are committed by blacks. Illegal drugs, especially crack cocaine, contribute to this. These numbers should be viewed from this economic alienation: half of black men, from ages 25 to 34-years of age, are either unemployed or earn wages below the poverty line for a family of four.

It should be added that white-collar criminals involved in financial crime face less imprisonment than blue-collar crimes involving a gun. For instance, in cases of fraud, insider trading, and tax evasion of a $1 million or more, there is a maximum of three years imprisonment (often not any), though these sentences may be increased to a 5.25 year maximum sentence in 2001.[30] For comparative purposes, one selling two ounces of cocaine in New York as a first-time offender can receive fifteen years to life.

Is anyone surprised that alienation/oppression, with its train of drugs and crime, takes such a heavy toll in lives and economic resources, especially savaging minority youth in the nation's inner cities? When Louis Chevalier, a French social scientist, observed that 10 percent of Parisians in the 1850s were criminals, poverty being the basic cause, is it unreasonable to claim that this also applies for street crime in American cities today?[31]

A substantial part of the damages related to pollution, including human illness and attempts to mitigate it, are also the resultant of a class-alienated society, with its particular technological structures and consumerist demands with their inherent waste. Certainly a cooperative world like socialism is more likely to solve these problems than the present order. The following statistics are generally annual ones for the early 1990s in the U.S.: Cancer rates climbed rapidly from 1950 to 1986, as reported in a 1989 study by the National

Cancer Institute. The figures depict an increase of 21.5 percent for children under age 14 and a 22.6 percent increase for adults. It may be argued that the rising adult cancer rate may be partly explained by an aging population, but this does not hold true for children. The work place itself, according to the National Safety Council, accounts for 23 to 38 percent of cancer deaths, or 150,000, which alone consumes $275 billion. As for other annual pollution costs in billions of dollars: air pollution from industry and transportation ($226 billion), on residential and industrial structures ($30 billion), the cost of polluted water on health ($1 billion), and $11 billion on recreational activity – they do not include the loss of irreplaceable natural resources in the many tens of billions of dollars. Finally, there is the toll of toxic microbes in food, which kills 9,000 people annually and causes illness in 80 million people, costing $7 billion in medical bills and work absences.[32]

According to Murry Weidenbaum, chairperson of President Reagan's Council of Economic Advisors, other wasteful annual expenditures in the 90s include $138 billion for advertising, $136 billion for deficient vehicle safety, as well as $300 billion for the military ($400 billion in 2003) and related areas.[33]

That the very wastes enumerated created jobs and great profits – not to mention special interest groups, which in an alienated class society are fearful of change lest they lost their jobs/profits – is obvious. But if class alienation can be overcome by socialism, the resultant should, within the context of contemporary technology, allow for a six-hour work day without the loss of jobs and present living standards in the U.S. and other developed nations within the near future.

In *The Culture of Narcissism*, history professor Christopher Lasch traced the American character from the 17th century Puritan centered on work as a "calling", to the 18th century "Yankee", personified by Franklin as more materialistic and individualistic but still related to some virtue and community; to the 19th-century one of unbridled individualistic success and self-improvement, to the late 20th century-one depicting the narcissistic "Happy Hooker," materialistic and acquisitive, living for the moment, consumerism equaling nirvana, but forced to conform, however, within the bureaucratic cage of monopoly capitalism, devoid of any sense of self-entitlement and power. His way out of this alienating impasse had a Marxian ring to it:

> The struggle against bureaucracy therefore requires a struggle against capitalism itself. Ordinary citizens cannot resist professional dominance without also asserting control over production and over the technical knowledge on which modern production rests...They [citizens] will have to create their own "communities of competence." Only then will the productive capacities of modern capitalism, together with the scientific knowledge that it now serves it, come to serve the interests of humanity instead.[34]

Lasch's consumerist nirvana is, of course, related to the alienation or essential meaninglessness of work for most of the work force, whose basic compensation now is to frequent the new temples/ pleasures of capitalism – the retail outlets, in frequent vacations, prompted by the new priests, advertisers and salespersons, who dispense the meaning of life.

Although Marx delved extensively into the various aspects of working-class alienation at work and outside of it, he did not do so for education. To be sure, the *Manifesto* favored "free education of all children in public schools," along with "abolition of child labor in factories," and the "combination of education with industrial production, etc." But, for most 19th-century thinkers, including Marx and Engels, it was assumed that education would not be of long duration for the masses at least for the immediate future – this in a society of yet primitive technology and great scarcity from our vantage point. In Western Europe, general literacy by the mid-19th century was widespread in France and Germany. The same could be said of Britain at a later period, with most workers and farmers having, at most, a primary education.

But Marxists and other progressives in the 20th century have delved into the problems of an alienating education in bourgeois society. In the economically advanced capitalist nations, education is, along with the family, the primary transmission belt to acculturate youth to society's norms. It is only vitally involved in determining the individual's life chances or socioeconomic success.

Not surprisingly, education, as part of an individualistic/ competitive society, is of a ferocious nature. Cooperation here is pictured as being friendly to one's peers and obedient to school authorities. But underneath this façade, there is the constant anxiety of being graded at every turn in relationship to the group or to long-established so-called objective criteria, a condition adversely affecting proper learning. Rewarding winners with good grades and accolades invariably humiliates average and poor students, while engendering pride among the former and resentment among the latter. This learning milieu, intrinsic to a bourgeois-dominated society, alienates in varying degree most of its students, as it is necessarily replete with boredom and futility associated with memorization and rote learning, restricting intellectual curiosity by emphasizing test grades.

With the importance of local taxation in funding education from kindergarten to grade twelve, there are also wide variations spent on children, obviously involved in the socioeconomic differences among various school districts. Socioeconomic alienation is less intense for the students of wealthier neighborhoods, allowing most of them to either attend college or to be accepted by the more prestigious colleges and universities. As observed at all levels, there is competition for grades, although in the higher socioeconomic groups it is muted with many good grades for most students as their academic intelligence, as indicated in tests, is uniformly high. In the working-class, especially its poorer half comprising a large proportion of blacks and Hispanics, great socioeconomic alienation impinges on a good education, with students buffeted by the usual problems associated with poverty, like poor academic performance and accompanying high dropout rates, in a milieu at school characterized by crumbling buildings, antiquated books, and lack of supplies – not to mention a home life encircled by economic insecurity and accompanying general chaos.[35]

Chapter 11: American Socialism

As a revolutionary nation founded by the American Revolution of 1776-83 within a frontier environment, in which land was inexpensive and allowed for rampant socioeconomic equality, the U.S. allowed many communistic religious, especially in the 19th century as the Shakers and Oneida, and the Icarians founded by Etienne Cabet.

A noteworthy utopia was New Harmony in Indiana, founded by utopian socialist Robert Owen in 1825. Another similar society was Brook Farm, near Boston, which remained in existence from 1841-47. Brook Farm's identity and structure closely mirrored Transcendentalism, which was the primary religious-philosophical current among the New England intelligentsia in the mid-19th century; its members included the novelist Nathaniel Hawthorne and editor/ writer Charles A. Dana. Visitors included Ralph Waldo Emerson and Horace Greeley.

It was Emerson, America's great sage of the 19th century, who proclaimed the essentials of socialism: "The union of labor and capital in the same individual through the cooperative principal." In connection with socialism there are three well-known utopian novels: Looking Backward (1888) by Edward Bellany; A Traveler from Altruria (1894) and Through the Eye of the Needle (1907) by William Dean Howell, an outstanding novelist and editor of periodicals, especially Harper's Monthly, 1900-1920. The first novel was very popular: 162 clubs carried its socialist message under the rubric of "nationalism."

In the American radical-socialist tradition, a principal father is the indomitable Radical Republican Thomas Paine, whose 1776 revolutionary pamphlet Common Sense helped spark the American Revolution. He was an arch-democrat, representatives served only short terms. An enemy of kings and aristocracy, he promoted state social services for the unemployed, universal education to age 14, maternity benefits, old age pensions and a graduated income tax. Importantly, he asserted in a socialist vein that wealth beyond personal individual effort "is derived to him by living in society." Or, great wealth comes from using/exploiting others. Nevertheless, he accepted some socioeconomic inequality.

An outstanding early American socialist pioneer was Wendell Phillips, a wealthy Harvard graduate. In his youth, he was an ardent abolitionist and insisted that government provide emancipated blacks with land to guarantee their new freedom. After the Civil War, he became involved in socialist activity. His good society included cooperatives run by workers, equalization of property and education, and ending the invidious wage system pitting workers against one another. His socialist ideas were similar to Marx's. He was an ardent supporter of the 1871 Paris Commune. He ran unsuccessfully for governor of Massachusetts in 1870 on the Labor and Prohibition Party ticket. His socialist newspaper was The National Standard.

The most important socialist after Eugene V. Debs in U.S. history is Daniel De Leon, a Marxist after 1890 who led the Socialist Labor Party (SLP), founded in 1877; in 1898, it had a membership of 80,000. De Leon attended European universities and was a graduate of Columbia University's Law School. He also led the Socialist Trade and Labor Alliance, the industrial union arm of the SLP, and was one of the founders of the syndicalist Industrial Workers of the World (IWW) in 1905.

Debs is the most well-known American socialist. A worker by the age of 15, he quickly engaged in union activity. He became president of the American Railway Union, leading it in the successful strike against the Great Northern Railroad, was involved in the 1894 Pullman Strike, was imprisoned and, while incarcerated, read Marx and became, ultimately, a socialist. He was one of the founders of the Social Democratic Party in 1898, which became the Socialist Party (SP) in 1900. Running on the SP ticket for the U.S. presidency in 1900, 1904, 1908, 1916 and 1920. He opposed U.S. entry into World War I, was tried under the 1917 Espionage Act and jailed, but later pardoned by President Warren Harding in 1921. He was also one of the founders of IWW in 1905, but he soon left it because he opposed its direct action tactics. He advocated socialism to be run from the bottom up, for participatory-democracy; not surprisingly, he was a fierce opponent of bureaucracy.

By circa 1914, the SP had over 126,000 dues-paying members, 31 mayors, and 1,200 lesser offices in 340 towns and cities; also two members in the U.S. House of Representatives, Victor Berger from Milwaukee and Meyer London from New York City. In the 1912 AFL Convention, the socialist Hayes Max received a third of the vote for the presidency running against Samuel Gompers. A socialist periodical, The Appeal to Reason, had a circulation of 300,000. Seventy cities had socialist mayors.

An important socialist periodical, The Masses, 1911-17, with a circulation of up to 20,000, was read by socialist intellectuals, activists, writers, and so forth. It featured articles on politics, art, literature and science. After 1912, it shed its democratic socialist stance for revolutionary action against capitalism. It was barred from U.S. mails when the U.S. entered World War I in April 1917, and its editor Max Eastman and staff were tried under the October 1917 Espionage Act. The case was eventually dropped by the government.

The Masses eventually continued as The Liberator, 1918-23. Among its contributors were Eastman, John Dos Passos, Carl Sandburg, John Reed, Mabel Dodge (from the rich Dodge auto family), Arturo Giovannitti, Upton Sinclair, Edmund Wilson, Bertrand Russell, George Bernard Shaw, Amy Lowell, Floyd Dell, Maxim Gorky, Roger Baldwin, and Stuart Chase.

"Gas and Water" Socialism, the municipal ownership of utilities, natural gas, street cars, water works, etc., was advocated in the 1890s and early 1900s in Toledo by Samuel Jones and in Cleveland by Newton Baker. Baker was successful in socializing water works, the Cleveland Transportation System and Muni Light, which provided electric power.

We should also note the importance of socialism in the early 20th century among reformers, intellectuals, and writers of the Intercollegiate Socialist Society (ICSS), founded in 1905 by the novelist Upton Sinclair, and whose first president was the novelist Jack London. It included such luminaries as Paul H. Douglas (later a U.S. senator from Illinois), Walter Lippmann, Randolph Bourne, Norman Thomas, A.J. Muste, Florence Kelley, Stuart Chase, Vida Scudder, Roger Baldwin, John Dewey, Selig Perlman, and John Sprago, among others.

The ICSS favored evolutionary democratic socialism, public ownership of large industry/banks but allowing for privately owned small business. After World War I in 1918, the ICSS called itself the League for Industrial Democracy. In addition to the preceding socialists (some later became progressives), others included outstanding economists, novelists, dramatists, and composers like Veblen, Ernest Hemingway, Maxwell Anderson, Clifford Odets, Eugene O'Neil, Arthur Miller, Aaron Copeland, and Leonard Bernstein, among many others.

American Socialism suffered a heavy blow with U.S. entry into World War I, with Germany as the primary enemy. This led to much discrimination against German-Americans, many of whom were socialists and viewed as un-American. Furthermore, Russian Communism was portrayed as dictatorial, against democracy and also un-American.

After the death of Debs in 1926, Norman Thomas assumed leadership of the SP. A graduate of Princeton Union Theological Seminary, he was a Presbyterian minister until 1931. He ran as U.S. president on the SP ticket in 1928, 1932 (garnering 880,000 votes, the highest he ever received), 1936, 1940, 1944, and 1948. He was a pacifist and, like democratic socialist Debs, he opposed communism, fascism and American capitalism.

In the 1930s, known primarily as the Great Depression period, the SP did stellar work organizing, establishing mass unemployment councils, and fighting for black equality.

The successful Russian Communist revolution in 1917 and a series of strike actions by American workers in 1919 brought about the First Red Scare of 1919-20. It was led by the Democratic Attorney General A. Mitchell Palmer in the Palmer Raids, which saw "Reds" everywhere, arresting more than 5,000 radicals and deporting 600 aliens. It aided the conservatism of the 1920s.

The 1917 Communist Revolution in Russia eventually led to the formation of the American Communism Party (CP). It was closely aligned to the Soviet Union, basically worker-centered, intimately involved in union activity, especially in the Congress of Industrial Organizations (CIO) with its membership of unskilled and semi-skilled industrial workers. In fact, during the Second Red Scare, the CIO in 1949 expelled all 11 of its CP-dominated unions.

The heyday of the CP was during the Great Depression of the 1930s because it was involved in union organization (half of its membership did so). It was also active in leading black sharecroppers in the South, forming councils for the unemployed and evicted tenants and fighting for improved government relief which resulted in large mass demonstrations in New York City, Chicago, Detroit and Chicago, inevitably battling police. It also aided Mexican farm workers in California and was instrumental in fighting for black civil rights and economic equality, even supporting a separate black nation in a caste-dominated south. The outstanding black leader, W.E.B DuBois, was a Communist, and the black actor, singer, and activist Paul Roheson was closely aligned with the CP. The CP attracted many intellectuals, writers and artists to its ranks as evidenced by its journal, The New Masses. Also, many immigrant workers were either members or sympathetic to the CP's workerism. It fared poorly, however, in presidential elections: William Z. Foster in 1932 garnered about 100,000 votes, the most ever by a CP candidate. CP membership was never large: 75,000 in 1938, 80,000 in 1947 and 17,500 in 1985. CP leaders included Earl Browder, Jay Lovestone, and Gus Hall.

As already noted, the CP played a major role in the 1930s; its influence among the masses should not be underestimated.

American socialism in the 1920s was involved in perhaps the most noted criminal case in American history: Bartolomeo Vanzetti and Nicola Sacco – known as Sacco and Vanzetti. These two Italian immigrant and anarchists were accused of killing two men in a robbery in May 1920 near Boston. They were soon tried, convicted, and sentenced to death for not only the murders but for their anarchist beliefs and the prevalent anti-foreign sentiment that was so prevalent and influential in the 1920s.

American liberals/socialists, including many in the artistic and literary community, fought to exonerate them. Upton Sinclair's novel Boston and Maxwell Anderson's plays, Gods of the Lightning and Winterest, addressed the case and its aftermath; the latter work, which takes place after the executions on August 22, 1927, had Dante Sacco as the main protagonist. Edna St. Vincent Millay, the brilliant poet, also wrote a sonnet for Sacco-Vanzetti. Exactly 50 years after the executions, Michael Dukakis, the Democratic governor of Massachusetts and presidential candidate, exonerated them, declaring their innocence.

The apogee of American social democracy was the 1944, second Bill of Rights Speech of FDR advocating for all the right to a job, home ownership and a comfortable retirement.

With the extension of Communism to Eastern Europe and China soon after World War II, the Second Red Scare of 1945-54 occurred against American Communism. It included the earlier Smith Act (1940) and the McCarran Internal Security Act (1950), spy cases of Julius and Ethen Rosenberg (both executed), and Alger Hiss, a prominent New Dealer and assistant secretary of state. Then there were the Truman Loyalty Program, the "Hollywood Ten" trial of alleged Communist writers, eleven Communist leaders tried and imprisoned, 2,700 Communists losing their jobs and blacklisted, and the CP losing legal status until the 1960s. Then, the Joseph R. McCarthy hearings occurred in the early 1950s in the Senate in which Communists were said to be in and hold offices within the United States government. McCarthy would overreach and discredited himself.

The two Red Scares were basically orchestrated by the conservative corporate elite, or groups of hysterically anti-communist members that smeared not only Communists but also socialists and progressives who wished to reform American society. The Communist threat was a fiction, a mirage like the McCarthy hearings.

While the Second Red Scare was developing in the 1948 elections, the CP supported Henry A. Wallace, FDR's Vice President in 1940-44. Wallace was in the extreme left of the Democratic Party espousing peaceful co-existence with the Soviet Union, which was spreading Communism to Eastern Europe, ending Jim Crow in the South, and expanding New Deal reforms to include universal healthcare, a guaranteed government job program and so on.

To the immediate right of Wallace's Progressive Party was the Americans for Democratic Action (ADA), whose pro-labor and pro-Civil Rights platforms and aims worked for black equality. Its members included Eleanor Roosevelt and Hubert Humphrey, among others. They accused Wallace of being a Communist dupe. Wallace received 1.15 million votes, mostly in New York State.

The ADA, socialists and other progressives did not wish to cooperate with an expansionist Soviet Communism, which was seen as anti-democratic and totalitarian. This view took precedence over Communist destruction of the nobility and capitalists in Czarist Russia and Eastern Europe and establishment of a society of general socioeconomic equality and extensive social welfare programs.

The rise of the New Left in the Students for a Democratic Society (SDS) in the 1960s occurred as living standards were rising – part of the post-war economic expansion in the midst of the Civil/Voting Rights Acts granting full citizenship to blacks in the South, all the while the unpopular war in Vietnam raged. Also, women and other oppressed groups were mounting movements for liberation.

Most SDS members were white middle-class students having a broadly socialist orientation. At its height in 1970, the SDS had about 100,000 members in more than a hundred colleges. It evolved from the older Student League for Industrial Democracy, a democratic socialist organization opposed to the authoritarian communism of the Soviet Union.

SDS aims are encapsulated in the "Port Huron Statement" (1962), written by Tom Hayden, and "America and the New Era" (1963). They include ending materialistic, alienating, war-obsessed and authoritarian capitalism for a decentralized socialist society based on participatory democracy which would eliminate sexism, racism, and discrimination against LGBTs. Furthermore, it would end the manual-mental labor dichotomy with integrated labor combining both as quickly as possible. The end result would be a society of educated people living in a milieu of general socioeconomic, cultural, and political equality. Also, it called for a quick end to the Vietnam War.

The student movement against the Vietnam War began in earnest with "Free Speech" actions at the University of California, Berkeley, in which students occupied the administration building and fought police. As many as 700 students were arrested, leading to a student strike. In April 1968 at Columbia University in New York, SDS-inspired students occupied the library and other buildings to protest the Vietnam War and the university's unsatisfactory relations with the nearby black community. After skirmishes with police, 800 students were arrested.

Another signal event against the war occurred at the August 1968 Democratic Convention in Chicago, where pro-war Hubert Humphrey was elected as its presidential candidate. Ten thousand SDS/leftist youth students converged on the convention, fighting 10,000 police, 6,000 National Guardsmen, and 1,000 FBI agents in a bloody melee. Hundreds were injured and arrested. A government report characterized the event as a "police riot" because police attacked not only students but bystanders.

The strong SDS chapter at Kent State University at Kent, Ohio, protested President Nixon's widening the war in Southeast Asia by invading Cambodia. Four students were killed at the university and nine wounded when members of the Ohio National Guard opened fire on a student demonstration on the campus on May 4, 1970. A few days later at Jackson State (a black college) in Mississippi, two black students were also killed in dormitories by police bullets.

These events triggered the greatest mass student strike in American university history: the closing of almost all universities by millions of students for months to protest the slaughter of students and the continuing Vietnam War. In Europe, French university students began the 1968 May events, whose aim was a new socialist-anarchist society.

In a 1969 SDS split, its left wing – the Weathermen, soon Weatherpeople – embarked on direct action to topple capitalism. Led by Bill Ayers, Mark Rudd and Bernadine Dohrn, its principal event was in "Days of Rage" in Chicago on Oct. 8, 1969, when 600 of them charged police, resulting in hundreds of injured but no deaths. The cops won.

By 1970, the Weatherpeople had launched 423 attacks against police stations and 101 against military bases, with bombings also in Seattle and Madison, Wisconsin. These actions are similar to anarchist "propaganda by Deed," to waken the masses against capitalism.

A Fortune poll in 1968 indicated that 20 percent of college students were favorable to the New Left.

The Black Liberation struggle in the 1960s, especially in the South, witnessed much violence: 37 churches were bombed, resulting in the deaths of many blacks, including children, thousands beaten and arrested. Also there were black city riots in New York, Detroit, Cleveland, and Los Angelas, among others.

These are some of African American organizations that participated in the struggle for justice and equality in the turbulent 1960s: the Southern Christian Leadership Conference of clergy whose chief spokesperson was Dr. Martin Luther King Jr., a democratic socialist; the National Association for the Advancement of Colored People; the Congress of Racial Equality composed of blacks and whites; the leftist Student Nonviolent Coordinating Committee which worked closely with SDS; the CP whose member Angela Davis was very active.

There was also the Nation of Islam and the indomitable Malcolm X who left it, and the Hispanic fight for justice led by Cesar Chavez of the Farm Workers Union, among others.

Native Americans, too, fought for greater rights under the banner of the American Indian Movement led by Dennis Banks and George Mitchell. By the end of the 1970s, Indians won many lawsuits to recover lands under earlier treaty rights. It was also in the 1960s that Gay, Lesbian, Bisexual, Transgendered (LGBT) liberation began in earnest.

Today, SDS and many of the other groups mentioned continue the struggle for more equality and justice. The Occupy Wall Street movement, which erupted in September 2011 with sit-ins in many cities was socialist, and its message drove home the shibboleth of "We are the 99 percent."

The Women's Movement also became prominent in the 1960s with the founding of the National Organziation for Women; it called for women's equality with men, including in pay, opportunity and so forth. Its founders included Betty Friedan, The Femine Mystique, 1963, a key work.

The proceeding leftist movements were well covered by the monthly *Ramparts*, 1962-75. It featured articles by such Leftists as Angela Davis, Noam Chomsky, and Christopher Hitchens, among others.

Closely allied to the New Left is the counterculture "hippie" movement of mostly young people who have dropped out of the capitalist rat races. They live a life of personal liberation/ nonconformity in dress, sexual behavior and values, and expression; they live outside of marriage, live in communes, and are immersed in music, art and illegal drugs.

Today, the large center-left is comprised of the Democratic Party House Congressional Democratic Caucus of 70 or so members whose electorate is largely from large cities, including blacks and Hispanics. It supports free state college tuition, a government job program, raising taxes on the rich and corporations, universal healthcare, increased social welfare benefits for the poor, ending endless wars, and clean energy.

Why has Socialism up to now been politically weak in America? First, slavery and Jim Crow have deeply divided black and white voters. In the South today, Republicans are the white party, blacks the Democratic Party. The racism of white workers allows for much conservative politics. Second, sharp class/status divisions among skilled and unskilled workers related to successive immigrant waves, compounded by ethnic and religious divisions, have also weakened working class unity. Third, relatively high wages/living standards compared to other nations, allowing until recently for some upward social mobility. Fourth, labor reforms via the ballot have led to less radicalism. Fifth, capitalist control of the media extolls capitalism while neglecting labor/socialist activity. Sixth, the class power flow in capitalist societies in which the subaltern workers wish to improve their socioeconomic circumstances, forces them to admire/emulate their class superiors as much as possible, again dampening their class struggle against capital. And of course, declining social mobility in the present age exacerbates the class struggle.

To be sure, underneath the American shibboleths of "democracy," "freedom," and "free enterprise," there is the authoritarianism/ totalitarianism of the economic whip of socioeconomic inequality at whose apex is a small capitalist oligarchy.

Today, interest in socialism in American society is widespread, especially in the age 18-29 category, a group that either favors socialism over capitalism or is equally divided over the merits of capitalism and socialism in opinion polls, as noted in: NYT, Jan. 19, 2012, p. A21; and The Nation, June 11, 2012, pp. 18-22.[1]

American Socialism received a great boost forward when Democratic Socialist and Senator from Vermont, Bernie Sanders, received 46 percent of the vote in the 2016 Democratic Party primaries. Also, there are now more than a hundred socialist chapters in American colleges and universities. In addition, Sanders' Our Revolution Movement, with its democratic socialist program, is now a significant political force.

Of great interest: the most important Socialist organization today is the Democratic Socialist of America, founded in 1982 by Michael Harrington, a college professor and author of The Other America: Poverty in the United States (1962), a key work on the war on poverty launched by President Lyndon Baines Johnson. The co-founder is Barbara Ehrenreich, a well known Socialist journalist. Its membership has grown from 5,000 in 2016 to 48,000-plus in 2018 thanks to the Bernie Sanders political phenomenon.

The DSA is not a party but charges dues. Its Socialist membership includes Marxists, Democratic Socialists who are against government-ownership of the economy but are for socio-economic reform, to be observed.

Also of importance are the present socialist periodicals <u>Dissent</u>, <u>Monthly Review</u>, <u>Jacobin</u>, <u>n+1</u>, <u>Z Magazine</u>, and <u>The Nation</u> (near Socialist).

Chapter 12: Labor, Socialism and Religion

As observed, Marx/Engels and other secular socialists recognized that in periods of historical transition religion itself as a major social institution was invariably involved in their socioeconomic and other tension points, for within its institutional structures the forces of change and the status quo clashed.

It was, therefore, not surprising that a formidable religious reformist and socialist tradition developed in the last two centuries within the world's major religions, such as Christianity, Judaism, Islam, Hinduism, and Buddhism. In other words, the proletarian class struggle to reform or change capitalism for socialism was reflected in either the reformist or totally socialist morality of individual theologians or parts of various religions, the latter, for instance, represented by Catholic Liberation Theology in Latin America.

The exploration begins with the social doctrines of Catholicism, the largest – indeed central – Christian group, fashioned by Catholicism's long history of being part of the governing order in the West, much of it under the rule of kings and nobility. Thus, its core social doctrines historically were of a conservative nature, based on Aristotle and Aquinas, defending private property, the male-dominated patriarchal family, and socioeconomic inequality, although generally antithetical to capitalist "usury," unbridled economic individualism, and large trade and industry, signifying the rise of the bourgeoisie.

Catholic social views often longed for a medieval past when everyone knew his/her place in villages/small towns, with their sense of community, the wealthier socioeconomic groups paternalistically looking after their socioeconomic inferiors under the rubric of "Christian charity."

It should also be pointed out that with few exceptions – Belgium, the Rhineland, northern France, and northern Italy – the Industrial Revolution came rather late to Catholic Europe, permitting the mindset of the Middle Ages to continue. Thus, even the more conservative side of Catholicism lodged in the papacy would decry capitalist evils, wishing to mitigate them while still upholding the new inequality ushered in by capitalism.

The landmark papal encyclical on the socioeconomic ravages that capitalism inflicted on the working-class was *Rerum Novarum* ("Of New Things"), issued by the progressive Pope Leo XIII in 1891. (Encyclicals or papal letters are position papers on Catholic views, which, although not binding on Catholics, carry great weight among them. Only in matters of dogma, like the Immaculate Conception of Mary, are popes considered infallible).

To begin, it lamented capitalist destruction of the medieval craft guilds and the present clearly inadequate social services for the working-class, as "workingmen have been surrendered, isolated and helpless, to the hard-heartedness of employers and the greed of unchecked competition." It, then, denounced the evils of usury and the fact that "a small number of rich men has been able to lay upon the teeming masses of the labouring poor a yoke little better than slavery itself." In appealing to Catholic social justice, it urged employers not to see their workers as slaves, but rather that work in itself was honorable, thus to treat them justly and to pay them a living wage, a wage not based on market-place bargaining, to end the brutality of children working in factories, and to lessen the burden of women's factory work and even eliminating it. It approved of the establishment of labor unions, with the right to strike, recognizing that the collective strength of workers was needed to improve their socioeconomic lot, permitting some form of institutional antagonism between labor and capital, but rejected the notion of a general class struggle advocated by socialists, especially Marxists. In this vein, it denounced industrial violence injuring capital, recommending local, state-sponsored arbitration boards to settle industrial disputes over hours of work and working conditions.

Nevertheless, *Rerum Novarum* accepted socioeconomic inequality as part of the natural order of things, for although God granted the earth to humanity, he left it to human institutions to determine its distribution, an approach related to an almost explicit social Darwinism, of natural inequality as a fact of life: "People differ in capacities, skills, health, strength; and unequal fortune is a necessary result of unequal conditions." Thus, a completely just world could never exist on earth. This defense of private property, insisted that without it "nobody would have any interest in exerting his talents or industry." But it also asked that private property heed the pleas of workers and render them social justice based on "Christian charity," quoting Aquinas that those who have goods share them "without hesitation when others are in need." To be sure, it also condemned an atheistic Marxian socialism. The immediate significance of this encyclical was the formation of Catholic reform parties, like the Catholic Center Party in Germany and the Popular Party in Italy.

*Rerum Novarum* was influenced by the efforts of earlier and contemporary Catholic social activists concerned with ameliorating the lives of workers, like Bishop Emmanuel von Ketteler in Germany and Cardinal James Gibbons in the United States: both favored labor unions – Gibbons, the Knights of Labor, the right to strike, worker-owned cooperatives, and state legislation to aid workers, like reducing working hours and promoting better working conditions.

*Rerum Navarum* was not only reaffirmed, but broadened in *Quadragesimo Anno* ("On the Fortieth Year" of *Rerum Novarum*), in 1931, when Pope Pius XI repeated Catholicism's commitment to more social justice through profit sharing for workers in industry to promote greater harmony between capital and labor, endorsing various forms of fascism, which through the corporate state sought to insure social peace between them.

In *Populorum Progressio* ("On Progress for the People"), Pope Paul VI, a noted liberal scholar whose ideas were very similar to Pope John's, again declared that private property was not an unconditional right without responsibilities, there being no justification for one to retain "what he does not need, when others lack necessities." Furthermore, he broke new ground in asserting the necessity of "building a world where every man, no matter what his race, religion or nationality, can live a fully human life, freed from servitude imposed on him by other men or by natural forces over which he had not sufficient control," castigating the "international imperialism of money," and decrying the increasing gap between rich and poor nations.

Pope John Paul II (the "Polish Pope") in various encyclicals, continued in this social tradition in works such as *Laborem Exercens* ("On Human Work") (1981) and *Centesimus Annus* ("the One Hundredth Year" of *Rerum Novarum*) (1991), allowing as a last resort for armed struggle against socioeconomic oppression. Although defending private property, socioeconomic inequality, free-market economics, and the profit system under capitalist auspices, he maintained that limits be placed on them, subordinated to social justice and to work itself, which played a central role in human development. In fact, he insisted on the "priority of work over capital," which "places an obligation in justice upon employers to consider the welfare of the workers before the increase of profits," and critical importance of unions in working-class life, to protect the "dignity" of workers, including their "participation in the life of the industrial enterprise so that, with others and under the direction of others, they can in a certain sense work for themselves through the exercise of their intelligence and freedom."

Furthermore, in the spirit of human solidarity, he urged society to provide everyone with various social services to insure their well-being, including pensions, health insurance, and workers' compensation. Although the state had a responsibility to bring about social reform, unions also had to be involved in this process. He also criticized a "sinful" and wasteful Western consumerism in a world of great poverty.

These encyclicals were reflected in the United States by The National Conference of Catholic Bishops' pastoral letter in *Economic Justice for All* (1986). It forthrightly declared that, "We feel the pain of our brothers and sisters who are poor, unemployed, homeless living on the edge," and for Catholics to "work actively for social and economic justice." It also affirmed "we judge any economic system by what it does for and to people and by how it permits all to participate in it," and that "all people have a right to life, food, clothing, shelter, rest, medical care, education, and employment."

Importantly, it allowed for the "socialization…of certain means of production" and "cooperative ownership of the firm by all who work within it," urging that "full employment is the foundation of a just economy," and insisting that the "highest priority" was to eliminate the poverty of those on welfare and the lowest income groups to end a "social and moral scandal." Then, too, the letter bestowed proper recognition on labor unions and advocated the strengthening of civil liberties and democratic institutions. These measures were to be undergirded by "an unalienable dignity that stamps human existence prior to any division into races or nations and prior to human labor and human achievement."[1]

Key individuals predated this progressive movement toward a full-fledged socialism in Catholicism. A precursor was the French cleric, Félicité Robert de Lamennais (he flourished in the first half of the 19th century), who attacked the privileges of kings/nobility and capitalists, fearing that the Catholic Church's close association with them would cause the masses to leave it. His solution called for Catholicism to disassociate itself from the ruling classes by accepting the separation of church and state and by supporting a democratic and egalitarian society, freeing the workers from their capitalist overlords through cooperative enterprises. For this and other views, he was excommunicated. Another was the socialist Charles Péguy, who was killed in World War I while in the French army. In his epic poem/drama, *Joan of Arc*, dedicated to individuals working for the "universal socialist republic," he synthesized a deep religious fervor with an equally great love for socialism. In his *Socialist City (De la cité socialiste)*, he sketched the outlines for a future democratic and socialist society whose economic parameters featured cooperatives run by workers, clearly in the tradition of Proudhon and revolutionary syndicalism.

Perhaps the most noted Catholic theologian of 20th century, the French neo-Thomist, Jacques Maritain, an intimate of Péguy, became a Christian socialist by the 1930s, inspired by *Rerum Novarum* and *Quadragesimo Anno*. In *True Humanism* (1936), he cogently spelled out the need for a "certain collectivization of ownership" in large enterprises inasmuch as it protected human dignity and solidarity. In citing Proudhon and Sorel, he upheld the principle of economic democracy, involving workers' ownership/management through unions, labor not to be regarded as simply a commodity by capital, socioeconomic arrangements to be so organized that a worker's job was a right. Then, too, the new society would guarantee all of its citizens a comfortably standard of life. These economic imperatives would take place in the context of an open and free democratic society in a "pluralistic commonwealth" of competing ideologies. He disseminated his liberal/socialist ideas in America as a professor at Columbia and Princeton.

Another prime example of Catholic socialism was the personalist (he stressed the primacy of the individual) Emmanuel Mounier, the founder and editor of *Esprit*, the leading French Catholic Journal, from 1932 until his death in 1950. Under Mounier, *Esprit* engaged in a serious dialogue with Marxism/Communism.[2]

Weil was another outstanding example of Catholic socialism, particularly of the anarcho-syndicalist variety; we have already discussed her book on working-class alienation under capitalism. Her influence on the Catholic left in Europe, the United States, and elsewhere was considerable, as on Pope Paul VI. Although never baptized as a Catholic, this upper-middle class French-Jewish professor of Greek at a lycée, after several mystical experiences, one in which she felt the presence of Christ, became a devout Catholic, thoroughly immersed in a Catholic milieu. Earlier, she had supported Communism, but was appalled by Stalinism, turning to revolutionary syndicalism, deeply involved in its Workers' Education Circle.[3]

In the United States itself, there is the well-known Catholic socialist-anarchist movement, The Catholic Worker (CW), founded in the early 1930s by Dorothy Day and Peter Maurin; its monthly journal, *The Catholic Worker*, which began publication on May 1, 1933, is still going strong. Day, born into a middle-class Episcopalian family, joined the American Socialist Party, became a reporter for the socialist *New York Call*, and was involved in the publication of the *Masses* and the *Liberator*. In 1927, she converted to Catholicism.

Maurin, born into a poor French peasant family, was a member of
the Christian Brothers for nine years, joined the *Sillon* (Furrow)
movement favoring workers and unions, farmed in Canada for many
years, and went to New York City in 1925 as an unskilled worker,
where he eventually met Day. The general socioeconomic views of
the CW were heavily influenced by Kropotkin, Tolstoy, Martin Buber,
the Jewish religious philosopher who contributed to their newspaper
(more on him soon), and the English Distributism of the Catholics
Hilaire Belloc and Gilbert K. Chesterton, espousing a return to a
medieval-like society of small towns and villages dominated by small
producers/property, honoring work, and not charging interest.

Specifically, Day and Maurin called for a decentralized society
based on mutual aid whose socioeconomic parameters combined
small private property in a communitarian setting of small farms
and factories. Tools, land, buildings, and machinery (the last kept to
a minimum) were to be held in common, wage labor and assembly
lines done away with, and crafts restored, freeing workers from
meaningless/alienating work. Furthermore, they would end racism,
anti-Semitism, all exploitation, and war. CW members are pacifists,
even refusing to fight in World War II. The CW combated poverty
with Houses of Hospitality, staffed by volunteers.

The influence of the CW on American Catholic intellectuals and
members of the Church's hierarchy should not be underestimated:
socialists and peace stalwarts, like Michael Harrington and Fathers
Daniel and Philip Berrigan, the last two imprisoned for anti-Vietnam
war activities, are closely associated with it.[4]

The importance of Socialism today within Catholicism is also
well illustrated by the splendid work of the Maryknoll Order among
workers and farmers in Latin America and by their outstanding
publishing house, Orbis Books, a valuable resource of Catholic
Socialism, emphasizing the social struggle in poor nations.

In Latin America, Catholic Liberation Theology, whose doyen
is Gustavo Gutierrez, today encompasses a large minority of the
Catholic clergy, playing a leading role in establishing more than
200,000 Basic Christian Communities or mutual-aid groups. It was

also much involved in the Sandinista Revolution in Nicaragua. Its theology, combining the revolutionary life of Jesus of Nazareth and revolutionary Marxist socioeconomic analysis, envisages a God of the poor and oppressed who encourages them to fight for a better life in the here and now.

An examination of Gutierrez's *A Theology of Liberation* (1973), a leading work of this movement, follows. To begin, Gutierrez categorically proposed a socialist solution to solve the manifold problems of contemporary society, based on the "social ownership of the means of production." In socialism's construction, he quoted Che Guevara on the importance of not only increasing material prosperity, but in transforming the human person for the better.

He also favored Marxian class struggle, which occurred within the "church itself," between the "oppressors" (the wealthy and their allies) and "oppressed" (workers and farmers), many of them living in "material poverty," a "scandalous condition," and in a "subhuman situation." Thus, "class enemies" existed and "it is necessary to combat them." In this regard, he asserted that "to love all men does not mean avoiding confrontations; it does not mean preserving a fictitious harmony." Indeed, the "liberation of the poor and the liberation of the rich are achieved simultaneously. One loves the oppressors by liberating them from their inhuman condition as oppressors." Anyone denying the existence of the class struggle, for him, including the Church, could only aid the "dominant sectors," there being no neutrality here. He charged the Catholic Church in Latin America with being part of the present capitalist and "alienating" social system, of upholding its "dominant ideology," based on the "worst kind of violence – a situation which pits the powerful against the weak." Only by severing its ties with this power structure, with a "radical critique" of it, could the Church properly fulfill its mission on earth.

In this vein, Gutierrez examined the concept of sin in human history, which he insisted was of an individual/collective nature, i.e., individual sin was related to the larger socioeconomic and other collective sins, to be "regarded as social, historical fact, the absence of brotherhood and love in relationship among men, the breach of friendship with God and with other men, and, therefore, an interior personal fracture." This "sin is evident in oppressive structures, in the exploitation of man by man, in the domination and slavery of peoples, races, and social classes." Sin was, thus, "the fundamental alienation, the root of a situation of injustice and exploitation." Only by overcoming this sin could humanity witness in history the "growth of the Kingdom," but itself is "not the coming to the Kingdom, not of all salvation." Thus, although allowing for the existence of a socialist humanity, he also saw that a supernatural occurrence was needed for complete human fulfillment/liberation.

The ending of class oppression and a classless society, for Gutierrez, was ultimately based on God's love for humanity, which literally demanded that humans love one another, for following the Hebrew prophetic tradition, "man is created in the image of God." Individual/class oppression was thus an affront to God, indicating alienation from Him and the general community, the Bible replete with denunciations of the wealthy oppressing the poor, insisting on a society of general equality and "common ownership of goods," as in Acts, instituting a proper *koinonia* (Greek for "community").[5]

Protestantism, no less than Catholicism, has been progressively involved in the socialist project. In mid-19th century England, the term "Christian Socialism" was first coined by two Anglican ministers, Frederick Denison Maurice and Charles Kingsley (both were professors at Cambridge University, the former in moral philosophy and the latter in history), and J.M. Ludlow, a lawyer. Their periodical, *The Christian Socialist*, condemned a selfish and predatory middle-class ethic for one based on political democracy and worker-run cooperatives.[6]

In the United States, the Protestant Social Gospel movement was especially influential in the 1900-1920 period, during the heyday of American socialism. It continued the earlier Christian utopianism of the first half of the 19th century, although different social and economic settings characterized the two movements: the first thrived in a basically rural milieu and was usually fundamentalist, while the second acted in the urban scene, coping with intense working-class poverty, generally accepting science, and Darwinian evolution.[7]

Two early exponents of this Protestantism were Washington Gladden, a Congregationalist minister from Columbus, Ohio, and Richard T. Ely, a professor of economics at Johns Hopkins, University of Wisconsin, and Northwestern. The former advocated a world without racial and religious prejudice – deeply aware of the plight of African-Americans and the wrongs perpetuated upon them by society and of prejudice between Catholics and Protestants – and took an active interest in alleviating working-class misery, to be remedied by extensive socialization of industry (mines, railroads, telephones and telegraph, gas, electricity, and water), and cooperative ownership of large business: "All people should unite to furnish the capital and direct the work," a view reminiscent of Emerson's dictum uniting labor and capital. The latter, a consistent advocate of labor, supported the eight-hour day, formation of labor unions, abolition of child labor, workers' compensation, and the nationalization of large industry, but allowed small private enterprise.[8]

The foremost proponent of the movement was Walter Rauschenbusch, who after graduating from a gymnasium in Germany, attended the University of Rochester, Rochester Theological Seminary, and the University of Berlin, concentrating on economics and theology; then, he went to London to study industrial relations, meeting members of the socialist Fabian Society.

Thus it was that when Rauschenbusch became the pastor of the Second Baptist Church in New York City, in a slum near Hell's Kitchen to minister to working-class German immigrants, his interest in socialism quickened. (In addition to Christ and the Bible, the other important ethical-intellectual influences on his socialism included Marx, Edward Bellamy's *Looking Backward*, Henry George's *Progress and Poverty*, Leo Tolstoy, and the Fabians). As early as 1900, he supported the Presidential runs of Eugene V. Debs, the standard-bearer of the American Socialist Party (ASP), although he never joined it.

The principle model for Rauschenbusch's socialism was primitive Christianity as practiced in the Book of Acts, buttressed by the belief that God worked in history for the growing perfection of human beings and their collective institutions. In the coming of socialism, he assigned to the working class the principal role because it suffered the most, the goodness-through-suffering theme.

In *Christianity and the Social Crisis* and *A Theology for the Social Gospel*, Rauschenbusch condemned capitalism as the greatest enemy of God, a system spawning great riches and its corollary of great poverty, "inherent in a social system that exalted profit and position above virtue, and an economy that taught us to approach economic questions from the point of view of goods and not of man," of treating people like things or commodities, encouraging a competitive spirit based on covetousness, invariably breeding fear and intolerance, in which the new machine technology, although leading to more economic abundance, also brought the specters of unemployment and ill-distribution of wealth. His remedy proposed a society of general equality, socializing large property under the control of the producers, alongside small private enterprise, to come through democracy and passive resistance; he influenced, for instance, Dr. Martin Luther King, Jr., also a democratic socialist.[9]

The socialist impulse of the Social Gospel extended to the 1930s depression period. One of its leading figures, Reinhold Niebuhr, a disciple of Rauschenbusch and a well-known theologian, joined the ASP, running once unsuccessfully on its ticket for the U.S. House of Representatives. He later became a left liberal, one of the founders of Americans for Democratic Action in 1940.[10] Norman Thomas, the chief spokesperson of the ASP after Debs' death, also entered socialism through the religious route, as a Presbyterian minister.[11] He ran for president in 1928, 1932, 1936, 1940, 1944, and 1948.

Today, the Social Gospel tradition continues in American life through mainline Protestantism and Orthodoxy in The National Council of the Churches of Christ in the United States, comprising progressive elements of both, which enunciates a left liberal, if not a moderate socialist, economic and social orientation. For instance, it envisages the possibility, with the recent, spectacular developments in technology/production, of "a world without hunger, nakedness or human beasts of burden," "participation" of the citizenry in the decision-making process in society, for all people "regardless of employment status" to have "an adequate livelihood," the vital importance of "human rights and freedoms," narrowing the income gap between the rich and the poor nations, and the diminution of the armaments race. It is also acutely aware of the "hazards of great wealth," holding that private property is not an absolute right, and of the dangers of pollution.[12]

In Europe, the two foremost Protestant theologians of the 20th century, Karl Barth and Paul Tillich (both also active ministers), were firmly lodged in the socialist camp. Barth, depicted as the "red" pastor in his native Switzerland, wholeheartedly assisted workers in their fight to establish unions and win higher wages and recognized the importance of politics to achieve socialism, becoming a member of the Social Democrats.

Tillich, author of *Systematic Theology* and a chaplain in the German Imperial Army in World War I, was so utterly appalled by the death and destruction unleashed by the forces of autocracy and capital, that he became a left-wing socialist. In fact, in the work that he was most proud of, *The Socialist Decision*, he emphasized the critical role of Marx in developing a working-class consciousness, realizing that under capitalist economic arrangements, workers were invariably condemned to an inherent inferiority. In the tradition of Marx and Proudhon, among others, he believed that socialism would at once "liberate the workers from having to work for someone else's profit," educate them in understanding the complexities of the new technology, and remove the curse of purely repetitive work through technological innovation. In the tempestuous period after the collapse of Imperial Germany shortly after the war, when Germany was on the brink of a social revolution, he rejected the Communists and reformist Social Democrats, only to endorse the revolutionary Independent Socialists. He also had the rare distinction of being the first non-Jew to lose his professorship at a Germany university with the advent of Nazism. With the aid of Niebuhr, he came to America to continue his teaching.[13]

Count Leo Tolstoy and Nicholas Berdyaev represented the radical Orthodox socialist tradition. Tolstoy, the author of *War and Peace* and *Anna Karenina*, enjoyed the wealth, power, and culture of one born into the Russian nobility in the 19th century, advantages gained at the expense of the peasantry that, until the 1860s, were serfs. In his middle years, Tolstoy experienced a religious conversion to imitate Jesus as a Christian anarchist, practicing an ascetic lifestyle, rejecting individual possessions, and identifying himself with the peasantry. He would change the world through non-violent resistance, by non-payment of taxes, and refusal to serve in the military, actions based on Christian love. The ultimate aim of these pursuits was to establish cooperative communes, devoid of private property, where people live and work together on the basis of equality and solidarity. This pervasive radicalism resulted in his excommunication from the Russian Orthodox Church.[14]

Berdyaev, the outstanding Orthodox theologian of the 20th century, enunciated a controversial theology that reflected an individualist view of religion – a personalist – embedded in a mystical eschatological vision. Since he regarded himself as a member of the Russian intelligentsia, in the legacy of Tolstoy and Dostoevsky in the religious realm, and of the Westernizer socialists, like Herzen, Belinsky, Chernishevsky, and Bakunin, his thought combined a deep religiosity to a basically Marxist/anarchist perspective; he loathed the authority of the state.

A rebel Marxist youth, Berdyaev repudiated the class of his parents, the nobility, for the working-class and Marxism. Although he later left Marxism for religion, he remained steadfast in his socialist convictions, including the cooperative ownership of the means of production, decentralist patterns to prevent authoritarianism, the abolition of wage labor, and participatory democracy. The end result of his socialism was the creating of a new working-class, akin to the old nobility, in which classlessness would still allow for some status differentiation. Berdyaev was expelled from the Soviet Union in

1922 because he refused to abandon religious activities, migrating to France to become a close friend of Maritain and Mounier.[15]

Principal thinkers of Judaism, Hinduism, Islam, and Buddhism have also embraced socialism. In Judaism, Martin Buber, a professor of religion and social ethics at the University of Frankfurt before spending the last years of his life at the Hebrew University in Jerusalem, was its leading, near-contemporary thinker. An expert on Hasidism, the widespread religious phenomenon gripping the Jewish poor in Eastern Europe in the last few centuries, he analyzed the connection between utopian longings and social misery.

The good society, for Buber, would be a socialist one whose socioeconomic parameters insured a general equality. But for it to flourish, its primary ethical values of cooperation in the spirit of equality and brotherhood must be daily experienced in the personal interactions of its citizenry, otherwise it would lack authenticity. Thus, he rejected the Soviet Communist experience/model for the anarchist-socialist one of Proudhon, Kropotkin, and especially of Gustav Landauer, a German-Jewish social philosopher and socialist who added to the views of the first two, the element of religion, in the sense of its being "a bond of common spirit in freedom."

Buber saw the best example of this good society in the Israeli *kibbutzim*, whose small-scale collectively-owned property allowed for participatory democracy at work and intense social engagement, all under the bonds of a shared historical heritage, of language/ ethnicity, and religious tradition. To be sure, *kibbutzim* personnel play a leading role in the Israel Labor Party today, including the staffing of its top leadership. But *kibbutzim* now are themselves important capitalist enterprises, hiring labor, losing, in the process, their earlier idealism.[16]

Mohandas K. Gandhi is surely one of the giants of our age. Born into an Indian Hindu family in the *Vaisya* caste, he led a life of privilege. His father was an important, local politician. Gandhi was educated in both India and in England, studying law in London and admitted to the bar. While in South Africa, practicing law in the 1890s, he encountered the systematic dehumanization of white racism, which he decided to change through *Satyagraha*, or love-force, a nonviolent resistance to evil.

Deeply influenced by Tolstoy, Gandhi founded a Tolstoy farm in 1910, a cooperative village based on the moral foundations of love-force to challenge racist South Africa. This utopian experiment embodied the key contours of his vision of the good society, of free individuals living in self-governing cooperative villages, where the work was of the cottage-industry variety (he opposed the dehumanization of Western industrialism) that would allow for not only full employment but the necessary smallness to promote human solidarity. He would even permit some petty capitalism, but at death, one's estate reverted to the community. In 1915, Gandhi returned to India to fight for its independence from British rule, spending many years in prison for practicing the passive resistance of love-force.

The social ethics of Gandhi, which obviously included his socialism (he once stated that everyone's time was equally valuable), were firmly based not only on the Hindu classics like the Bhagavad-Gita, but on the Bible and Koran, which he read daily. Under the inspiration of the love-force, he also became a determined champion of the *Dalits*, whom he called *harijans*, or "Children of God." In 1948, Gandhi was assassinated by a Moslem zealot whom he forgave as he fell to the ground.[17]

Islamic societies, no less than those of other religions, have also been active participants in the modern socialist project: to be sure, secular socialism in its Marxist form has not influenced their peasant masses, although it has had some impact in urban areas among workers and middle-class intellectuals. Early Islam, like Christianity, attempted a radical reorganization of society, with its precepts of a fraternal and generally egalitarian community based on social justice, with no interest on loans.

Recent Islamic socialism has both a fundamentalist or theocratic bent (under the Ayatollah Ruholla Khomeini in Iran), and a generally secular current under Gamal Abdul Nasser in Egypt, Mu'ammar Qaddafi in Libya, the ruling Ba'th socialist parties in Syria and Iraq, and in the governing parties of Algeria and Tunisia. Its hallmarks are widespread nationalization of industry and banking, cooperatives in the countryside, and extensive social welfare. Concerning women, the Iranian radical fundamentalists have championed the veil or traditional sexism, although the Libyans, the Ba'th group and the Algerian and Tunisian socialist have a liberal position toward them.

The most thoroughgoing socialist party in the Islamic world was that of Libya under Qaddafi, which has socialized the means of production and exchange, with people's committees running society, resulting in a pervasive egalitarianism so intense that any business outside of small family has employees who are partners. To promote women's equality, Qaddafi and the left of the revolution have also consciously and successfully integrated women into economic life outside the home, even attempting, without success, to let them serve in the military.

The handbook of this revolution is Qaddafi's *Green Book*, a fiercely anti-capitalist and pervasively socialist tract. Examples: "No individual has the right to carry out economic activity in order to acquire more...wealth than is necessary to satisfy his needs, because the excess amounts belongs to other individuals"; "Whoever works in a socialist corporation is a partner in its production"; and, "Whoever works for a wage has no incentive to work."

This tract challenges the traditional conservative Moslem clerics, or *ulama*, for a socialist Islam based on the communal/egalitarian scriptures of the Koran, disregarding the *hadith* or narratives of Mohammed, in agreement with some Islamic and many Western scholars who question its authenticity, akin to Moslem *Shii* views.

The success of this revolution was based on the support of the impoverished Libyan masses whose Bedouin egalitarianism and sense of individuality within the communal boundaries of family, clan, and tribe are proverbial. Furthermore, a weak bourgeoisie and large oil revenues aided in the generally weak resistance to socialism associated with modernity. Then, there was the key influence of the anti-imperialism and socialism of Nasser on Qaddafi and the revolutionary youth of his generation. The official name of Libya is the Socialist People's Libyan Arab *Jamahiriyyah*; the last word denotes "people's democracy." But Qaddafi became dictatorial and was deposed.

Another outstanding Islamic socialist was the Iranian intellectual/ teacher, Dr. Ali Shariati, one of the principal inspirers of the 1979 Islamic Revolution in Iran. His education, including studies at the Sorbonne in Paris, synthesized traditional *Shii* concerns for social justice, as embodied in the return of the Twelfth Imam to usher in the definitive era of social justice, with world socialist thought. He was an enthusiastic supporter of the Cuban and Algerian socialist revolutions and admirer of the now-legendary Third-World-revolutionary Communist, Che Guevara.

To be sure, Shariati was an ardent proponent of the centrality of the class struggle in history waged by the masses (peasantry and workers) against their governing elites (landlords and bourgeoisie), and within this model opposed Western imperialism, along with its junk consumerism and racism. Furthermore, like Rauschenbusch and Gutierrez in their studies of Christianity, he contrasted early revolutionary Islam under Ali, one of equality and brotherhood, with the later one of the Savafid dynasty, of sharp class divisions and concomitant socioeconomic oppression.

A final remark on political Islam: Jon Obert Voll, an authority on the subject, noted that its radical fundamentalist current has both a "long-term durability" and ability to "inspire revolution." [18]

Buddhism was founded by Siddhartha Gautama (563-483 B.C.), called the Buddha or Enlightened One. The religion of Buddhism is yet another philosophy/religion compatible with Socialism. The Buddha, a prince from the *Kshatriya* Hindu caste and from what is now Nepal, renounced family, wealth and power after observing the great disparities between his privileged life and the socioeconomic misery of the masses. In attempting to understand why the elite enjoyed wealth and power, while the masses suffered, he became an ascetic for six years, living in a forest, but eventually concluding that this did not lead to wisdom in changing society. His solution called for a peaceful social revolution, of nonviolence or *ahimsā*, rejecting the Hindu caste system, but still adhering to its reincarnation cycle.

The Buddha conceptualized a deep dichotomy in the human condition, of injustice and strife, but also goodness that promised liberation. On the one hand, life was pervaded by general suffering, physical illness, death, and psychological anguish/alienation from thwarted desires and disappointments in seeking wealth/power to gratify the senses, related to individual-social selfishness. On the other hand, there also existed a strong desire for justice and equality within the human condition, to be attained through the "four noble truths," "eightfold way," and compassion and loving kindness for all living creatures.

Thus it was that the Buddha established *sangha* chapters, akin to Christian monasteries, admitting even *Dalits* to practice a communist poverty and celibacy in equality. The Buddha himself was ultimately a communist, calling nothing his own, and in anticipating the early Christians, deemed begging meritorious, encouraging the first general strike of the masses against their wealthy exploiters. Furthermore, he viewed great wealth as wicked, the only decent thing being to give it to the poor, thus indicating his abhorrence of wealth and power.

Early Buddhism today is best represented by its *Hinayana* or *Theravada* form (strong in Southeast Asia, Sri Lanka, Myanmar, Cambodia, Thailand, and Vietnam), which regards the Buddha as a great human reformer, denies the existence of a personal and omnipotent/omniscient god/force, including one creating the universe, and rejects the immortality of the soul. But there is still a transcendent and all-powerful supernatural force permeating the universe, which judges, as already observed, human and other living beings according to their *karma.*

The *Mahayana* version of Buddhism, which continues in India, China, Tibet, Taiwan, and Japan, regards the Buddha as a god-like figure and believes in *bodhisattvas*, human beings achieving moral perfection returning to Earth to further everyone's salvation.

Buddhism itself suffered greatly in India and China where it was once strong. In India, the invasions of the White Huns in the 6th century and Turkic Moslems in the 11th century, in addition to the Hindu counterattack, terminated Buddhism as a viable force.

But it survived as part of Hinduism, the Buddha becoming one of the avatars of the god Vishnu. Recently, Buddhism gains strength there, especially among the *Dalits*. In China, Buddhism had many adherents, but waned in strength when the emperor Wu-Tsung in the 9th century, fearing the growing power of the tax-exempt *sangha* chapters, abolished many of them.

Buddhism, like other religions in their accepting the patronage of kings, implicitly reinforced the status quo of class and attendant oppression, in the process of which *sangha* chapters became corrupt. This state, in turn, was often related to focusing on individual salvation, tending to minimize or ignore the broader socioeconomic causes contributing to individual-social alienation. Indeed, only *sangha* members could generally escape the deadly grip of real-existing life, of brutal exploitation of the many. Not surprisingly, Buddhism often magnified the small sins of the poor, while the large individual and collective socioeconomic ones of the ruling elite were often downplayed, indicating their hegemony.

The *karma-nirvana* doctrine (in some degree related to family *karma* and even beyond in some Buddhist texts) ostensibly rewards the rich and powerful while condemning the poor for former-life sins: in Tibet, prior to their liberation by Chinese Communism, slaves of the feudal aristocracy and monasteries were told by them that this was the why of their lowly status. Furthermore, are the people of the First World more virtuous than those of the Second and Third? But from the perspective that members of the *sanghas* attempt to escape exploitative/alienating society – this can never be done completely – the *sangha* counterculture is potentially revolutionary.

Buddhism along with other major religions today emphasizes the importance of the socioeconomic element in the makeup for some happiness, itself in Buddhism texts and in recent Buddhist lay movements, like the *Soka Gakkai* ("Value Creation Society") in Japan, with its more than one million well-organized followers (this is a tightly-knit mutual-aid society): A formidable force in contemporary Japanese politics, it firmly endorses a form of a this-world paradise, its followers urged to strive for wealth and all that goes with it, like good health and many friends.

To be sure, Buddhism, along with other religions mentioned, has now many socialist adherents. Sri Lanka, a predominantly Buddhist nation, has a powerful Buddhist socialist tradition, leading to extensive nationalization of the productive forces undergirded by democracy. Its official name is Democratic Socialist Republic of Sri Lanka. In Myanmar, organized Buddhism is the principal force bringing about its socialist character, of large-scale nationalization of commerce, industry, and land, undergirded by peasants' and workers' councils. This nationalization for U Nu, a Buddhist and former prime minister, was in accordance with Buddhist principles: "Property is meant not to be saved, not for gains. It is to be used by men to meet their needs in their journey to Nirvana." But he rejected state socialism for one in which workers and peasants actively participated in running the economy.

Regarding the key question involving relations between Marxism (and Soviet and Chinese Communism) and Buddhism, the views of D.C. Vasayavardhana (*The Revolt in the Temple*, 1953), a prominent Sri Lankan Buddhist intellectual, are representative. He noted the many similarities between the aims of Marxism and Buddhism, like human brotherhood and equality, international peace, and their shared rationalism, but disapproved of Marxian class struggle and dictatorship of the proletariat, opting instead for an evolutionary road to socialism through "discussion, cooperation, agreement." Buddhism itself suffered greatly under a militantly atheist Chinese Communism, but the Chinese government has now restored many previously destroyed Buddhist temples and monasteries.[19]

To be sure, Marx's prophecy of traditional religion's becoming progressively irrelevant, predicated on the increasing importance of science/technology, itself associated with the rise of the city and mass secular education, is partly correct. The following in percentages for contemporary regular church attendance on any given Sunday: the United States, 44; Ireland, above 50; 5 or under in Germany and Scandinavia; 27 in the UK; 21 in France; and 40 in Italy. In former

Communist Eastern Europe/Soviet Union, 2, but more than 50 in Poland. Outside these areas, Communist China is officially atheist, but India is very religious. Indeed, as already observed, in the Islamic world, Catholic Latin America, and in Hindu and Buddhist nations, where religion is important, it itself must become ever more socialist to survive.

Other statistics on religion are in order: on acceptance of life-after-death for selected nations in percentages: the U.S. and the two Irelands, 80; Italy, 65; Poland, 60; West Germany, 55; former East Germany, 12; UK, 50; Israel, 42. As for belief in God (not only a theistic one), for selected nations in percentages: the U.S. leads with 94, followed by Italy, the two Irelands and Poland, from the mid-80s to low 90s; UK and Israel, 70; West Germany, 65; East Germany, 32; Norway, 60; Russia, 54. Belief in traditional Christianity in the U.S. varies widely, highly correlated with the amount of general education, socioeconomic status and region. For instance, in a survey after World War II, among four denominations, in percentages: on belief in Jesus as God's divine son – Congregationalists, 40; Methodists, 54; Catholics, 86; Southern Baptists, 99. On belief in life after death – Congregationalists, 36; Methodists, 49; Catholics, 75; Southern Baptists, 97. And on the belief in the definite second coming of Jesus – Congregationalists, 13; Methodists, 21; Catholics, 47; Southern Baptists, 94.[20]

In discussing the major religions, we observed their double standard with respect to worldly wealth and power. For instance, they allowed their average adherents to engage in war and to succeed in business, thus permitting the economic exploitation of labor, including the employment of slavery – although Buddhists were admonished not to engage in the slave trade – and were not too kind to unbelievers or members of other religions, invariably condemning them to the fires of hell or to deferred salvation. Thus, it is neither surprising that when members of different religions wish to marry one another and have children, "religious" disputes typically follow, nor is it surprising that various religious-social associations themselves invite conflict in business and other areas of life as they usually favor their co-religionists at the expense of others, nor that religiously-inspired warfare among and within religious groups, is a common occurrence.

Penultimate remarks on religion in the U.S.: the progressive elements of it have been catalogued, but the Catholic Church's position on abortion and sexuality is still reactionary, although 85 percent of Catholic couples use contraceptives and many approve of abortion, especially in the first trimester.

There is also a conservative white Protestant fundamentalism, most of whose adherents are from the white working and lower-middle classes, which is highly racist, homophobic, sexist, and opposes abortion. They staunchly resist civil rights for blacks and other minorities. Their leading conservative ministers, all Republicans, include Pat Robertson, Jerry Falwell, and Donald Wildmon. The Reverend Billy Graham does not endorse Presidential candidates, but he gave an unofficial nod to George W. Bush in the 2000 election. To be sure, the many Black Protestant fundamentalists are on the left of the main political spectrum; Dr. Martin Luther King Jr. was a democratic socialist and many others are near socialists. The historically sharp socioeconomic differences between the two groups explain their respective politico-religious orientations.[21]

Will alienated institutional religion escape its exclusiveness, with its bigotry and parochialism (the Unitarian Universalist Association has), and even unite to establish a world which the great religious prophets were pointing towards a worldwide fraternal society of general equality, fraternity, and liberty based on pervasive democratic norms? Perhaps, but only if they become more spiritual, which includes embracing more tolerance and more socialism.

Postscript

An important religious development is its concern with global warming and its dire consequences for humanity. In this regard, Pope

Francis' 2015 encyclical, <u>Laudato Si (Our Care for Our Common Home)</u> is a milestone.

To begin, Francis particularly acknowledges the work of Orthodox Patriarch Bartholomew's concern with global warming and ills of a profligate consumerism which is intimately related to them, to be replaced "with a spirit of sharing" worldwide.

Pope Francis, also a scientist with an MA in chemistry, describes greenhouse gases, especially carbon dioxide, caused principally by technology employing fossil fuels, cause global warming, rising sea levels and so forth imperiling humanity. To end this scourge, he calls for a concerted worldwide effort to convert to clean energy, like solar and wind power.

In this endeavor, the wealthier nation's most responsible for global warming should aid the poorer ones. Also, Francis urges that the neoliberal/capitalist economic model based on mass consumerism and conspicuous consumption be replaced with one embodying "the principal of the common good," which would end poverty and unemployment and terminate the world's militaries, which, based on budgets and annual spending, are significantly costly – and wasteful, according to its critics.

Francis' attack on neoliberalism does not do away with private property, but he warns that "it must serve the common good, that it is not absolute or inviolable."

Francis also decries capitalist financial bubbles, leading to economic downturn and increasing unemployment/socio-economic misery. He is also aware of how technological changes lead to unemployment.

Francis' deep concern for social justice is also amply indicated in a March 2015 speech to the Italian cooperative movement. Specifically, he condemned widespread unemployment caused by capitalist market economies, horrific working conditions/long work days, workers easily replaced, and so forth, and workers submitting to "hunger."

To end these horrid conditions, Francis calls for "new models and methods" to end a throw-away system by those that control the economy – who, I should add, are a capitalist oligarchy.

The proper economic approach to the new society, according to Francis, is one which men have control over capital, not vice-versa; and that would be accomplished through cooperatives presumably and, ideally, under workers' control.

An ardent opponent of contemporary Global Capitalism, Pope Francis condemned it in 2013, claiming it embodied the "survival of the fittest where the powerful feed upon the powerless" and "where masses of people…are excluded…without work, without possibilities, without means of escape." In addition: "While the earnings of a minority are growing exponentially, so, too, is the gap separating the majority from the prosperity enjoyed by those happy few. This imbalance is the result of ideologies which defend the absolute autonomy of the marketplace and financial speculation."

The thirst for power and possession is limitless. In this system, which tends to devour everything that stands in the way of increased profits, whatever systems (like the environment) are defenseless before the interests of a deified market which becomes the only rule. In a speech to the association of Italian cooperative movements, Pope Francis landed more attacks on contemporary neoliberal global capitalization: 1) high chronic unemployment; 2) insufficient healthcare funding; 3) concern for the poor without hope, forced to work long hours in the underground economy at low wages, who are readily "replaceable" by others in desperate economic straits.

These workers labor simply to avoid "hunger."

Then, he praised the Italian cooperative movement as a path to obviate "the throw-away culture created by the powers that control the economic and financial policies of the globalized world." He cautioned, however, that in these cooperatives "capital does not command over men, but men over capital," a thoroughly socialist notion.

Laudato Si draws upon previous Papal encyclicals, including Pope John XXIII's Pacem in Terris, (Peace on Earth), rejecting war for peace; of Pope Paul VI, awareness of ecology of destruction by "human activity"; of John Paul's II first encyclical on the dangers of unrestrained human consumption on earth's environment; of

Pope Benedict XVI's calling for the elimination of global economic "dysfunctions" and to protect a severely damaged nature; of Orthodox Patriarch Bartholomew for protecting the natural environment by clean technology, and to replace consumption with sacrifice, greed with generosity, wastefulness with a spirit of sharing" and so on.

In some detail, Pope Francis describes devastation caused principally by carbon dioxide producing global warming and leading to great "climate change and unprecedented destruction of ecosystems with serious consequences for all of us," like rising sea levels endangering "a quarter of the population" and the "majority of our megacities" on the coasts. The poor themselves are especially affected by water deterioration caused by mining, chemical products, water shortages, ocean acidification, threatening marine life, forest and biodiversity losses. Francis noted the technological impact not only on nature, but on its socioeconomic ramifications touching unemployment, social breakdown and so forth.

Pope Francis then decries the foreign debt of poor nations as a means of controlling them. To end uncontrollable pollution, Pope Francis calls for a society to reject consumerism for its own sake ("a throw-away culture which affects the excluded just as it quickly reduces things as rubbish"). This condemnation of contemporary capitalism also includes financial bubbles and overproduction of commodities to more chronic unemployment. Indeed, he challenges capitalist orthodoxy, that profit alone is the sole criterion in economic relations. Economic progress itself should be related to protecting the environment.

The solution: An immediate effort worldwide for clean energy, in which rich nations, indeed the most responsible for climate warming, should aid poor ones to develop it, while simultaneously ending poverty. To aid this endeavor, wasteful world armaments should end.

To carry out this ambitious program, "a true world political authority" is needed to coordinate the various activities required. This paradigm, however, does not exclude the importance of local initiative provided by cooperatives "to exploit renewable sources of energy which ensure local self-sufficiency and even the sale of surplus energy."

Cooperatives owned by worker of Catholic cooperatives is a long-held Catholic view, related to monasticism and secular enterprises, like the many Mondragin collectives cooperating together in private property, which is not "absolute or inviolable," and which should not "favor only a few." In general, Pope Francis' proposals lead to transformative changes in present social economic and political arrangements specifically, they envisage that the contemporary neoliberal capitalist model by modified drastically and are obviously in the cooperative socialist tradition.

In Pope Francis' papal visit to the U.S. in late September 2015, in a speech before Congress, he mentioned four Americans whom he particularly admired: Abraham Lincoln, Dr. Martin Luther King, Dorothy Day and Thomas Merton, the last two being Catholics; the first a co-founder of the Catholic Worker Movement, and the second a Catholic Trappist monk and mystic interested in Buddhism.

The anarchist-socialism of Day has already been delved into and the mentioning of Merton indicates Catholicism's generous spirit of openness to understand and appreciate other religions. Pope Francis's mentioning King indicated his approving Black Liberation in a racist nation and concern with workers' struggles for higher wages, benefits, unions, not surprising because of his democratic socialism. As for Lincoln, he is related to black emancipation from slavery and generally progressive socioeconomic views related to the time.

Also, Pope Francis called for protecting the earth's environment and social justice. Then, to indicate Catholicism's preference for the poor, he visited them to share their pain and vulnerability.

Pope Francis' close proximity to Liberation Theology: celebrating mass with Gustavo Gutierrez, a Peruvian priest and one of its founders; reaching out to Leonardo Boff, a former Brazilian Franciscan friar and another of its founders; and appointing Cardinal Gerhard Muller as perfect for the doctrine of the faith, who co-authored with Gutierrez, On the Side of the Poor: The Theology of Liberation.

Chapter 13: Ecology and a Proper Socialism

Ecology

Anarchists and socialists are now deeply concerned about and wish to reduce global pollution/climate warming – 60 percent of which is caused by the richest 10 percent of the world's population and eighteen percent by the bottom 60 percent. If the world's present population of approximately 7 billion (or 10 billion by 2100) were to live like its richest 10 percent today, it would require "four earths to supply the resources and assimilate pollutants," according to Fred Magdoff (Monthly Review, Jan. 2013, p. 22).

In May 2013, carbon dioxide levels in the earth's atmosphere reached 400 parts-per-million (ppm). Not long ago, it was an acceptable 350 ppm. The last time 400 ppm was reached in the earth's atmosphere was 3 million years ago when the polar ice caps were smaller and sea levels were 60-80 feet higher than currently. At present rates of increase, by the early 2040s, carbon dioxide in the atmosphere will reach 450 ppm, increasing under 2 ppm annually.

In the 1750-2014 period, from the first Industrial Revolution in Britain to the present, 580 billion metric tons of carbon dioxide entered the earth's atmosphere from the burning of fossil fuels; at that rate, by the 2040s, approximately a trillion metric tons will have entered the atmosphere.

Also of note is the world's fossil reserves, which have as much as five times the carbon that can be safely burned for a planet habitable by humans, according to climatologists.

The world's largest fossil fuel producers circa 2016 (in percentages) include: China, 22; United States, 16; India, third. China has made great progress to reduce carbon dioxide; in 2015 levels were lower than those of 2014, but India will increase them threefold by the 2030s.

Indeed, that there will soon be acute global warming with grave consequences is also the warning by the United Nations 2014 report of the Intergovernmental Panel on Climate Change (IPCC). Its conclusion is that if the fossil fuels problem is not solved in the next 15 years, carbon dioxide will approach 500 ppm in the atmosphere by 2100, forcing humanity to quickly embark on a program to employ clean energy or else build costly at yet-unproven technologies to store carbon dioxide underground.

Furthermore, warming climate will melt the arctic permafrost and warm the ocean floor, releasing large amounts of methane gas that will accelerate global warmth, which in turn will rapidly increase the acidic content of the oceans, endangering sea life. Carbon dioxide increase in the atmosphere, according to the preceding climatologists, will inevitably lead to climate extremes, including droughts, heat waves, heavy rains, storms, flooding and rising sea levels – initially from 2 to 4 meters before, ultimately, reaching 230 feet in the next 9,000 years.

Jason Box, an Ohio State University glaciologist, anticipates catastrophic climate changes and consequences, including lower food production and famines; increased physical damage to farms and cities requiring great population displacement. Indeed, a 2-4 foot sea rise by or before 2100 would inundate low-lying areas in Eastern (Florida especially) and Western U.S., as well as Eastern China, Bangladesh, several Pacific islands, Europe, Africa, and so forth, engulfing such cities as New York, Miami, New Orleans, Tokyo, Shanghai, Venice, and Washington D.C., among others. This will result in the relocation of hundreds of millions of people.

Kevin Anderson of Britain's Tyndale Centre for Climate Change Research avers that to prevent catastrophic climate change, the EU and U.S., which claim to accept it, need to cut fossil emissions by 80 percent below 1990 levels by 2030. He also warns that climate warming is "incompatible for...an equitable and civilized global community."

Of note: 97 percent of climatologists promote anthropogenic climate warming; the remainder 3 percent who do not are tied to the fossil fuel industry.

Presently, about 80 percent of the world's energy is from fossil fuels, only 7 percent from renewables. In poor nations today, 3 billion people add to pollution by heating and cooking on open fires and with inefficient stoves. Wealthy nations, having the financial means and innovative powers to improve society as a whole, should not only convert to clean energy but also aid poorer ones to utilize it.

There are now many proposals to reduce carbon dioxide emissions in the atmosphere, including reforestation, conservation, storing carbon dioxide underground, and increased reliance nuclear power (which I reject), a progressive reduction of population, and an increase in clean energy, including the complete replacement of fossil fuels in the next 20 to 40 years.

According to the UN Department of Economic and Social Affairs, it will cost $1.9 trillion a year for the next 40 years to convert to clean energy, end poverty and avoid the catastrophe of global warming.

One such plan to convert to clean energy within 20 to 40 years comes from two professors: Mark Jacobson, a professor of civil and environmental engineering and a Senior Fellow at Woods Institute for the Environment at Stanford University; and Dr. Mark Delucci of the Institute of Transportation Studies, University of California-Davis.

Jacobson/Delucci posit that it is now technologically and economically feasible to convert to clean energy (50 percent wind, 40 percent solar and 10 percent hydro, wave and biomass); to provide the necessary electric power for industry, dwellings and transportation (vehicles, shops and trains), and aircraft powered by liquid hydrogen.

A super electric grid would handle energy variability of solar and wind power via a sophisticated and computerized system already available. Space used by the plan: less than 1 percent of the earth's surface. Of course, the earth's climate would continue to become warmer, but its worse affects may be mitigated if quick action for clean energy is undertaken.

Clean energy itself should reduce the ill effects of asthma, chronic obstruction pulmonary disease (COPD) and emphysema caused partly by fossil fuels (an eighth of the world's deaths are caused by dirty air).

Converting to clean energy will require three stages. The first two would reduce fossil fuel consumption by 80 percent and be executed in decades. They involve using clean energy (mainly solar and wind power) to electrify motor vehicles and fuel cells for heavy trucks. Then, increase reliance on organic farming for local food consumption; manufacture more efficient appliances and construct energy-saving housing to be serviced by clean energy electricity for heating and cooling (electricity accounts for almost a fourth of energy used in the U.S.). Furthermore, mass transit is employed to replace individual motor vehicle use.

Level three should eliminate most of the remaining 20 percent of carbon pollution; it will be longer to complete, necessitating more research and development to eliminate carbon. Now, all agriculture is organic, including its delivering to consumers. New processes employing electricity, hydrogen and so forth will be used in construction, including cement, paving roads and so forth.

But in the communications area – phones, computers, wires – mining and continued fossil-based plastics continues; they should be made to last longer and be recycled.

City planning should lead to higher population density to encourage walking by reducing transportation. This may require new architectural designs.

Also, future technology may allow for manufacturing and even mining to be almost non-polluting through sophisticated filtering systems. Indeed, moon-based manufacturing and mining could further spare the earth from pollution.

In the meantime, reforestation, reduced population, and technologies to capture carbon pollution may be employed.

Of interest regarding fossil fuel use in the U.S., 90 percent is caused by power plants and vehicles. To accelerate clean energy, 40 nations have already passed a carbon tax, the US should follow, but its political climate makes it problematic.

A promising development: clean energy costs to generate electricity from 2000 to 2015 have been sharply lowered: solar power by 82 percent, wind by 61 percent. Of new energy sources in 2014 in U.S., 36 percent was of the clean variety, a promising development.

Clean energy itself should provide more jobs than fossil fuels: examples in jobs per million dollars of GDP: U.S., 8.7 versus 3.7, + 135 percent; China, 132.1 versus 74, + 79 percent.

To be sure, the conversion to clean energy will lead to lay-offs of fossil fuel workers. The Democratic Socialist Senator Sanders, with two other Democratic colleagues, has introduced legislation to aid these workers by providing them unemployment insurance, healthcare, job retraining and living expenses, and provides employers who hire them with tax incentives. Furthermore, it protects workers' right to join unions. The cost is over $40 billion.

According to the economist Paul Krugman, from both economic and technical perspectives, it is now feasible to drastically reduce fossil fuel emissions that could be achieved by presidential executive order if not barred by the Supreme Court.

Examples of clean energy progress: Jerry Brown, the Democratic governor of California, launched a clean-energy program in which a third of the state's energy by 2020 will be produced by renewables. Portugal's energy needs are now mostly powered by solar clean energy. Germany is a quarter satisfied by clean energy, 80 percent by 2050. Wind power now comprises 20 percent of Texas' energy.

Also, divestment in various stages of fossil fuels is now in progress at Stanford, Oxford and other universities, by the Rockefeller Foundation, the Deutsche Bank, World Bank and International Monetary Fund, the United Church of Christ, the Unitarians, Church of England and Episcopalians, the Catholic and Orthodox churches, Judaism, Islam, Buddhism, and Hinduism are also in the forefront advocating for clean energy. A hopeful development is a carbon tax (some nations have it), which should accelerate clean energy conversion.

On a hopeful note: A USA Today poll in late January 2016 had 80 percent of American youth, ages 18-34, wishing for a rapid transition to clean energy to fight the threat of climate warming. There is a large worldwide movement favoring clean energy.

On the whole, a clean energy economy focuses on conservation and rejection of producing more goods for more capitalist profit. As such, mass consumerism will be replaced by manufacturing fewer products which are designed to last longer. Furthermore, economic localism is stressed at the expense of the national and international varieties now prevalent.

The current population explosion is a contributing factor to global climate warming. Contraception to prevent births are forbidden by Catholicism, although most American Catholics use them. Protestantism generally accepts them as do other religions. There are now, in 2016, 7.4 billion people on earth, 9.6 billion expected in 2050. In February 2016, Pope Francis allowed contraception in sexual intimacy in Latin America because of the Zika mosquito scourge; perhaps this may be extended.

Of the two major American political parties, Democratic and Republican, the former is greatly concerned with global climate warming as both of its presidential candidates in the 2016 elections, Hillary Clinton and Bernie Sanders, have plans to mitigate it with ambitious clean energy programs. The latter, or Republican view, is that anthropogenic climate warming is a hoax to please the fossil fuel industry, one of their main electoral campaign contributions. All other world parties, except the conservative Australian one, accept it. Also, there is formidable economic/political opposition to clean energy from the power fossil fuel industry and its workers, including Exxon Mobil, Chevron, privately-owned in the US, and state-owned companies like Gazprom (Russia), Aramco (Saudi Arabia), Petrobras (Brazil) and so forth.

In early December 2015, 186 of the 195 world leaders met in Paris to curb global climate warming with its consequences already observed. Since the beginning of the Industrial Revolution in the 1750s to the present, average temperatures rose 0.8 degrees centigrade, or 1.5 degrees Fahrenheit. The aim of the summit is to keep the temperature rise below 2 degrees Celsius or 3 degrees Fahrenheit by 2050 to prevent horrendous climate disasters. Better yet, a 1.5 degree Celsius by the 2030s-40s would slow the melting of the Greenland ice sheet. Temperature rise will continue for a time, but its terrible affects will be more manageable.

The summit is not a binding treaty, but does have the force of national commitment. Signatories will meet every five years to report progress.

In a pessimistic vein: pledges to reduce fossil fuels by individual nations at the Paris Summit would increase global warming by about 3.7 degrees Centigrade, resulting in a climate catastrophe.

Indeed, James Hansen, the leading U.S. climatologist, calls the Paris Summit as being worthless. As for Anderson, the summit's proposal that a balance be achieved in 2050-2100 by fossil fuels and their removal by reforestation and carbon capture and storage by technologies to store it underground are unrealistic or utopian fixes.

Others now predict that climate warming and its consequences will spell the end of civilization as we know it. One of the many examples include Naomi Oreskes, a Harvard University professor of the history of science and technology, in The Collapse of Western Civilization: A View from the Future, which outlines the progression of this disaster, which in turn leads a beleaguered humanity to adopt neo-communism.

The U.S. in 2015 by an Obama executives order will cut carbon dioxide by 26 percent to 2005 levels. But the U.S. Supreme Court in 2016 has temporarily blocked this directive, the issue in doubt.

Circa 2015-2016, OPEC and other oil producing nations have greatly reduced oil prices, which should also negatively impact clean energy advances.

Ultimately, I agree with Naomi Klein in This Changes Everything: Capitalism vs. The Climate that only a worldwide socialism largely based on economic localism run by workers' collectives featuring participatory democracy can rapidly convert to clean energy, and save humanity from the worst of global climate warming. Otherwise, humanity will face disastrous consequences.

In October 2018, climate scientists at the UN's Intergovernmental Panel of Climate Change (IPCC) reported that unless action is taken now to reduce carbon dioxide emissions by 2030, global temperatures will rise from the present degree centigrade to 105 degrees centigrade to 1.5 degrees centigrade which will bring climate catastrophe.

Thus it is imperative to rapidly deploy clean energy (70 percent electrical) by 2050, underdake mass reforestation and employ technology to capture carbon.


A Proper Socialism


A socialist society would strip capitalists to make ever more money and also from these free gifts: a well-educated workforce through public-financed education; government research/development of new technologies like computers and in drugs; the military-industrial complex (very costly) that protects corporate investment abroad; through PACs/lobbyists, low taxes, tax havens' limited corporate liability; bailouts in economic downturns; lax federal regulatory agencies and so forth.

Socialism would raise the wages of most blue-white-collar and service workers by eliminating high salaries/perquisites of the higher managerial elite and their investment income; as already observed the richest 1 percent had 22.5 percent of the income in 2012 U.S. Then, the conspicuous consumption of the wealthy (richest 10 percent to 60 percent of consumer spending in the U.S. circa 2010), would cease, diverting these resources into constructing better housing and so forth to the lower half of the population and improving social services. Also, the bloated military-industrial complex, including the intelligence agencies, would be eliminated, their funds again diverted to social welfare. Then, too, the waste of economic downturns with their high unemployment would be replaced by steady growth. To be sure, the wealth of the rich would be confiscated by taxes democratically.

A halfway house to socialism is in such social-democratic nations like Germany, France, Italy, Norway, Sweden, Denmark and Finland with their extensive social welfare programs, having more socioeconomic equality than the U.S., and some government ownership of industry, also heavily regulated, labor/socialist movements in these nations often govern. Nevertheless, a capitalist class is the dominant one. Further left would be deformed socialist nations like the Soviet Union and China in which capitalism has now prevailed.

My proper socialism would correct the patterns of the failed socialist experiments by having, at its core, democratically self-managed worker collectives, closely cooperating. This socialism is greatly indebted to utopian socialism/anarchism, John Stuart Mill, and Marx himself ("united cooperative societies working on a common plan.") In 19th century U.S., such stalwart thinkers/reformers, as was Ralph Waldo Emerson, Horace Greeley and Wendell Phillips, also advocated this collective view, as did labor unions like The Knights of Labor.

But in the 20th century, where industrial bigness/complexity prevailed, it was indeed folly to imagine that a workers' cooperative had the economic resources to challenge General Motors. Also, the two large communist experiments of the 20th century among developed nations, the Soviet Union and China, subjected workers to state bureaucrats acting like capitalists to create rapid surplus-value. Thus, the idea of workers' collectives running society is less prevalent today than previously, but the Mondragon collective in Spain and the many workers collectives in Italy and the U.S. are models for a future socialism.

In my proper socialism, social services will be free and expansive: as in education, including college, healthcare, daycare, maternity leave, disability payments, vacations, and so forth; many to a large extent are already in place today in social democracies like France, Germany, and Scandinavian nations, among others.

Alongside the producers' collectives stand consumers' collectives, the two negotiate between themselves transparently to determine price/quality of goods based on material/labor costs, profit expanding the means of production and so forth. This dynamic economic model allows for planning and consumer free choice to be complementary, assuring a balance between production and consumption. Computers and a pricing system are employed to ensure maximum efficiency. (In developed nations, like the US, consumer consumption is the largest part of GDP, 70 percent in the U.S.). This producer-consumer system is akin to an expensive wrist watch with its many complications. To be sure, there are economic safeguards in place in case of unforeseen shortages and so forth, like stockpiling raw materials and other resources.

"Government" exists to levy taxes, allocate resources to the social-welfare sector, plan for national projects, and so forth; it operates locally, regionally and nationally (in the future perhaps internationally). Its work is overseen by committees elected and supervised by the electorate. There are no elected executives or legislatures. In this society, socioeconomic and political power is diffused, the media playing an important informational role. Voting is conducted via computers.

Regarding property arrangements, this author would allow private personal dwellings/contents/transportation and small privately owned cooperatives, the remainder being socially-owned locally, regionally, nationally and even internationally to be run by democratic self-managed collectives.

Regarding present wage differentials, they are decided democratically and following the successful Mondragon collective, should be about 6.5 to 1. With technological advances and so forth, the dichotomy between manual and mental labor should be progressively erased, integrated labor becoming the norm, a development reducing wage differentials eventually to zero. Ultimately, this author envisions a society of technical, educational, socio-economical, cultural and political co-equals.

An advanced technology and reforms already suggested should lead to a shorter workday/week, increased levels of education, social welfare and so forth.

Savings accounts exist at no interest. Regarding artists and other unusually gifted individuals, they would be granted royalties/ bonuses, but are heavily taxed.

It may be asked if scientific/technological dynamism would be impaired under an egalitarian socialism which supposedly might stifle initiative and genius. I would think not. Even in capitalist United

States, for instance, most of the advanced research is conducted through the aegis of public monies in government/university complexes before being presented, especially government gratis to business for commercial development. Scientific discoveries are now highly cooperative, usually employing a team approach, often interdisciplinary, and unthinkable without the contributions of past generations.

Socialism itself will terminate consumer choice of a restrictive capitalism bounded by class and myth of the free market, actually oligopolistic, whose manipulative advertising employs the conditioning techniques of the psychologists John B. Watson and Edward Bernays and utilizes the socioeconomic insights of Veblen as depicted in The Theory of the Leisure Class, which emphasizes "invidious distinction," of identifying the buyer, consonant with the amount of money spent, with the "better people," who set the standards of "excellence," itself related to planned obsolescence of goods for more profit. It is, thus, a myth that consumers today have free choice. A socialist market transcends these capitalist parameters/ criteria for those of technical excellence and utilitarianism, combined with a proper aestheticism, while ending the accumulation of junk goods for the sake of profit.

International trade is allowed, but not to cheapen labor as does contemporary capitalism. But economically advanced socialist nations will surely aid poorer ones with appropriate economic assistance of a non-exploitative nature.

As for gender relations, socialism decrees social equality. Indeed, in wealthier capitalist nations, women today have achieved great gains: in the U.S. today, they are the majority of college students, many now in high prestige occupations, like law and medicine.

In the realm of sexuality, consensual sex prevails and transgendered, gay and lesbian relations are celebrated as part of the human condition. Twelve states, including California and New York, and the District of Columbia, recognize same-sex marriage, encompassing half the U.S. population by 2013, a great boost to gay liberation; in Western Europe, many nations, like France, Britain and the Scandinavian ones, also have legalized it. As for the nuclear family, its future becomes ever more problematic, but various combinations of it may endure.

Finally, a proper socialism rejects Aldous Huxley's <u>Brave New World</u>, a society genetically-based on intelligence-class.[1]

Chapter 14: The 2016 Election and its Candidates

A great boost for Democratic Socialism in the U.S. in 2015-16 was the presidential run in the Democratic primaries of Bernie Sanders, an independent U.S. Senator from Vermont who caucuses with the Democrats.

Sanders' aim is to replicate and extend the social welfare programs of Franklin Delano Roosevelt's 1930's New Deal, which included government jobs programs, Lyndon Baines Johnson's in the 1960s and of socialists in Europe. Furthermore, he would fulfill FDR's Second Bill of Rights of 1944 which called for the government to guarantee all Americans full employment, good education and medical care, and a decent home. This presupposes that economic security and wellbeing is a precondition for authentic freedom and democracy – for the good of society.

Sanders' political career included being mayor of Burlington, U.S. House representative and U.S. Senator from Vermont. His political runs were financed by small donors and unions. Of his top 20 donors in recent election, 19 were unions, the principal one being the International Association of Machinists and Aerospace workers. He himself in 2015 has only a net worth of $340,000. He will not accept PAC money from corporations or the wealthy.

Background of Sanders' democratic socialist credentials: as a teen, his brother, Larry, acquainted him with works of Karl Marx and Sigmund Freud, a formidable combination. As a student at the University of Chicago in the 1960s, he joined and became a chapter leader of the Congress of Racial Equality, a black civil rights organization, helping launch such occurrences as a sit-in at president's office to end housing segregation. He supported Jesse Jackson in the 1988 Democratic primaries and was actively opposed to the Vietnam War.

Sanders also joined the Young People's Socialist League ("yipsel"), which advocated a society of the "social ownership and democratic control of the means of production and distribution."

Yipsel was against Soviet Communism and Western Capitalism. For them, socialism could be achieved only via the democratic route. They vehemently opposed the Vietnam War.

Like many leftists, Sanders went to Vermont, a sparsely populated state, hoping to allow it to drift politically leftward. There he joined Liberty Union, a progressive leftist party. He was twice its candidate for governor and senator, at most garnering only 6 percent of the vote. He left it in 1977 because of disagreements among the leadership.

Biographically, Sanders is a non-practicing Jew; his wife, Jane, is an Irish Catholic, both from Brooklyn.

In 1977, Sanders embarked on producing educational films and a documentary on the left of Eugene V. Debs, an outstanding American Socialist whom he admired. The program was shown on Vermont PBS. Sanders' big political break occurred in 1981 when he became mayor (by a narrow margin) of Burlington, Vermont's largest city.

Politically, Sanders has attacked the plutocracy and advocated for social reform, while also being pragmatic, such as supporting the F-35 Lockheed fighter plane beset by many problems because of its base in Burlington. He supported the Afghanistan invasion but opposed the Iraq War.

Other proposals and platform(s) (17 of which are listed here) of Sanders include: 1) Expand Social Security by raising payroll taxes of individuals earning more than $118,000 annually (now the limit); this measure would protect its viability indefinitely, and payments to retirees also would be raised up to $65 monthly; 2) taxes: individuals annually earning $250,000 to $500,000 to pay a federal income tax of 37 percent; top rate, 52 percent if one earns $10 million or more – in 2013, 13,000 households; also, raise corporate and estate taxes and terminate tax havens; 3) free college tuition for undergraduates (seven million) in public colleges and universities; annual cost would be approximately $47 billion by the federal government, 23 billion by the state, to be paid by taxes on Wall Street trades of stocks, bonds derivatives; 4) a federally mandated $15 an hour minimum wage phased over five years; 5) lower military spending; 6) a massive jobs program: $1 trillion for crumbling infrastructure, a 4-year $5.5

billion youth jobs program to create 14 million new jobs; 7) universal healthcare (savings $900 billion annually). To be financed by a payroll tax, 2.2 percent on employees, 6.2 percent on employers; no income tax on people earning under $28,000 annually; earners of more than 1 million annually would pay a 5 percent sur-tax and a small tax on traded bonds and stocks; 8) a supporter of LGBT rights (the Supreme Court legalized gay marriage in June 2015). Additionally, he is pro-choice regarding abortion; 9) for public financing of elections, ending the tyranny of big money; 10) for a small (0.01 percent tax on stock/bond transactions to raise $185 billion over 10 years to finance prekindergarten programs for 3- and 4-year olds and restore college aid for poor students; 11) break up Too-Big-To-Fail Wall Street banks and reinstate Glass-Steagall. Hopefully, he should extend rules on "Shadow" banking, like hedge and money market funds, short-term lenders; limit risky bank debt; and shift corporations to investments, not payouts; 12) end job-killing free trade; 13) aid unionization with card check; 14) expand the means-tested programs like HUD and food stamps; 15) federally-mandated maternity leave of one month with pay and yearly 10-day vacation time and sick leave; 16) protection for undocumented workers and path to citizenship; 17) economic aid to worker-owned cooperatives to foster more economic equality.

Sanders' program should be popular with the public, according to a recent New York Times/CBS news poll conducted in May 2015: 66 percent favor more socioeconomic equality; 67 percent agree that the gap between rich and poor is increasing (65 percent that it should be addressed immediately); 68 percent are for raising taxes on annual income of income of more than 1 million; 80 – 85 percent call for paid sick and maternity leaves; 71 percent favor raising the $7.25 an hour minimum wage to $10.10, but 60 percent so far oppose a $15 an hour minimum wage; 58 percent in a recent Kaiser Poll favor universal healthcare.

These polls indicate a left-leaning opinion of Democrats in a 2015 Pew Research poll; 41 percent liberal, 35 percent moderate, but in a 2014 Gallup Poll of all Americans: 24 percent liberal, 34 percent moderate, 38 percent conservative. If the nation as a whole tends to be conservative, why does it favor discrete left measures? The answer is the conservative class/caste-like U.S. class structure. Also, low voting participation by the lower income half of voters favors conservatives.

But the 2014 Gallup Poll mentioned has been superseded by a Nov. 16, 2015 one reported in The Nation (Nov. 16, 2015) where 47 percent of the public and 59 percent of Democrats would vote for a socialist president. Sanders' democratic socialism is of a mild form because it does not propose any nationalization of industry or banking.

By March 2016, Sanders had a sizeable war chest of over $125 million, contributed by 3.5 million individuals who, on average, donate $30. He also has about 200,000 volunteers.

To be sure, there are a few progressive capitalists who support Sanders' primary presidential run like Ben Cohen and Jerry Greenfield of Ben and Jerry's ice cream fame. But Sanders insists that they only contribute the maximum $2,700 limit because he is against any super PAC support.

In November 2015, Sanders' presidential run received a great boost forward when the Postal Workers' Union endorsed him, as did soon afterward the Communication/Workers of America, National Nurses United and Social Security Workers. These unions have more than a million members. By contrast, Hillary Clinton has the support of 18 unions, representing 12 million workers whose leaders view her as beating Sanders in the Democratic primaries and winning the presidency, thus currying her favor.

The Presidential candidacy of Sanders is in the tradition of American radicalism: of labor struggles/Paine, Abolitionism, Transcendentalism, of the 1900-20 socialist upsurge featuring Debs, among many others; the New Deal, and the 1960 upheaval of feminism, black and Native American liberation movements and the anti-Vietnam War student upsurge.

Among democratic voters in January 2016 opinion polls, as in the CBS/New York Times one, Sanders leads Hillary Clinton by 60 percent to 31 percent of those under age 45, but of those over that age, Hillary leads by 2 to 1. Of Democratic voters under age 30, Sanders won 84 percent in Iowa and 83 percent in the New Hampshire 2016 primaries. Why? Many youth are in low-wage jobs (real wages for men have remained flat since c. 1980); college debt is now at $1.5 trillion; 40 percent are children of divorced and poor parents, thus receiving scant family economic assistance – 40 percent live with parents/relatives. Their chances for upward social mobility are slim. As already observed, half the youth are favorable to Socialism.

In his presidential primary run, Sanders faces a serious challenge in that 20 percent of delegates in the 2016 Democratic Convention are super-delegates (party officials and some lobbyists), almost all of whom are pledged to Hillary Clinton at least on the first ballot if she is in front.

Lastly, the mainstream capitalist media seldom mention tax and other issues, focusing only on candidate popularity and only give grudging exposure to Sanders because of his Democratic Socialism, which they abhor.

Sanders' principal opponent is Hillary Rodham Clinton, wife of former President Bill Clinton, former New York state senator, former secretary of state under President Obama and the presumptive favorite to win the Democratic nomination for president. A liberal, she favors paid sick and 12-weeks maternity leaves, universal pre-kindergarten for all 4 year olds, a general $12 hour minimum wage ($15 in urban areas phased over five years, profit sharing for workers, 2-year free tuition in public colleges (annual cost $35 billion), and more college student aid to decrease college costs.

Clinton supports expanding the ACA, strengthening means-tested social programs, legal protection for undocumented workers and a $275 billion infrastructure program that would create 3.25 million new jobs.

Unlike Sanders, however, she would not break up large Wall Street banks and is against universal healthcare. Fearing Sanders' strong popularity, she now opposes the TPP. Along with Sanders, she is a proponent for a strong clean energy program, and following Buffett, proposes that the very rich pay at least a 30 percent income tax and would raise income taxes on individuals earning more than

$250,000 annually and a 4 percent income tax surcharge if one annually earns over $5 million. But she favors the rich with a lower long term capital gains tax. The Clintons have earned about $125 million from speeches to corporations and Wall Street since 2001; Bill himself from 2001-14 earned $82 million and Hillary alone, in 2014, $1.2 million, including $325,000 from Cisco Systems, $675,000 from Goldman Sacks for three speeches, $225,000 from General Electric and so on. She is a war hawk, supporting the Afghanistan and Iraq Wars, and agrees with strong intervention against ISIL and the Syrian government.

Since the Bill Clinton presidency of the 1990s, with the decline of unions, Democrats via Democratic Leadership Council are closely tied to big business and Wall Street campaign contributions.

As already observed, she has great labor union support. Finally, her presidential run is well funded: her Super PAC of $100 million includes $15 million from Wall Street in early 2016. Clinton has a commanding lead over Sanders on early primaries, helped by overwhelming black support, about a fourth of Democratic voters. But Sanders' run still has garnered sufficient votes, pushing Clinton politically leftward.

There are several leading Republican presidential candidates in the 2016 primaries, one of whom, Jeb Bush (President Bush I, father; Bush II, brother), may perpetuate the family political presidential dynasty. He is an example of one using his family's economic political connections to run for public office in an effort to amass great wealth and political power.

After serving two terms as governor of Florida, leaving office in 2007, he embarked on his quest for wealth. He gave 260 speeches from 2007 to 2015 to business groups earning $9.95 million, served on the board of Tenet Healthcare and made a tidy $462,000 profit in purchasing its stock in 29 months. He also managed a private investment firm, whose net worth was $2 million in 2007 and $22 million in 2015.

Jeb Bush is a fiscal conservative except for the military and follows closely the Republican 2015-16 agenda. He is somewhat favorable to undocumented Mexican workers (his wife is Mexican and he is a Catholic Convert). His conservative credentials are evident – in July 2015 he remarked that workers should work longer hours to gain more income (American workers already have a very long work week).

Ever a plutocrat, Bush would reduce the top income tax of 39.6 percent to 28 percent, cut maximum corporate tax from 35 percent to 20 percent, and terminate estate taxes on the very rich. Overall, the richest 1 percent would receive half of these tax reductions. Federal revenue would decline $3.4 trillion in the next decade if his program is enacted. Voodoo economics.

He is also against a clean energy program and would repeal the ACA and Dodd-Frank – the first maneuver an unmitigated attack on poor workers and the second hastening another economic disaster.

After spending the majority of his $130 million war chest (the most of any Republican), Bush quit his campaign on February 20, 2016, after losing badly in early primaries.

Donald Trump, a billionaire magnate and television personality, is by far the Republican frontrunner in the 2016 primaries. He appeals to a large crosssection of the electorate: white male blue-collar workers, middle-class and rich. His program includes lower taxes on everyone, anti-black, anti-undocumented, mainly Mexican workers, anti-Moslem rhetoric (racism and homophobia), xenophobia; end job-killing free trade with a 45-percent tariff on Chinese goods and a 35 percent of Ford's manufacturing in Mexico. This is an attack on TNCs, a key Republican constituency. Congressional approval is needed to approve Tariff changes. He also angers "God" Republicans because he supports Planned Parenthood, which aids poor women with medical problems, contraception and abortion.

Among his most outrageous and divisive proposals is his proposal to deport 12 million undocumented, mostly Mexican, workers to Mexico and requiring Mexico to build and finance a wall between it and the United States in an effort to prevent undocumented workers from coming into the United States; Trump also proposed acts and/or legislation that would prevent Moslems from entering the U.S. for a period of time because of their domestic and other terrorist activities.

Trump would propose large tax cuts on the poor, middle and wealthy classes; reduce the top federal income tax rate from 39.6 percent to 23 percent to couples earning over $300,000 annually and eliminate the estate tax on the rich. Also, there would be no federal income taxes on individuals earning under $25,000, couples under $50,000. A couple now earning $100,000 pay an approximate $11,437 income tax; that would be reduced to $5,000, a 56 percent reduction. The top corporate tax of 35 percent would fall to 15 percent. Overall, the richest 1 percent would receive half of tax reductions.

Contrary to other Republicans, Trump would not reduce or privatize Social Security/Medicare, though he would rebuild a crumbling infrastructure, but in a Republican vein he would terminate ACA and replace it with another means-reducing program, and would increase military spending and is against clean-energy conversion.

Overall, Trump's tax cuts and massive military spending increases, as well as infrastructure programs, would lead to large federal budget increases. He believes, however, that the tax cuts alone would increase economic growth by 6 percent annually. Such beliefs and estimations translate to Voodoo economics.

Previously, he supported Canadian universal healthcare and a federal tax on wealth to reduce federal budget deficits. As a billionaire, he has contributed money to both Democrats, like Hillary Clinton, and Republicans for business favors.

Trump is prepared to spend $100 million of his own money to become president, a mere pittance of his up to $4-8 billion fortune.

Although Trump is popular with Republicans, a November 2015 ABC news/Washington Post poll found that he is unfavorably regarded by 64 percent of women and 74 percent of non-white voters.

Florida Senator Marco Rubio, a Cuban American, has a tax platform featuring sharp tax reductions. He would eliminate taxes on investment income favoring the very rich like Mitt Romney who would not have to pay any federal income taxes.

All in all, the taxes of the richest 1 percent would decrease by

11.2 percent, the largest gainers. Taxes on the lower half of income earners: for the bottom 10 percent, a steep use in tax credits to increase their income by 44.2 percent; those of 40-90 percent of average to have a 1-3 percent reduction. He would also reduce and privatize social welfare programs.

Rubio, a Protestant Christian conservative, would ban abortion, repeal the ACA and the nuclear deal with Iran. He is also a war hawk who would increase military expenditures. As almost all other Republicans, he regards human-induced climate warming as a hoax, and as such is against clean energy. His leading patrons are billionaires: Sheldon Adelson, Paul Stringer and the Silicon Valley ones. Overall, Rubio was the conservative favorite until he dropped from the race in late spring.

Dr. Ben Carson, an African-American neurosurgeon, is a Seventh Day Adventist who believes the Bible literally, including the six-day world creation. He appeals to Republican "God" fundamentalists. Carson is against any Moslem becoming a U.S. president and believes that if German Jews had guns they would not have been easily led by the Nazis to the death camps, statements approved by Protestant Fundamentalists. His tax and social welfare plans are typically Republican. Taxes: a 15 percent flat tax on personal and corporate income, the rich inevitably paying lower taxes. Social welfare: the ACA would be repealed and social welfare programs would be cut/privatized. His Biblical creationism runs against a federal clean energy program. In late October 2015, he was the most popular Republican candidate in the primaries, but his popularity would eventual fade until he dropped out of the campaign.

Senator Ted Cruz of Texas, a Cuban American, proposed a 10 percent flat tax on income; a 16 percent value-added tax; a return to the gold standard, a discredited idea; abolishing the IRS and terminating the corporate income tax – recommendations especially that would please the rich. As an Evangelical he believes in imminent Armageddon (his father was an Evangelical minister). He opposes abortion and same-sex marriage, although both are legal, and he would repeal ACA and eliminate/reduce social welfare programs.

He believes climate warming is a hoax and is against clean energy programs. He would "carpet bomb" ISIS and consider sending more American troops to the Middle East. He opposes citizenship for undocumented immigrants and to not allow them legal status. He also is popular with tea-party crowds who abhor "big government." About 40 percent of Trump's supporters would vote for Cruz as a second choice. He has a $65 million electoral campaign war chest in January, second only to Bush. He is backed by many wealthy, including billionaires. If Trump stumbles, Cruz becomes the front-runner overall as a far-right Republican.

In fearing Cruz as his principal rival, Trump is questioning his religious faith, his being disliked by many other Republican politicians, and his citizenship (he was born in Canada to an American mother); legal experts maintain that this allows to be a natural-born citizen.

Ohio Governor John Kasich proposed to cut the top marginal income tax from 39.6 percent to 28 percent, reduce the corporate income tax from 35 to 25 percent, the capital gains tax from 23.8 to 15 percent, thus further enriching the wealthy. Kasich is an unusual Republican who extended Medicaid expansion in Ohio, part of the ACA. Previously, he attempted to destroy collective bargaining in Ohio, which was defeated in a statewide referendum. He does accept human activity causing climate warming, an exception to the Republican views and beliefs. He is viewed as a "reasonable" Republican.

The tax plans of the two leading Republican candidates – Trump and Cruz – favor the rich and corporations and cutting/eliminating Democratic tax increases and social welfare programs; they occur in the midst of increasing economic inequality and aging population reaching retirement which will put more financial demands on Social Security/Medicare, Medicaid and other social welfare programs. According to the liberal citizens for Tax Justice, which I prefer, the tax plans of the two in the next decade will reduce federal coffers in the following trillions of dollars: Trump 12; Cruz, 16.2. The conservative Tax Foundation and the centrist Brookings Tax Policy Center generally project smaller, but still substantial budget deficits.

To be sure, the two believe that these massive tax cuts will promote economic growth. Tax cuts on workers will spur their consumption thus increasing economic activity. But tax reductions on the rich/ corporations, already flushed with money, will simply be sent to tax havens (half the cash hoard of U.S. corporations is deposited in them).

Sadly, some Republican presidential candidates are demonizing/ scapegoating Moslem Americans, about 1 percent of the American people. Examples: Rubio would close their mosques, cafes and restaurants. Trump would impose special ID cards on them. Carson called some Syrian Moslem refugees "rabid dogs." Bush would prefer Christian Syrian refugees. Cruz views Shariah Law as dangerous. Half of Iowa Republican voters would make Islam illegal. To be sure, the Republican presidential candidates are parroting the prejudices of Fundamentalist Protestants and may other Christian bigots.

The "God" Republican constituency, already observed, also demands that the 1973 Roe vs. Wade court decisions allowing for legal abortion in early pregnancy be repealed or more severely restricted and following the Bible, condemns homosexuality. These wedge (non-economic) issues are prominent and effective in Republican campaign rhetoric. Although 78 percent of the public favors abortions with restrictions, the 22 percent opposed are a large Republican voting bloc. Of note: 40 percent of American women by age 49 have had an abortion, and not surprisingly, Cruz, Rubio, and Carson oppose all abortions, while Trump and Kasich allow them only for rape and incest. Republicans are obviously staunchly anti-labor, wishing to end collective bargaining, and oppose raising the $7.25 an hour minimum federal wage.

Republican presidential candidates in the 2016 primaries are bankrolled by a few dozen very wealthy families and others less wealthy. Of 358 individuals contributing more than $100,000 in early primaries, most went to Republicans (The Nation, March 14, 2016, p. 8). Indeed, the activity/money contributions of the very wealthy to the radical right is amply documented by Jane Mayer, Dark Money (New York: Doubleday, 2016).

With half the Republican primary races completed by March 1, 2016, Trump is leading, followed closely by Cruz and Kasich.

Part of the Trump program is inimical to the Republican/corporate Establishment (TNC's Wall Street, Big Oil, Big Pharma, and so forth), by its ending free trade with tariffs, protecting Social Security/ Medicare, blaming George Bush for the Iraq invasion and for not preventing the Sept. 11, 2001 terrorist attack in New York City killing thousands. Also Trump is verbally abusive to his Republican primary opponents. This has caused deep fissures among Republicans.

The hope of the Republican insiders is for a brokered convention if Trump does not secure a majority of delegates. But Cruz, who is running second to Trump, is also disliked by the Republican establishment.

The political stances of Trump and Sanders appeal to an increasing economically marginalized working class. In the last few decades, 90 percent of the income was redistributed to the richest 1 percent, workers being the biggest losers (NYT, March 9, 2016, B7). But Trump, contrary to Sanders, is against unions and a higher minimum wage.

The Sanders political phenomenon signals a leftward Democratic trend, which reverses a rightward one after the 1972 and 1984 McGovern and Mondale defeats and rise of the Democratic Leadership Council under Bill Clinto; Obama moved slightly leftward with the ACA, but is still beholden to corporate interests as evidenced by his promotion of the TPP.

Looming over Democratic and Republican prospects in the 2016 general elections, whose cost was the highest in history, was the reality of the importance of big money to both parties from the wealthy/corporations to protect their interests. To be sure, minor parties, like the Greens and Libertarians, fielded presidential and other candidates with scant chance of success.

To be sure, as already observed, there is in the U.S. a sizeable democratic left consisting of the House Congressional Progressive caucus (72 members in 2016), the various socialist parties/groups, and the Democratic Socialist Bernie Sanders' run itself. It is driven by continuing capitalist dysfunctions, such as increasing socioeconomic inequality, periodic downturns, stagnant/falling real wages, lower upward social mobility, high real unemployment, and the crisis of global warming. Sanders' presidential candidacy itself signaled the beginning of a movement which continued after his primary run whose aim is to propel the Democrats leftward. Sanders would again seek the Democratic nomination in 2019 on much of the same platform.

The preceding elements challenged the Regan neoliberal era of 1980 to the present, for one of the 1930s New Deal Keynesianism and labor militancy. As it turned out, the 2016 election, which saw Trump win the presidency, ushered in a increasingly divided government, destructive attempts at reform and a blurring of political party identity.

These scenarios lead me to believe that it will take many, many decades or even longer before working class political power can defeat the capitalist class to usher in a socialist society, featuring Marx's worker-controlled united cooperatives working together.

For Democrats, in addition to Clinton's proposals, Bernie Sanders' strong showing influenced some policy inclusions, including a federal $15 an hour minimum wage, a four-year college tuition for students of parents earning under $125,000 annually, and a public option for many individuals/families to enroll in Medicare, substantially reducing their medical insurance costs. Also of importance: Sanders' strong popularity in the Democratic primary is not a fluke. In two July 2016 polls by On Message Inc. and The American Action Network, 60 percent of Democrats have a favorable view of socialism (David Brooks, "The Materialist Party," NYT July 26, 2016, p. A 27.

The Republican platform would butt heads with Trump but, in the end, would present him as its nominee. He would eventually win the presidency.[1]

# Chapter 15: 2016 Election Results and Early Trump Presidency

Demographic and socioeconomic realities regarding the November 8, 2016, election for president between Democratic center-left Clinton and right-wing populist Republican Trump, were stark and telling. In population percentages, 64 percent were white, 18 were Hispanic, 12 African-American, 6 Asian-American, and 1 Native American.

In voting percentages, Clinton collected 42 percent of white votes, 64 percent Hispanic, 92 percent African American, and a large majority Asian-Americans. Trump, meanwhile, collected 58 percent of white votes, 6 percent Hispanic, 8 percent African Americans and small minorities among others. Among college whites (about a third), 48 percent voted for Trump, for reasons mainly related to lower taxes, fear of blacks/Hispanics and a reduction to social-welfare spending; 45 percent voted for Clinton, many being government workers (teachers and feminists), favoring free college tuition in state schools, higher taxes on the rich and clean energy.

Among non-college white workers, 67 percent voted for Trump, many of whom had lost well-paying manufacturing union jobs with benefits that went to Mexico and China, as well as to automation. In turn, these workers entered low-wage, non-union jobs without benefits, usually in the service sector. They approved of Trump's plan to raise tariffs on goods from China and Mexico. Their favored status/job position is now also eroding to black militancy for equality/jobs and to the massive influx of undocumented Hispanic workers. Trump's rhetoric of anti-black and anti-Hispanic undocumented workers has wide appeal among these working class whites. Clinton received only 29 percent of their vote.

These working class whites delivered Trump the election in three key Rust Belt states – Pennsylvania, Michigan, Wisconsin – by the thin margin of 72,000 votes while Obama won these states in 2008 and 2012, Trump's economic pledges were the difference-maker. Moreover, Trump's obvious misogyny did not prevent his garnering

53 percent of the white women's vote. Obviously economics overrode sexism.

Clinton, however, received 2.9 million more votes than Trump but lost the election in the Electoral College vote. Indeed, if Clinton would have embraced high tariffs as Trump did, I believe she would have defeated him. As Secretary of State, she supported free trade TPP, but running as president she opposed it; this was not enough to win workers. She was also sabotaged by Obama who strongly supported TPP to the bitter end. Trump has indicated he will withdraw from the agreement.

The 2016 elections were dominated by the great television exposure of Clinton and Trump, and to a much lesser extent of Sanders, the socialist outsider. It also consisted of free television time worth $2 billion for Trump. In the 2016 elections Clinton outspent Trump 2 to 1, and their total cost was $9 billion. Sanders' war chest was over $200 million and he got some television time as his primary campaign against Clinton gained momentum, receiving 46 percent of the Democratic vote. The conclusion is clear: the corporate PAC's and control/ownership of television by the plutocracy dominated the viewing of the 2016 elections, with corporate TV giving Trump three times more airtime than Clinton and six times more than Sanders.

Trump beat Clinton depsite Obama creating 11 million more jobs and enrolling 20 million more in healthcare insurance, although real wages generally have fallen since 1979; more women entered the workforce to compensate for this.

Outsourcing jobs by U.S. corporations is objectionable, but a greater threat is loss of jobs to rapid technological change: Trump beat Clinton by stressing the first, but not mentioning the second. Clinton herself opted for ethnic/racial unity but Trump scapegoated Hispanics and blacks. But Clinton did not promise to correct anti-union laws and belatedly called for tariffs, losing the working class vote and election to Trump.

Since 1979, median wages adjusted for inflation have not risen. Indeed, those in manufacuring experienced large wage losses and high unemployment because of automation/robotics and jobs going abroad. The 2008 Great Recession and its aftermath exacerbated these conditions. Furthermore, 40 percent of U.S. jobs are now contingent (temporary and of limited contracts), according to a 2015 Government Accountability Office report. A 2013 Oxford University study has 47 percent of U.S. jobs at risk because of technology.

Specificity on imports to the U.S. in 2015: Trade deficits on Chinese products, $336 billion; on Mexican goods, $58 billion. Half of imports from China are from American corporations with large investments there.

In early March 2018, Trump's slogan to "Bring Jobs Back to America" defied the free-trade Republican and Democratic Parties: he decreed a 25 percent tariff on steel and a 15 percent one on aluminum, exempting Canada and Mexico and possibly other U.S. allies (Progessive Democrats and Sanders are also against free trade). As a result, the Chinese announced their own tariffs in early April, and its trade surplus to the U.S. will be reduced by $60 billion annually on Chinese steel, electronic products, clothing, shoes and so on. Trump may also impose tariffs on the European Community and others. They, of course, will retaliate with tariffs on U.S. products if this occurs.

Since the Reagan Presidency, the U.S. has had large annual trade deficits: In the 2017 period, $745 billion, about half to China in which U.S. corporations there account for half. Trump's tariffs will aid U.S. manufacuring/jobs but raise consumer prices generally.

Until the Regan presidency, the U.S. normally did not have any annual trade deficits, but with the advent of free trade, they increased significantly. This trend allowed foreign-owned companies to increase their share of U.S. business assets: 1 percent in 1980 and 14 percent today. Trump also states that his $1 trillion 10-year infrastructure rebuilding plan will not primarily come from federal government spending but rather from tax cuts to involved corporations. This is "doublethink" because lower taxes on them would increase federal budget deficits. This Trumpian Keynesianism favors the corporations and the rich.

As for preventing entrance of 11 million undocumented workers to the U.S.: Since 1986 and the President Reagan administration and succeeding ones (both Republican and Democratic), there has been no enforcement of the law to levy stiff fines on employers who hire them. If the law isn't enforced, economic need will continue the flow of undocumented workers, mostly Hispanic, in the U.S.

If Trump extends the wall separating the U.S. from Mexico, human ingenuity may still largely overcome this obstacle. Indeed today, half of Hispanic undocumented workers enter the U.S. legally with a Visitor's Visa before they disappear. Parenthetically, Trump himself has hired undocumented Polish and other workers, outsourced the fabrication of shirts and ties to low-wage nations and has purchased building materials from them.

Trump will have difficulty expelling undocumented Hispanic workers from the U.S. to Mexico. To begin, there are increasing numbers of sanctuary cities like Los Angeles and San Francisco, among others. Furthermore, it will cause considerable economic dislocation and transform the U.S. into a police state, unpopular with many Americans. Of note, millions of undocumented Hispanics over the years have been deported to Mexico, but many sucussfully return to the U.S.

A favorite Republican tactic is to allow seniors age 65 and older to remain in Social Security, but with people under 65 not contributing to it; its funds will repaidly deplete effectively, quickly destroying it. The same applies to Medicare. Privatizing Social Security and Medicare will enrich Wall Street and the healthcare insurance companies.

As for the disabled and poor, Trump and Republicans would reduce such programs as Medicaid, Supplemental Security Income and others, transfering them into state block grants, further weakening them because they will not keep up with inflation.

Welfare recipents have scarcely any voice in Congress. Trump intends (and as of this writing is putting in motion) to repeal Obamacare, which, as imperfect as it is, allowed 20 million poor people to have healthcare insurance. There is some sign, however, that he may extend its life.

Trump, like most Republican legislators claiming that global warming is a hoax, will disengage from United Nations efforts to combat global warming caused by fossil fuels.

Interestingly, the war-hawk Clinton's enmity to Russia will end because Trump wants peaceful relations with it, opposed by the Military Industrial Complex; but Trump would placate them with increased funding. To be sure, Trump is an unmitigated reactionary, anti-union, resisting through the years demands that he unionize his companies. .

In the short run, Trump's programs will greatly increase federal budget defts but lead to more jobs. In the long run, however, it will result in an economic crash. Since Trump is so extreme regarding climate warming, deporting millions of Hispanics, slapping high tariffs on imports from China and Mexico, and slashing EPA regulations protecting the public, he may partly or completely backtrack on some or all of them.

Trump claimed to have saved 1,000 jobs going to Mexico from the Carrier Corporation in Indianapolis, Indiana (a subsidiary of United Technologies, a large military contractor). What happened was that only 700 jobs were saved, with 400 going to Mexico. The state of Indiana then compensated Carrier with a $7 miillion tax reduction. Also, the United Tecnologies' CEO plans to invest many millions of dollars to automate production in Carrier, thus eliminating most of its jobs. In this scenario, workers invariably lose more jobs.

Trump's cabinet appointments are typically Republican, from Wall Street and other large corporations; others are billionaires, supporters of privatizing Social Security and Medicare and other social programs, schools, slashers of the EPA, global warming skeptics and outright deniers. To be sure, the massive tax cuts of Trump's agenda will further enrich them.

The only hope for Democrats in future elections is to adopt a progressive Bernie Sanders' platform of democratic socialism, one modeled on the 1930s New Deal. To be sure, it should be deepend with plans to nationalize industry and be operated by worker councils.

For working class whites, legal and illegal immigrants break unions, leading to lower wages and increasing unemployment. If present U.S. population trends continue, by 2050 non-whites will become the majority, many of whom will become citizens and with their U.S. born children will vote for the Democrats. These immigrants are mostly concentrated in California and Texas, but also in southern cities, New York City, and many other cities.

Although Trump appealed to white workers through his promise (slogan) of "bringing back jobs to America" and to expel undocumented Hispanic workers, he is, as will be observed, an unmitigated reactionary Republican.

To begin, Trump appointed a wealthy/reactionary cabinet closely tied to Wall Street and other large captialist corporations, promoting their interests at the expense of the general public. Trump did not "drain the swamp" as he had promised before the election; he added to it. Trump is an example of George Orwell's <u>1984</u> term of "doublespeak," or the opposite of truth. Both Trump and his spokespersons, in fact, promoted the term "alternative facts" early in his presidency.

Contrary to Trump, the Republican Party wishes to privatize Social Security/Medicare to enrich Wall Street and health insurance corporations.

The 2018 Trump federal budget increases military spending by \$52 billion, a 10 percent increase, and reduces social welfare by 1.7 trillion in the next decade. Spcific cuts include: planned parenthood providing life-saving services to poor women, food stamps, infant nutrition, day care, rent support, public housing, meals on wheels, home heating, job training, and grant-aid for college, among others.

Also, the important National Institutes of Health's budget will be slashed by 18 percent, endangering research for cancer and other cures. Lastly, there are plans to end government funding for the Corporation of Public Broadcasting, National Endowment for the Arts and Humanities, and the Legal Services Corporation aiding the poor, as well as Americorps. A Congressional budget resolution restored some of the preceding cuts, especially for the National Institutes of Health.

The Trump/Republican budget also slashes the EPA by 31 percent.

Importantly, it also cuts the Office of Science in the department of Energy, engaged in climate research, by $900 million, almost 20 percent of its budget. Also, there are deep cuts in the Oceanic and Atmospheric Adminstraton and the NASA's earth science.

Fossil-fuel pollution will worsen the health of people. The Republican Party is the only major political party in the world favoring the increase of fossil fuels. However, Trump, seemingly contradicting himself on global warming, may approve geo-engineering projects with sulfur and other particles in the atmosphere to counter solar warming. But these schemes may change the climate in unforeen ways, including droughts, excessive rainfall and so on.

These quick and problematic fixes will allow fossil-fuel production to increase continuously with consequent increases in carbon dioxide and methane, which, if not checked, may lead to the extinction of humanity and other life forms – a consensus of most climate scientists.

Trump would also sign the "working families act" passed by the Republican House. It would allow workers laboring overtime to choose paid time off rather than receive time-and-a-half wages. But it would be at the convenience of the employer within a 13-month period. This favors wage theft. The naming of this legislation follows, once again, "doublethink."

That most white workers voted for Trump depsite his anti-worker actions has already been observed; most workers were not even aware of them and/or behaviors. In comparison, Obama expelled 2.5 million Hispanic undocumented workers, but Trump promised many more.

Regarding the 11 million undocumented Hispanic workers in the U.S., Trump plans to spent $25 billion to extend and strengthen the wall on the US/Mexican border to prevent their entering the U.S., and would then expel 2-3 million of them quickly, the approximate 8 million workers later (5 percent of the work force). But Trump in late April 2017 announced that he would let the 800,000 "dreamers," young children who came to the U.S. with their undocumented Hispanic parents, to stay in the country.

These undocumented and terribly exploited Hispanic workers

earn close to the minumum wage or even below it, supporting through their work the many industries like farm labor, fast food, construction, meatpacking, hospitality – among several. If they are deported, these areas of the economy will become more expensive because American workers who replace them will demand higher wages.

This author very much doubts that the Trump plan of massive expulsion of undocumented Hispanics will succeed because of great opposition to it: The Democratic Party has voted for many sanctuary cities and states for the undocumented, making it more difficult to deport them. Furthermore, the Catholic Church, main-line Protestantism and other religious denominations, as do the American Civil Liberties Union and capitalists who thrive and depend on cheap labor.

The undocumented workers' problem can be solved by enforcing existing law which imposes heavy fines on employers who hire them. But because capitalist need to thrive on cheap labor, the law will not be enforced. Any employer concerned about the status of an employee can check green-card foreign workers.

Regarding education, Betsy DeVos, Trump's education secretary, is from a billionaire family. She is an ardent proponent of charter schools, many of which are for-profit in her home state of Michigan. The aim here is for a capitalist takeover of public education and destruction of public teachers' unions contributing heavily to Democrats. As of now, there are 2.5 million students in the K-12 charter schools nationwide. Also, Trump and Republicans will subsidize private schools by $1 billion annually, 5 percent of the total.

In the middle of May 2017, Trump dismissed James B. Comey, the FBI director investigating the Trump 2016 electoral campaign and its Russian connection. Comey angered Trump because he asked Congress for more funds to pursue the preceding investigation and would not give to Trump his personal loyalty. Then when Trump asked Comey not to investigate Michael J. Flynn (an impeachable offense), Comey refused. Flynn, Trump's former national security adviser, did not disclose that he was a paid lobbyist for Turkey.

Some of Trump's lies, or Orwellian "doublespeak," include such claims as: U.S. has the world's highest taxes, though the truth is that it ranks 32$^{nd}$ among the 35 advanced nations, according to the Organization of Economic Cooperation and Development). He began his campaign by stating that Obama was not born in the U.S., that Obama wiretapped Trump Tower; that after the 2016 presidential elections, the 2.9 million Clinton voting margin over him was committed by fraudulent votes of blacks and Hispanics, a claim that was never formally investigated, though Trump claimed he would. Many reputable studies indicate that voting fraud is extremely rare. Politifact (a Florida-based Pulitzer Prize winning website) claimed that about 80 percent of Trump's public statements are untrue. A May 2017 Quinnipiac University poll found Trump's approval rating at a low 36 percent, with the leading answer to describe Trump as an "idiot."

On May 16, 2017, David Brooks, a noted conservative columnist of the New York Times, in a column titled "When a Child is Leading the World," mercilessly attacked Trump, labelling him "an infantalist," "ill-informed" concerning his own policies, "desperate for approval," believing to invent an old economic phrase "priming the pump;" that he mastered the complexities of health care quickly, and of knowing "more about aircraft carrier technology than the Navy." Ultimately for Brooks, Trump is a "hollow man."

Bob Woodward, in Fear: Trump in the White House (New York: Simon and Schuster, 2018) pp. 212-44, describes Trump as an ignorant, bumbling person whose staff behind his back call him "a moron" and an "idiot."

On May 17, Rosenstein appointed former FBI director, Robert S. Mueller III, as special counsel to investigate links between the Trump presidential campaign and Russia and Trump's abrupt dismissal of Comey.

Trump as president is attempting to govern like he did in running his own enterprise without any interference. As yet, he seems not to realize that American politics are closely watched by most of the media, which reports many, if not most, political missteps – especially by the president. Trump defends himself from negative news stories with claims of "fake news," thus diverting and distorting public attention.

Did Russians intrude in the 2016 U.S. elections? Yes, but it was amateurish, inept and ineffective, not influencing electoral results. The Department of Justice has recently indicted 13 Russian individuals and three Russian companies for this interference. (Amy Goodman interview with Masha Gessen expert on Russia, Free Speech TV, Feb. 23 and 24, 2018: She authored, The Future is History: How Totalitarism Reclaimed Russia, the 2017 National Book Award Winner).

Regarding workers, Trump is basically anti-worker, the proof of which is found in his fighting a certified union in one of his casinos, by weakening health and safety standards at work and betraying poor white Appalachian workers who voted for him by calling for the elimination of funds from the Appalachian Regional Council. He is also against raising the $7.25 federal minimum wage.

On June 1, 2017, Trump withdrew from the 2015 Paris Climate Accords (PCA), an agreement adopted by 195 nations that promotes the reduction of carbon dioxide emissions. He immediately suspended the United State's voluntary involvement and commitment to fulfill its quota of a 28 percent reduction by 2025. He thus canceled Obama's Clean Power Plan by executive order. U.S. withdrawal will add 3 billion tons of carbon dioxide to the atmosphere by 2025. Formally, it will take four years before the U.S. leaves the PCA. While the PCA itself will not rapidly solve climate warming because its goals are too modest and because it has no enforcement mechanisms, it is a constructive step towards solving a global issue that scientists have proven to be true.

For Noam Chomsky, a noted leftist activist and intellectual, Trump's decision to leave the PCA signified that the "United States is the most dangerous country in the world," a statement made in Z Magazine in June 2017.

Trump's decision to leave PCA was opposed by the majority of the American people, the Democratic, Green and Socialist parties, the Secretary of State Rex Tillerson, the Defense Department and many large U.S. corporations, including Apple, Walmart, General Electric and Exxon Mobil (the giant oil company), among others.

Abandoning the PCA, however, will not prevent Democratic party states like California (the world's sixth largest economy), Hawaii, Oregon, Washington and New York, among others, as well as 200 cities, from continuing with clean energy (wind and solar) programs. In fact, Republican-controlled party states, including Texas and Iowa, are already heavily invested in clean energy.

Finally, some of the dire consequences of climate warming include the rising of ocean levels, which threaten coastal cities and low-lying ground areas, droughts, excessive rainfall, deadlier storms and release of deadly methane gas which will be released from the ground and oceans. Civilization is now in danger and life may even become extinct.

This author's view to combat climate warming involves worldwide cooperation of nations to drastically reduce military resources and transfer them into rapidly building clean energy programs and methods.

Concerning health insurance, Trump supports the reactionary House Republican American Health Care Act (AHCA), which would replace the Democratic ACA. Attempts to pass revisions thus far (September 2017) have failed, with Senator John McCain casting a decisive "no" vote. Outraged, Trump lashed out at Republican senators and leaders, including the Mitch McConnell, majority leader.

The third revision of AHCA transfers under $600 billion in the next decade from the poor to the richest 2 percent who earn $250,000 annually. It will cut Medicaid over the next 10 years by $772 billion. Medicaid itself under the ACA covers the low income, disabled, and the elderly in nursing homes. They will be economically savaged. Let them die as quickly as possible. About 22 million poor individuals in the next decade will lose ACA insurance. Also it would somewhat reduce the 3.8 percent sur-tax imposed by the ACA on the 20 percent capital gains tax paid by the rich to finance extended overage for private insurance – not Medicaid. It also has cheap health insurance for the young and poor with few benefits and raises insurance premiums for the elderly. They may, of course, go to a hosptial emergency room and then face bankruptcy. The AHCA also increases premiums by a 5-to-1 ratio between young and old, versus the 3-to-1 ratio of the current ACA.

Also, the third version would aid individuals purchasing their own insurance plans but risks workplace insurance of 170 million workers, which is tax-free and tax deductible for employers. This might encourage more of the self-employed to purchase insurance, but it may undermine employee insurance plans since it would repeal ACA requirement that larger companies provide healthcare or face stiff fines.

To be sure, there is formidable oppisition to the AHCA: the Democratic and Green Parties, the American Medical Association, U.S. Hospital Associations, the Conference of Catholic Bishops, private corporate insurance companies like Aetna, which will lose revenue if the AHCA passes, and the National Association for the Advancement of Colored People. Also, in public opinion polls, less than 20 percent of the public support it. With all its defects, the ACA is incomparably better for the poor and the disabled than the AHCA, which drops many millions of people from having health insurance. Also, some Republican state governors have accepted expanded Medicaid. Should the AHCA pass, some Republican senators and governors may lose the next election to opponents.

Currently, the U.S. has a hybrid system for medical care costs comprising individuals, federal and state governments, and employers in which government in its various levels pays half of the annual $3 trillion cost. The AHCA still (2018) endures, but has been severely hurt by Republicans.

Following World War II in 1945, the United States emerged as the world's hegemon, its economic and military influence and power unequalled among the world's nations. Thus it is that the U.S. engaged in an aggressive foreign policy that would ultimately protect the investments of its TNCs overseas; to prevent Communist/leftist expansion and to maintain reactionary governments in poor nations threatened by various socialist groups including Communists.

Why so? Because the foreign policy primarily serves the interests of those political and social classes at the top, the wealthy elite of its corporate and financial sectors. Thus its two principal enemies were the state socialist/Communist Soviet Union and the People's Republic of China. This animosity would then extend to Communist Vietnam, Cuba, North Korea and even Democratic Socialist Chile and Venezeula. Even when Russia succeeded the Soviet Union, there is now ill-will against it. This, of course, has resulted in a huge MIIC, the world's largest by far.

Since the end of World War II, the U.S. has steadfastly opposed Communism and even Democratic Socialism: the Marshall Plan for Western European economic recovery prevented it from becoming Communist. Positioning an American fleet near Italy in the Italian elections of 1948 indicated that if the Communists would have received the majority of votes (they received 33.4 percent), the U.S. would have intervened militarily to support the anti-communists. At this time, U.S. aid to Greece defeated the Communists.

Several other examples of U.S.-led campaigns against such governments are scattered throughout pre- and post-war history: In the Chinese civil war, pitting Communists against the reactionary Kuornintang, the U.S. supported the latter but the former won. The U.S. tried in 1962 to defeat, unsuccessfully, the Communist Fidel Castro in Cuba. In 1961, an American fleet aided the Brazilian military to overthrow the populist president Goulart. In 1973, with U.S. approval, the Chilean military overthrew the freely elected government of the Democratic Socialist Salvador Allende. In Nicaragua, the U.S.-supplied the Contra army and was instrumental in the 1980s in defeating its socialist president Daniel Ortega, who later again assumed the presidency with a moderate economic program. The U.S. successfully aided the reactionary large-landlord governments to maintain power against popular populist forces in Guatemala and El Salvador in long civil wars in the 1950s and afterward. It aided these reactionaries with economic assistance and by training their military officers in the School of the Americas in Fort Benning, Georgia. In Venezuela, the U.S. supported a coup attempt by part of the army against the socialist democratically elected Hugo Chavez, which ultimately failed. The U.S. was also involved in the overthrow of progressive governments in the third world of Patrice Lamumba in the Congo, Mohammad Mossadegh in Iran and Sukarno in Indonesia.

As an authoritarian billionaire, Trump likes his counterpart in Russia, Vladimir Putin, president of the Russian Federation under the tyranny of capitalistic oligarchs. But in April 2017, Trump became a hawk by threatening war with Syria/Russia and North Korea in an effort to show the American public that he can be tough against other nations.

On April 6, 2017, Trump ordered a missile attack on the Syrian government airfield used by one of its airplanes that supposedly dropped a chemical gas bomb in a rebel-occupied area. This action, killing 87 within a sovereign nation, was an illegal one, an act of war under international law.

The Syrian government of President Bashar Al-Assad and its Russian ally (Russia has a naval base in Syria) claimed they bombed a nearby warehouse holding chemical gas which spread to kill nearby people. The incident prompts a stark question: Why would the Syrian government commit this illegal/barbaric act while it is winning the war against the Jihadists and peace and reconstruction talks of war-torn Syria are occurring in Geneva and Brussels?

Indeed, just days before the supposed chemical gas attack, the U.S. announced that it did not wish to topple the Syrian government. Also, the Syrian government in 2013-14 destroyed its chemical gas stock, later verified by United Nations inspectors. The Jihadists, or ISIS, also have employed chemical gas attacks against the Syrian government. The ten Syrian chemical gas sites again have recently been inspected by the UN, with no chemical gas found; the two others in Jihadist territory have not been inspected.

The Syrian gas attack has been disputed by three reputable sources, including Professor Theodore Postol, an intelligence expert at the

Massachusetts Institute of Technology, who opined that the supposed bomb of the Syrian government airplane was actually ignited by an explosive device on the ground because of the crater's shape. Furthermore, retired U.S. Colonel Lawrence Wilkerson asserted that the Syrian government airplane tracked by U.S. intelligence indeed bombed a warehouse containing chemical gas, spreading and killing people. The well-known journalistic investigator Seymour Hersh has also debunked the al-Nusra/U.S. view.

Trump in an abrupt about-face following the supposed Syrian chemical gas attack found a convenient excuse to demand the overthrow of the Syrian government. This deflects attention from Democratic Party criticism of Trump: his possible commercial ties to Russia, which federal investigators and others have said hacked into the U.S. electoral systems, but which did not, according to Trump and supporters alike, influence the 2016 elections. Also Trump's dismissal of Comey, as already observed, may be an impeachable offense.

The Russians preferred Trump over Clinton in the presidential race because Clinton would have imposed a no-fly zone on Syria, effectively preventing Russian airplanes from aiding the Syrian government. This would have resulted in a confrontation between the U.S. and Russia. In late June 2017, tensions have increased between the U.S. and Syria/Russia with the downing of a Syrian airplane in a U.S.-occupied zone in Syria. Also, Trump gratuitously warned Syria not to drop another chemical gas bomb on its rebels.

The Syrian government/Jihadist conflict is largely a religious one with social class overtones. The Syrian government rules over 18 million people consisting of Shia, Christians and moderate Sunnis supported by Shia Iran and Iraq and Shia groups in Lebanon. To be sure, the al-Assad government is a brutal dictatorship, but religiously tolerant; ISIS is not.

The Jihadists, mainly ISIS with two million people under their control, are funded by Saudi Arabia, the center of Salafism, other Sunni Salfist gulf principalities, to an extent by Turkey and even the

U.S., which spent $500 million to fund a rebel group fighting the Syrian government, resulting in recruiting five fighters.

I add that the Jihadist Sunni Moslem state in Iraq and Syria was basically a reaction to the unprovoked U.S. attack on Iraq and consequent occupation, although Sunni/Shia conflict also played a role.

Wahhabi (Salafist) Saudi Arabia, influencing many Moslem nations, practices a bigoted Islam which hates Jews and Christians: the U.S. itself fights against the Wahhabi Moslems in Iraq by supporting the Shias, while fighting against the Shia's in Syria.

The U.S. is now involved with Islam by invading/attacking Afghanistan, Iraq, Libya and with drone attacks against radical Moslems in Pakistan, Somalia, Yemen and elsewhere with no end in sight.

On the 19th of April 2017, the Trump administration signaled that it would reverse Obama's policy for détente with Iran in exchange to freeze its nuclear program for ten years. Russia, Great Britain and others approved and supported the move. Details of this stance as of this writing are scant, but they basically involve trade sanctions. U.S. animosity toward Iran is based on its support of Palestinian statehood, opposed by Israel, the principal U.S. alley in the Mideast, joined by influential conservative Jewish-Americans.

North Korea, a poor Communist nation of 26 million people, is heavily armed because it fears an invasion from the US, which has 28,500 troops along with many South Koreans under U.S. commanders on its southern borders. In late July 2017, North Korea successfully launched an ICBM capable, according to military officials, of reaching the United States mainland with nuclear warheads.

The Trump presidency now nonsensically views North Korean testing of missiles as a great threat to South Korea and Japan. In response, the U.S. is sending extensive anti-missile systems to them.

North Korea invaded South Korea in 1950 and the U.S. intervened to help the South. An armistice was reached in July 1953 that ended the hostilities, but there is yet no peace treaty.

From 1994-2001, President Bill Clinton and North Korea agreed for the U.S. to purchase its missiles and that neither nation would be hostile to one another. But in 2002, President Bush declared North Korea a part of a group of nations comprising his "axis of evil." In 2005, Bush against almost reached a non-aggression pact with North Korea in which the latter would suspend further development of nuclear weapons and missiles and in return would receive a light-water reactor for medical purposes. But Bush, with an excuse, changed his mind. North Korea then resumed its nuclear weapons and missile programs. Obama then conducted a secret war to disrupt the North Korean missile program – an illegal war act.

North Korea itself would not add to its nuclear bomb and missle programs if the U.S. would agree to a nonaggression pact with it. So far, the U.S. has refused. Why? I believe that the U.S. wishes to impoverish North Korea by spending much of its resources on the military. Its people then may revolt against its Communist government, which would in turn prompt South Korea to annex the country. But this author doubts that the Chinese Communist government would allow it.

The U.S. and South Korea twice annually conduct provacative war games on North Korea's southern border, continuously exacerbating war tensions.

In early July 2017, war tensions between the U.S. and North Korea increased significantly after a North Korean ICBM achieved range to strike Alaska. A subsequent missile launch proved to have even more range. Trump was enraged, warning North Korea of dire consequences.

If a war breaks out between North Korea and U.S./South Korea, the former will be olbiterated by the latter, but the former will inevitably cause heavy damage to South Korea, killing millions of people. To be sure, a U.S. attack on North Korea would be an illegal war act. Finally, to ever believe that North Korea would ever attack the U.S. is an utterly silly notion.

North Korea itself is heavily armed with the world's fourth largest army, along with 200,000 special troops, 10,000 artillery pieces within range of Seoul, the South Korean capital, 15 large nuclear weapons with twice the destructive power of the Hiroshima bomb, many missles that can attack American bases in South Korea and Japan. It also has 15,000 underground installations for protection. Again, these North Korean military means are of a defensive nature.

During the U.S. war with North Korea, U.S. bombers not only devastated military targets but also civilian ones, as large dams regulating the growing of rice, flooding large areas of the countryside causing severe food shortages, a criminal act under international law. The Korean "Menace" is pure Orwellian "doublethink."

In the February 19, 2018, edition of Time, pp. 5-6, a mainstream magazine, one of its influential columnists Ian Bremmer urged that Trump learn to live with a nuclear-armed North Korea and negotiate a permanent peace treaty with it.

A possible war between the U.S. and North Korea may be avoided because Trump in March agreed to meet the North Korean leader Kim Jong-Un by May to resolve differences. But if there is no agreement, hostile military action by the U.S. may proceed. Also, the recent appointments of Mike Pompeo, former CIA director, as Secretary of State, and John R. Bolton as National Security Advisor, both of whom are hawks, may lead to probable wars with North Korea and Iran.

The United States' policy today has two principal enemies which it monitors closely: Russia and China. Russia annexed the Crimea from Ukraine, an area of 71 percent ethnic Russians, with its strategic Russian naval base in Sevastopol. Crimea traditionally was part of Russia until Nikita Khruschev, a Ukranian and a First Secretary of the Soviet Communist Party and after 1953 premier of the Soviet Union, gave it to Ukraine.

Ukraine, traditionally and ethnically close to Russia, has always been in Russia's sphere of influence. Russia annexed Crimea after the U.S. aided Ukranian dissidents to overthrow a pro-Russian government with one friendly to the European Union/U.S., which may enable the country to join the EU and North Atlantic Treaty Organization.

This author does not regard the Russian action as threatening NATO, which believes otherwise. Subsequent economic sanctions on Russia by the U.S./EU have caused increased tensions between the two superpowers.

Also ethnic Russians in Eastern Ukraine, wishing more self-government, are now engaged in intermittent warfare with the Ukrainian military. The ethnic Russian rebels are receiving aid from Russia.

China is building military bases in the South China Sea islands, the area of which is contested by neighboring nations and the U.S. This author views this action as basically defensive.

In the meantime, the U.S. has a string of military bases near China, principally in Okinawa, a Japanese island, and in Japan itself, among other places, reinforced by its pacific fleets. China itself is under constant U.S. military surveillance.

In late Spring 2017, Trump went to Saudi Arabia, an absolutistic monarchy and center of Islamic Wahhabism. Trump praised the Saudis as "great friends" of the U.S. and erroneously blamed the small emirate of Qatar as the principal funder of Jihadism. In what world is he living in? Saudi Arabia/U.S. friendship is based on U.S. dependence of its oil, its huge purchases of U.S. military equipment and its large investments in the U.S.

Apropos of Saudi Arabia, it is now engaged in the civil war in Yemen fighting its Shia with U.S. assistance, resulting in a probably mass famine as a result of its heavy bombing and naval blockade.

Recently, Obama opened diplomatic relations with Communist Cuba. But Trump will now impose trade and travel restrictions on Cuba and will not do business with the Cuban military which operates many economic enterprises.

This author believes that there now should be a détente by the U.S. with Russia and China because Russia, since 1992, has been ruled by a capitalist oligarchy and the Chinese Communist Party has allowed a capitalistic oligarchy to run China economically. Also, U.S. corporations have heavily invested in China. Also, these nations do not basically have territorial ambitions. Then, too, NATO has overwhelming economic/military superiority over the two combined.

But will the U.S. plutocracy with its bloated military complex allow this detente? As of now, this author doubts it.

Constant wars and foreign crisis reinforce the rule of the plutocracy who fear socialism, branding it as un-American. But any serious reading of American history should reveal that socialism played an important role in 1900-20 and in the New Deal in the 1930s, especially in the labor and intellectual areas. In 2016, Senator Bernie Sanders, who ran as a Democratic Socialist, did very well in the Democratic Party presidential primaries, amassing a large following throughout the country that to this days endures.

The endless wars/crisis, as in the Korean War, the long war in Vietnam, the invasions of Afghanistan and Iraq, the crisis with Syria/ Russia and North Korea now have produced a war psychosis among the American people, principally abetted by television. These wars/ crises enhance the power of the U.S. capitalist oligarchy over the working class by diverting attention to pressing domestic needs such as poverty and income inequality. This is reminiscent of Orwell's <u>1984</u>.

A study of history indicates that war is a constant in human affairs; that leaders are not always rational and foreign crises may esculate to probable wars. This belief was demonstrated in October 1962 during the Cuban missile crisis between the U.S. and Soviet Union. Nuclear war was avoided by a narrow margin.

If a nuclear war ever occurs between the U.S. and its allies against Russia alone, or a Russia-Chinese alliance, the nuclear intercontienental ballistic missiles of the belligerents will utterly destroy the U.S., Canada, Russia, Europe, and China.

But today the U.S. has modernized its nuclear arsenal, while after the implosion of the Soviet Union, Russian development of its nuclear arsenal eased for many years. Thus, the U.S. can almost certainly destroy Russia's nuclear force with a first strike. But knowing this, Russia might be tempted to strike first. Also, Russia's nuclear submarine force has enough power to destroy the U.S. Recently, President Putin of Russia announced that Russia now has ground-hugging nuclear-powered intercontinental cruise mussles with warheads based on land and unmanned submarines.

Also, there is now cyber warfare and perhaps it may occur in space. Will the big-power armaments race even end with its prodigious waste and possible war to destroy civilization and humanity?

The latest estimates of nuclear arsenal warheads, according to *Time*, Feb. 12, 2018, pp. 22-23): Russia, 7,000; France, 250; U.S., 6,800; China, 270; Great Britain, 215; Pakistan, 140; India, 130; Israel, 80; North Korea, 15. The U.S. now is engaged in a $1 trillion multi-year program to upgrade its nuclear warhead capabilities. Then, there, is cybernetical and bacteriological warfare. Madness indeed reigns.

The Trump/Republican tax bill became law in late December 2017. It was basically formulated by three former Goldman-Sachs senior executives: Trump's Treasury Secretary, Steve Mnuchin; Gary Cohn, director of Trump's Economic Council; and Bill Dudley, president of the New York Federal Reserve Bank.

According to the Tax Policy Center, the richest 1 percent would receive half the tax benefits in 2018, while middle-class families would receive about 25 percent, but by 2027, the last year of the tax plan, the former would receive 80 percent, the latter 5 percent. For Bernie Sanders, 80 percent of the 2017 tax cuts go to the richest 1 percent in its first year, with first year tax cuts earning $25,000 annually, $60; for the richest 1 percent, $57,000. The rich, including the real estate mogul Trump, will benefit significantly. Total ten-year tax deductions will be $2.4 trillion which at the least will add $1.5 trillion debt to the federal budget during this time.

The Trump/Republican tax law is a tax cut for corporations from 35 percent to 21 percent. Before, with loopholes, average corporate tax was 14 percent, a fourth paying 0 percent. Since the richest 1 percent own 40 percent of stocks (the bottom 80 percent only own 7 percent), the rich are the great benefeciaries. Furthermore, these tax cuts raise income taxes for the lowest tax bracket (the poor) from 10 percent to 12 percent, savaging them even more economically.

Also, the personal income tax was cut to 36 percent for the rich, who actually pay, after loopholes, 20 percent.

The ultimate Republican aim is to privatize all social welfare programs to further enrich the wealthiest 1 percent who, from 2009-2017, have acquired 95 percent of new income.

The tax cuts will further enrich the wealthy/corporations with more investments in already very high stock prices, becoming even higher with stock buybacks in a period of high corporate profits. (Tax cuts should come only in economic downturns to aid economic activity). Five percent will go to higher wages/bonuses.

In conjunction with these tax cuts, benefits for Social Security, Medicare (cut 4 percent in 2018), and Medicaid will be reduced; Trump promised on the electoral campaign platform not to touch them. He lied.

According to Paul Krugman (already identified), of forty two economists of various views surveyed recently by the University of Chicago, only one asserted that the Republican tax plan would promote economic growth, while all agreed that it would increase the federal budget deficit. (Krugman, "The Biggest Tax Scam in History," NYT, Nov. 8, 2017).

As already observed, the horrid exploitation of the world's working class by the rich, aided by their legislative muscle of tax avoidance, has allowed for the proliferation of tax havens, legal and illegal, about $30 trillion.

One such legal tax haven recently exposed is Appleby, located in Bermuda, Cayman Islands and other locations: it caters, of course, to the very rich worldwide, including 31,000 Americans, the most common nationality discovered. Their tax avoidance involves complex accounting practices and depositing money in nations with zero or low tax rates.

The international "very" rich today, with more than $50 million in wealth, now number 140,900, half of whom are from the U.S. Recently, the wealth of the rich increased by 7 percent annually, while, overall, it increased by 3 percent. The richest 1 percent now have half the world's wealth and the richest 10 percent owns 90 percent. (On Appleby and Wealth, <u>NYT</u>, Nov. 8, 2017, pp. A1 and A16).

As for the economic future, I foresee an economic crash in the U.S. in the near future. Corporations borrow money very cheaply because of low interest rates, which also, having high earnings and paying low taxes, allows them to increase their stock prices with corporate buy-backs. Add to this the high incomes and low taxes of the richest 1 percent which also fuels stock and derivatives speculation.

Simultaneously, the falling real wages for most of the workforce in the last almost 40 years is depressing consumer demand and working class consumers are also heavily in debt. Corporate debt itself is at an all-time high with corporate buy-backs of stocks and high executive salaries. Add to this factor the Republican gutting of the Dodd-Frank Act, a watchdog on capitalist speculative activities, and you have a time bomb.

A Republican victory in late 2017 is the FCC's 3-2 vote ending internet neutrality relative to users (large and small) with no price discrimination now favors the former over the latter regarding speed of access and per-unit time price charges.

The internet industry itself is dominated by three giant corporations (Comcast, ATT, Verizon) which have a monopoly or duopoly in most markets, creating an imaginary atmosphere of competition and thus being able to increase users' prices at will.

Indeed, the claim of the giant internet corporations of ending internet neutrailty will allow for more corporate competition and encourage technological innovation is blatantly false because their sole purpose is simply to increase high corporate profits.

In early January 2018, a tell-all book appeared by journalist Michael Wolff, <u>Fire and Fury: Inside the Trump White House</u>. Wolff had close cooperation in writing it from the conservative white populist, Stephen K. Bannon, who was Trump's chief advisor in the 2016 presidential contest and chairman of the reactionary Breitbart News.

He argued that Donald Trump Jr. committed, along with others, probably treasonous acts when meeting with Russians offering unfavorable information concerning Hillary Clinton. Furthermore, this work characterizes Trump as not well-informed, presiding over a dysfunctional staff. Trump himself is seen as lazy, not even reading brief memos or policy papers and abuptly leaving meetings. His advisors in private describe him disparingly as an "idiot," "stupid," "crazy" and so forth.

Enraged by the book, Trump angrily severed relations with Bannon. Trump's supporters and wealthy conservatives bankrolling Breitbart pressured Bannon to apologize to Trump which he promptly did. Nevertheless, Bannon was forced to leave his position at Breitbart News.

On Februrary 9, 2018, Republicans and Democrats passed another $300 billion two-year tax cut to increase military spending by another $160 billion and social welfare and other programs by $140 billion. The latter includes $5.8 billion for the Children's Health Insurance Program for 9 million children; $7.8 billion for community healthcare centeres serving 27 million patients, regardless of ability to pay; $6 billion for the opioid crisis; $90 billion for disaster relief, and $20 billion for infrastructure, among others.

The two tax acts will raise the annual federal debt from $800 billion in 2018 to $1.2 trillion in 2019 and beyond. The federal debt will thus rise rapidly, imperiling social welfare reforms to reduce the federal deficit. Rising federal budget deficits owned mostly by the rich are an additional tax on the working class.

Trump's $4.4 trillion 2019 federal budget plan: Ten-year cuts of $490 billion to Medicare, $250 billion to Medicaid and $213 billion to food stamps (30 percent); one-year cuts include: $494 million (4 percent) to Social Security; 34 percent to EPA, 5 percent to the Education Department, and federal funding for Planned Parenthood providing abortions, cancer screenings and so forth for poor women, and reduced housing/heating assistance for the poor. Also, there are budget gains for the military, already observed, the Department of Homeland Security to prevent illegal immigrant entry and to construct a $25 billion wall over 10 years on the U.S-Mexico border.

Trump's rebuilding plan for the crumbling U.S. infrastructure includes a ten-year plan of $1.5 trillion – the federal share being $200 billion and the remainder from private, city and state investment, the private sector to enjoy the tax breaks – another giveaway to the rich. Customarily, the federal government contributes 80 percent and cities/states 20 percent for infrastructure funds; at times there is also private capital investment. Trump reverses this ratio to 20 percent federal government to 80 percent cities/states and large private investment, the last owning a large part of the infrastructure, resulting in more tolls to use roads, bridges and tunnels.

But cities/states have less tax revenue than previously because of declining real wages and continuing poverty. The federal government itself receives less tax revenue because the rich pay much lower taxes than previously and because of sluggish economic growth. Also, there are less funds for the civilians sector because of wasteful military/war spending. Trump's infrastructure plan will most likely not be enacted.

Trump broke his promise that he would not touch Social Security, Medicare and Medicaid. Also, as already observed, Republicans in office favor wars and military more so than the Democrats; they slash social welfare programs; they spend recklessly and cut taxes on the rich. And once out of office, they scream for thrift.

Since judicial conformation of federal circuit appeal court judges cannot be prevented by Senate filibuster, Trump and Republicans have elected scores of conservative judges. They want to limit abortion, maintain/expand gun rights, gut environmental protections, workplace safeguards and make union organizing even more difficult.

A hotly debated February 2018 issue in Congress and by Trump is the fate of 1.8 million young children, or "Dreamers," who came illegally to the U.S. with their Hispanic parents. If their legality to stay in the U.S. and also to becoming citizens is not resolved by Trump/Congress, it could be so by the courts or a presidential decree. Their legal status as of March 2018 is in doubt and the target of frequent outbursts by Trump on Twitter.

Readily available guns in the U.S. has made it into a battle zone, with the easily acquired semiautomatic AR-15 becoming a favorite rifle for mass killings. Since the 2012 killings in Newton, Conn., there have been 239 school murders until Feb. 14, 2018, in Parkland, Fl.

Trump/Republicans, lavished by National Rifle Association-electoral funds, blame school and other mass killings only on mental illness (most murderers are not psychotic but are disturbed/violent persons), but not on the readily-availablity of guns. Democrats themselves are for stricter gun controls. Of interest: 75 percent of households do not own guns (3 percent of them own half of them and 95 percent of the people are for stricter gun control). All other economically developed nations have strict gun laws and are thus spared of mass killings apart from Islamic terrorist ones.

On March 24, 2018, in the March for Our Lives, hundreds of thousands of high school and other students marched in Washington D.C., joined by many hundreds of thousands in up to 800 towns and cities in the U.S. and elsewhere as in Paris. The protests were against lax U.S. gun laws, including the legality of semi-automatic rifles. Politically these demonstrations were directed against the Trump/Republicans under the thrall of NRA money.

On April 7, 2018, an alleged chemical-gas bomb killed about forty people in Sunni-rebel-held Douma, which fell to Syrian Government/Russian forces a few days later.

On April 13, the allies (U.S., Britain, France) with missles struck various Syrian targets to punish Syria for employing an internationally banned weapon: chemical gas. But international law regards this action by the Allies as unlawful because Syria did not attack them.

The Allies asserted that photography from the air indicated a chemical gas attack dropped by a bomb; they also used other friendly sources to confirm it. This was disputed by the Syrian Government/Russians who claimed that the attack did not take place, that the rebel source was a falsehood. A third source stated that the attack was staged by rebels in an act of desperation. Recently, the BBC claimed the Douma bombing was a U.S./allies hoax.

The missle strikes in Syria were launched before an independent neutral agency could investigate the disputed chemical attack: On about April 20, the Organization for the Prohobition of Chemical

Weapons is examining the alleged chemical gas site and will send its findings to the Netherlands for analysis. To be sure, the rebels have also used chemical gas against the government and fasely blamed it at times for its use against them. Both sides have dirty hands, but the government more so than the rebels. According to Human Rights Watch, which I trust, the Syrian government is guilty of more than fifty chemical gas attacks against the rebels. (On the chemical gas attacks, see <u>NYT</u>, Ap. 19, 2018, p. A4 and <u>The New Yorker,</u> Ap. 23 2018, pp. 25-26.

Trump met chairman Kim Jung-Un of North Korea on June 12 2018 to start a peace process and also he pulled the U.S. out of the Iran Nuclear Deal, involving Britain, Germany, France, Russia, and China, which remain with it.[1]

Conclusion

Despite ethnic, religious, "racial" and ethnic arrival time to the U.S. divisions, the American working class has played an important role in American history: in forming unions, conducting strikes, in political activity, as in the 1900-1920 Socialist Party upsurge; in the 1930s New Deal of President Franklin Roosevelt, in which labor strikes and ferment played leading roles, the Great Society of President Lyndon Baine's Johnson, and the 1960s-70s upsurge aainst the Vietnam War and struggles for black, women's, Native American, and LGBT liberation. Indeed, in securing the 40-hour week, Social Security, Medicare and Medicaid, organized labor was in the forefront, as it is to secure future passage of universal health care. Indeed, union/socialist activity helped to bring about the 1940-80 relatively good years for many workers, with strong unions at their height in the 1960s representing a third of American workers. But the American labor movement, the spearhead of American workers for reform, has now reached a ninety-year nadir, almost to the pre-1930s New Deal. Since the election of Republican President Ronald Reagan in 1980 until now, 2018-19), American workers have lost ground economically because the union movement has become much weaker, representing only 10 percent of the workforce.

Why weak unionism? Capital moved jobs from the U.S. North to its South, then abroad to China and Mexico among other nations, automation, and anti-union legislation/judicial decisions being the principal reasons.

As unions became weaker, their contributions to the Democratic Party fell and the party relied more on Wall Street/corporate money. In turn, the Republican Party became more conservative. Liberal Eisenhower Republicans no longer exist.

Futhermore, a conservative U.S. Supreme Court in various decisions, culimating in Citizen United has allowed the richest 1 percent/corporations and unions to spend unlimited funds to defeat political candidates, the former contributing 80 percent of them, outspending the latter by 15 to 1.

Other developments exacerabating differences between the rich and workers in the last half century: taxes on the rich/corporations have declined by more than half and funds for higher educations have been reduced greatly, resulting in higher tuition costs and student debt, ulimately reducing worker upward social mobility.

Regarding social welfare progress, the U.S. lags far behind Western European and other democracies, the only one of 35 wealthy OECD nations without universal health care, insurance, although in an October 2018 poll, 70 percent of its citizens support it, as well as 120 Democrats in the U.S. House of Representatives (who, in the November 2018 election won back the House), according to Thom Hartmann, Free Speech TV, Oct. 17, 2018.

Working class defeat has led to the U.S. being under the control of a rapacious capitalist oligarchy, also involved in an aggressive foreign policy of endless wars. Thus, there is only one political party now – the Corporate Pary – comprised of all the Republican Party and the majority of the Democratic Party.

American democracy itself is less than desirable. Gerrymandering and suppression of black and Hispanic voters is widespread by the Republican Party. Also with each state having two U.S. senators and two votes in the electoral college to vote for the presidency, voters in sparsely populated states have greater voter clout than in states having large populations.

Also, the winner-take-all of the electoral college votes to elect the president, in hotly-contested battlground states is involved in the spectacle of Trump winning the presidency while having 2.9 million fewer popular votes than Hillary Clinton. The presidency is the only elective American office where this occurs.

Because of the legacy of black slavery/Jim Crow and consequent poverty of blacks and up to 11-13 million of Hispanic undocumented workers in the U.S. which have destroyed unions and lowered wages of about 10 percent of blue-collar workers, the American working class is now divided: the wealthiest white workers overwhelmingly vote Republican, while the poorer black and Hispanic ones by large margins vote Democratic.

In allying themselves with Republicans, white workers, largely evangelicals, aid the Republican Party to enrich the rich with lower taxes, gut social welfare programs, pass anti-union legislation/court decisions, and increase a bloated military budget.

The white evangelical workers, almost a third of the U.S. population, supposedly interpret the Bible literally, against other Christians, Jews, Moslems, Hindus, the LGBT community and abortion, but they forget the Hebrew prophetic tradition and Christ's castigating the rich and his favoring a society of general economic equality.

White evangelicals also believe that Christ will soon return to save only them from an unjust workd, while others go to hell. Christ will then usher in a Christian utopia of equality and justice.

These preceding evangelical views have an anti-capitalist sentiment where the wealthy oppress the poor, but in the meantime evangelicals wish to maintain their socioeconomic advantage over blacks and Hispanics.

The Trump/evangelical electoral alliance will fracture in the long run because the former enjoy the perogatives of the rich while the latter endure the disadvantages of relative poverty.

The losers of the preceding developments are American workers: their incomes since 1979 to 2018 adjusted for inflation for most of them have either stagnated or declined; to keep up with labor productivity in this period, they should be earning three-quarters more. Also, tragically the bottom 40 percent of the people (workers live in poverty/near poverty, earning only 12 percent of all income. The winners: the richest 1 percent. In the 1980s with 8 percent of all income and 18 percent of all wealth; now, 20-22 percent of income, 42 percent of wealth.

As already noted, half of American youth and blacks are favorable to socialism. But capitalist economic, political, and cultural hegemony still prevails especially among whites.

The popular media (television, press, periodicals, radio), basically owned by corporate capitalists, favor the capitalist ethos of "free enterprise," possessive individualism, incessant consumerism, and violence in its many forms to perpetuate a mindset and news programs lacking meaningful information to question the capitalist status quo. In fact, the working class usually lacks the economic and cultural means to question it.

Nevertheless, as already observed, a large section of the working class is progressive as indicated in the Democratic Socialist Bernie Sanders upsurge and the wide acceptance of socialism among youth and blacks.[1]

An economic downtown is not far off. To begin, total U.S. debt has risen from $50 trillion in 2008 to $80 trillion (approximately quadruple the U.S. GDP) at the end of 2017. It includes $21 trillion of federal government debt now increasing about a billion dollars annually because of the 2017 Trump/Republican tax cut which gave 83 percent of it to the richest 1 percent/corporations already waxing fat. The economic crash, precipitated and caused in part by massive debt, likely will also come from derivatives gambling in junk bonds or in the other debts mentioned. A strong warning sign of an impending economic downtown: In late 2018, short-term bond yields are higher than the more risky long-term bonds.

Most of the debt now is by non-financial corporations borrowing money at low interest rates. Other debts include $1.5 trillion in student debt; $1 trillion in autos; $1 trillion in credit cards; $7-8 trillion in home mortgages, and $6 trillion in the Federal Reserve Bank's QE program.[2]

# Endnotes

## Chapter 1: Increasing Economic Concentration

1) John Bellamy Foster and Robert W. McChesney, "The Endless Crisis," Monthly Review, May 2012, p. 20. Bernie Sanders, The Speech (New York: Nation Books, 2011), p. 37 on mortgages and credit cards. Thom Hartmann, Free Speech TV, Jan. 29, 2013, on 12 banks having 69 percent of assets. Anat R. Adamatt, "We're All Still Hostages to the Big Banks," NYT, Aug. 26, 2013, p. A21 on the assets and liabilities of the 6 largest banks. On the top 200 corporations' revenue and profit, John Bellamy Foster. "Monopoly Capitalism," Monthly Review, April 2011, pp. 6-7. Louis Patsouras, Marx in Context (New York: iUniverse, 2005), pp. 290-91. Robert W. McChesney, Blowing the Roof Off the Twenty-first Century (New York: Monthly Review Press, 2014), pp. 74-86. Jacob S. Hacker and Paul Pierson, Winner-Take-All Politics: How Washington Made the Rich Richer – And Turned its Back on the Middle Class (New York: Simon and Schuster, 2010), p. 25. William K. Tabb, "The Crisis," Monthly Review. Sept. 2012, p. 18. On mergers and acquisitions, NYT, Jan. 2, 2015, B4.

2) Gary B. Nash, et al., The American People, 3$^{rd}$ ed. (New York: Harper Collins, 1994), pp. 1053-58.

3) Jack Rasmus, "Income, Inequality...Recession," Z Magazine), Dec. 2012, p. 26, Steven Rattner, "The Rich Get Even Richer," NYT, March 2, 2012, p. A21. NYT Jan. 26, 2011, p. B5. PBS News, Nov. 22, 2013. Hacker and Pierson, pp. 22-23, on lower income/longer hours for lower income quintiles; p. 39 on national income shares of US and other nations. Steven Greenhouse, The Big Squeeze: Tough Times for the American Worker (New York: Anchor Books, 2009), p. 39. For 2009-12 income, see Paul Krugman, "Free To Be Hungry," NYT, Sept. 23, 2013, p. A21. On more estimates on income and wealth, see Rob Larson, "Home Is Where The Empty Investment Property Is," Z Magazine, Dec. 2013, pp. 32-35 and John Bellamy Foster and Michael D. Yates "Piketty and the Crisis of Neoclassical Economics," Monthly Review, Nov. 2014, p. 11.

4) Robert Reich, "Inequality in America," The Nation, July 19/26, 2010, pp. 13-15. Anne Lowrey, "Top 10% Took Half of US Income in 2012," NYT, Sept. 11, 2013, pp. B1 and B3. Rasmus, "Income Inequality." On falling incomes (2010-13), Steven Rattner, "Inequality, Unbelievably, Gets Worse," NYT, Nov. 17, 2014, p. A23.

5) On Gates, Buffett and other net worth's of billionaires, NYT, July 27, 2011, p. A6. On household wealth percentages in the US in 2012, see Peter Coy, "The

Richest Rich Are in a Class by Themselves," <u>Bloomberg Business Week,</u> pp. 7-13, 2014, pp. 16-17. Also, see Hacker and Pierson, P. 32 and 16-17; on world's rich, Chrystia Freeland, <u>Plutocrats</u> (New York: Penquin Books, 2034 ff. and p. 193. For an older estimate of household wealth in the US, John M. Shepard, <u>Sociology,</u> 11th ed. (Belmond CA: Wadsworth, 2010), p. 206. On Credit Swiss Weath Report, Thom Hartmann, Free Speech TV, Oct. 20, 2014. On <u>Forbes</u> 400 billionaires circa 2014: Eric Alterman, "What Are They Thinking?" <u>Nation,</u> Nov. 17, 2014, p. 6. On increasing wealth gap among the top, middle, and lowest quintiles: Patricia Cohen, "Fueled by Recession, U.S. Wealth Gap Is Widest in Decades..." <u>NYT,</u> Dec. 18, 2014, p. B3. On dynasty trusts, Mike Konczal, "Immortal Fortunes," <u>The Nation,</u> Aug. 17/24, p. 5. For John Bellamy Foster and Robert W. McChesney, <u>The Endless Crisis</u> (New York: Monthly Review Press, 2012), p. 122, the world's richest 1 percent had 42 percent of its wealth. On other statistics on world wealth-inequality, see Matthew Schofield, "Richest 85 people have as much as half of world," <u>Akron Beacon Journal,</u> Jan. 21, 2014, p. A5. On the world's $30 million wealth group, Julie Creswell, "If the Very Rich Were Like Wine...Vintage," <u>NYT,</u> March 5, 2014 p. B3. On the world's richest 1 percent having more than half its wealth circa 2015 and so forth, see Patricia Cohen, "Study...Richest," <u>NYT,</u> Jan. 19, 2015, p. B6. Again, Joseph F. Stiglitz, <u>The Great Divide: Unequal Societies and What We Can Do About Them</u> (New York: W.W. Norton, 2015), pp. 69-132 on growing economic inequality. On the richest 400 Americans owning $2.2 billion, etc., "Bernie" Sanders newsletter, June 2015. On 25 hedge fund owners earning $24 billion, Bernie Sanders, Free Speech TV, Aug. 23, 2015, <u>ibid,</u> on Waltons' wealth.

6) On 2012, CEO salaries, David Carr, "For Media Moguls...Out," <u>NYT,</u> May 6, 2013, pp. B1 and B9. On 2007 earnings of Soros and two other billionaires, Henry A. Giroux, <u>America's Education Deficit and the War on Youth</u> (New York: Monthly Review Press, 2013), p. 85. On 2013 top earners, William Alden, "Market...Year," <u>NYT,</u> March 5, 2014, p. B3. On percentages in salaries 1978-2011, Annie Lowrey, "Even Among the Richest...Diverge," <u>NYT,</u> Feb. 11, 2014, p. F2. On undeserved high CEO salaries, Paul Krugman, "We are the 99.9 %," <u>NYT,</u> Nov. 23, 2012.

7) On luxury consumption by the wealthy and upper-middle class: "Even Marked up Luxury Goods Fly off the Shelves," <u>NYT,</u> Aug. 4, 2011, p. A3, quotes Zandi. Jack Rasmus, <u>Z Magazine,</u> July/August, 2011, p. 29. <u>NYT,</u> Feb. 3, 2014, pp. A1 and A11.

8) Paul Krugman, "The Show-Off Society," <u>NYT,</u> Sept. 26, 2014, p. A27. On various income groups, Annie Lowrey, "Income...Talks," <u>NYT,</u> Dec. 13, 2012, p. A20. On tax havens, Naomi Klein, <u>This Changes Everything: Capitalism vs. The Climate</u> (New York, Simon and Schuster, 2014), p. 114.

9)   On the wealthy/power elite: C. Wright Mills, <u>The Power Elite</u> (New York: Oxford Univ. Press, 1959, pp. 3-29. G. William Domhoff, <u>Who Rules America? Power and Politics in the Year 2000</u> (Mountain View, CA: Mayfield, 1998), pp. 105-15.

10)  On the income of the richest 10 percent, see Greenhouse, <u>Big Squeeze</u>, p. 40. Sabrina Tavernise, "Survey Finds Rising Strain Between Rich and Poor," <u>NYT,</u> Jan. 12, 2012, pp. A11 and A13. Rattner, <u>NYT</u>, March 26, p. A23. <u>NYT</u>, Nov. 16, 2011. Lowrey, "Top 10 % Took Half of US Income in 2012." On racial discrimination to accumulate wealth, Patricia Cohen "Racial Wealth Gap Persists…Says," <u>NYT</u>, Aug. 17, 2015, pp. B1 and B2.

# Chapter 2: Lower Middle/Working Classes and Poverty

1) Jon Shepard, Sociology, pp. 202 ff. on class; p. 206 on income of bottom 40 percent and wealth of bottom 50 percent. For a Marxist view of class, Harry Braverman, Labor and Monopoly Capital: The Degradation of Work in the Twentieth Century (New York: Monthly Review Press, 1974). Robert Pear, NYT, Sept. 17, 2014, p. A19 on lower-middle class income.

2) On national minimum wages, Eduardo Porter, "Dwindling Tools to Raise Wages," NYT, Dec. 11, 2013, pp. B1 and B2. On doubling the poverty line, John F. Schwarz, "Let's Draw an Honest Poverty Line," Akron Beacon Journal, Oct. 27, 2013, p. A13. Shepard, pp. 217-23 on the poor. Leonhardt and Quealy, "America's Middle Class…" On increasing healthcare and costs, Christopher S. Rugaber, "Middle Class Feels Squeeze," Akron Beacon Journal, Sept. 28, 2014, D1 and D2.

3) On lower US income percentile levels than in other selected nations, David Leonhardt and Kevin Luealy, "America's Middle Class Is No Longer Richest in the World," NYT, April 23, 2014, pp. A1 and A14.

4) Annie Lowrey, "Household Income Flat Despite Sunnier Economy," NYT, Sept. 18, 2013, p. A15.

5) Eduardo Porter, "Inequality in America: The Data is Sobering," NYT, July 31, 2013, pp. B1 and B3.

6) Nelson D. Schwartz, "Recovery…Profits," NYT, March 4, 2013, p. A3. Fred Magdoff and John Bellamy Foster, "Class War and Labor's Declining Share," Monthly Review, March 2013, pp. 1-11. Joe Norcera, "No Respect for Unions," NYT, June 5, 2012, p. A21. Lowrie, "Household Incomes Flat Despite Sunnier Economy." On falling salaries for four-year college graduates, Jack Dickey, "I'm 24…Again," Time, Oct. 27, 2014, p. 40. On adults living with parents, Victoria Stilwell, "Multigenerational families…" ABJ, July 20, 2014, p. A5.

7) Roger Bybee, "Insourcing Trend Strictly a Myth," Z Magazine, March 2013, citing Stiglitz in NYT, January 20, 2013, p. 23. Mina Kimes, "King Cat," Bloomberg Businessweek, May 20-26, 2013, p. 71. On the $3,105 income loss: Eduardo Porter, "Rethinking…Inequality," NYT, Nov. 13, 2013, pp. B1 and B8. On the Federal Reserve Bank of San Francisco, statistic and of falling share of wages worldwide, see "Notes from the Editors," Monthly Review, vol. 65, Nov. 8, January 2014. On median income of lowest 90 percent falling in last thirty years, Robert Reich, "The Middle Class Squeeze," NYT, Jan. 23, 2014, p. A22.

8) Catherine Rampell, "Big Income Losses Hit Those Near Retirement," NYT, Aug. 24, 2012, pp. B1 and B2. Binyamin Applebaum, "For US Families Net Worth Drops to 1990 Levels," NYT, June 12, 2012, p. A1. On median income decline, Annie Lowrey, "Household Incomes Flat Despite Sunnier Economy,"

NYT, Sept. 18, 2013, p. A15. Paul Krugman, "Money and Morals," NYT, Feb. 10, 2012, A23. Jack Rasmus, "Obama's Economy," Z Magazine, May 2012, p. 31. 2011 NYT Almanac, p. 520. On starting wages in manufacturing recently falling by half: Roger Bybee, "The War on Wages," Z Magazine, Dec. 2012, p. 25. Greenhouse, Big Squeeze, p. 39. Lowry, "Top 10 % Took Half of Income in 2012." On lower wages for men with at least a bachelor's degree, see Eduardo Porter, "Rethinking the Rise of Inequality," NYT, Nov. 14, 2013, pp. B1 and B8. David Leonhardt and Keven Quealy, "America's Middle Class...World," NYT, Ap. 23, 2014, pp. A1 and A4.

9) Greenhouse, Big Squeeze, p. 5. 2011 NYT Almanac, p. 349. Richard Wolff, Capitalism Hits the Fan (Northampton, Mass.: Olive Brand Press, 2010), p. 83. Lawrence Mishel, "Even Better Than a Tax Cut," NYT, Feb. 23, 2015, p. A17.

10) NYT, Nov. 16, 2011. Ariana Huffington, Third World America (New York: Crown, 2010, p. 48. Eduardo Porter, "Inequality in America?" NYT, July 31, 2013, pp. B1 and B9.

11) Dionne Searcey and Robert Gebeloff, "More Fall Out As Middle Class Shrinks," NYT, Jan. 26, 2015, pp. A1 and B4.

12) Greenhouse, Big Squeeze, p. 43.

13) Rana Foroohar, "Tilting at Hillary," Time, Jan. 26, 2015, p. 28. Mishel, "Even Better Than a Tax Cut."

14) Steven Rattner, "Inequality, Unbelievably Gets Worse," NYT, Nov. 17, 2014, p. A23. Mishel, "Even Better Than a Tax Cut."

15) Sabrina Tavernise, "Reversing Trend, Life Span for Some Whites Shrinks," NYT, Sept. 21, 2012, pp. A1 and A3.

# Chapter 3: Social Welfare

1) Tavis Smiley and Cornell West, The Rich and the Rest of US: A Poverty Manifesto (Carlsbad, CA: Smiley Books 20has a plethora of information on poverty and other related subjects.

2) For the New Deal, and Great Society programs, see Garry B. Nash, The American People: Creating a Nation and a Society, 3rd ed. (New York: Harper Collins, 1994). On recent social welfare programs, see 2011: NYT Almanac, pp. 173 ff. For elderly income dependency on Social Security, Paul Krugman, "The Insecure American," NYT, May 29, 2015, p. A23.

3) T.R. Reid, The Healing of America (New York: Penguin Books, 2010), pp. 9 ff.

4) Public Citizen, Sept. 2010.

5) Steven Brill, "Bitter Pill," Time, March 5, 2013, pp. 16-18 on a dysfunctional US healthcare. On healthcare bankruptcies and deaths without it annually, Reid, p. 31 and Senator Bernard Sanders, Free Speech TV, Aug. 23, 2012. On Gov. Rick Scott, Mike Papantonio, Free Speech TV, Feb. 6, 2014. On the Commonwealth Fund statistics, editorial, NYT, June 17, 2014.

6) Many articles of the ACA in NYT; one of many, Robert Pear, "Data on Health Law Shows Largest Drop in Uninsured in 4 Decades, the U.S. says," March 17, 2015, p. A12. On two 2015 reports on high hospital costs, NYT, June 16, 2015, p. A22.

7) 2011 NYT Almanac, pp. 173 ff. Paul Krugman, "Hunger Comes to USA," NYT, July 15, 2013, p. A17. On the GOP's attack on the poor, see Jonathan Weisman, "Republicans...Deep Cuts," NYT, March 18, 2015, p. A16; and Elizabeth Drew, "The GOP's War on the Poor," Rolling Stone, Nov. 7, 2013, pp. 35-39. Jonathan Weisman, "Increased Military Spending...House," NYT, March 26, 2015, p. A13 on House Republican attack on welfare.

8) On French social welfare, see NYT, Nov. 8, 2013, pp. A4 and A8.

9) On social welfare benefits for individuals, families and society in general, see Eduardo Porter, "In the War on Poverty, A Dogged Adversary," NYT, Dec. 18, 2013, pp. B1 and B3. Nicholas Kristof, "Progress in the War on Poverty," NYT, Jan. 9. 2014, p. A21. Jason Furman, "Smart Social Programs," NYT, May 11, 2015, p. A19.

10) On current poverty in America, see Sasha Abramsky, "The Other America, 2012," The Nation, May 14, 2012, pp. 12-14. On childhood poverty: NYT, Jan. 15, 2014, pp. A1 and A4. The Nation, Jan. 20, 2014, p. 3.

11) On indebted poor, see Benedict Carey, "Life in the Red," NYT, Jan. 16, 2013, pp. B1 and B6. Thom Hartmann, Free Speech TV, Aug. 5-7, 2014. On large expenses of the poor, Charles M. Blow, "How Expensive...Poor," NYT, Jan. 19, 2015, A19.

12) Eduardo Porter, "Broader Tax for Fighting Inequality," NYT, Nov. 28, 2012, p. B8. Leonhardt and Quealy, "America's Middle Class...World," EU average in social protection circa 2003, 27.3 percent. New Left Review, no. 90 Nov/December 2014, p. 57.

13) See Chapter Four on social mobility and education.

14) Tom Stieghorst, "Vacations...Europe," Akron Beacon Journal, July 15, 1996, p. D1. Greenhouse, Big Squeeze, p. 187. On US vacations, Jack Dickey, "Save Our Vacation," Time, June 1, 2015, pp. 46-49. On social welfare spending, The Nation, June 20/27, 2016, p. 6.

15) On sick and maternity leaves: Julie Hirchfield, "Obama...Workers," NYT, Jan. 15, 2015, p. A14. Claire Suddath, "Mother of a Problem," Bloomberg Businessweek Jan. 19-25, 2015, pp. 56-59. On 2009 government GOP spending HUWs, pp. 132-33.

16) NYT, Jan. 22, 2015, p. A18

17) Toli Mendelberg and Bennett L. Butler, "Obama Cares. Look at the Numbers," NYT, Aug. 22, 2014, p. A21.

18) 2011 NYT Almanac, p. 163. Various articles in NYT, The Nation, Z Magazine. For instance, Paul Krugman, "Slavery's Long Shadow," NYT, June 22, 2015, p. A17; slavery/racism is the single principal cause for lagging US social welfare programs; Paul L. Morgan and George Farkas, "Is Special Education Racist?" NYT June 24, 2015, p. A21. The Nation, Aug. 15/22, 2016, p. 29.

Chapter 4: Social Mobility and Education

1) Jason DeParle, "Harder for Americans to Rise from Economy's Lower Rungs," NYT, Jan. 5, 2012, pp. A1 and A12. Hacker and Pierson, pp. 28-29. Paul Krugman, "Oligarchy, American Style," NYT, Nov. 4, 2011, p. A21. Eduardo Porter, "Inequality Undermines Democracy," NYT, March 21, 2012, pp. B1 and B4. Christopher Hayes, "Why Elites Fail," The Nation, June 25, 2012, pp. 14-15. Monthly Review, July-August 2011, p. 64, military spending exceeds that of K-12 education. Joe Nocera, "Filling the Skills Gap," NYT, July 3, 2012, p. A19. On the study of Chetty, Saez and others on social mobility, see David Leonhardt, "Upward Mobility Has Not Declined, Study Says," NYT, Jan. 23, 2014, pp. B1 and B4.

2) "College Loans Are Weighing Heavier on Graduates," NYT, June 11, 2011, A section. Brian Williams, NBC Evening News, March 22, 2012. Eduardo Porter, "Dropping Out of College and Paying the Price," NYT, June 26, 2013, pp. B1 and B5.

3) 2011 New York Times Almanac, p. 373. "Default," Link TV, March 22, 2012. On technology and wages and so on, see William Julius Wilson, "The Great Disparity," Nation, July 30 – August 6, 2012. For many statistics, see Amanda Ripley, "College is Dead. Long Live College!" Time, Oct. 29, 2012, pp. 36-37. On Pell grants, Richard Perez-Pena, "Rising College Costs...," NYT, Oct. 18, 2012, p. A14. Katherine Rampell, "A Sharp Rise in Americans with Degrees," NYT, June 14, 2013, p. A1. David Leonhardt, "Though Enrolling More Poor Students, 2-Year Colleges Get Less of Federal Pie," NYT, May 23, 2013, p. A18. Scott Ross and Mike Browne, "Sentenced to Debt," The Progressive, Nov. 2013, pp. 32-34. On wage premium in 20013 salaries for bachelor's degree students, Shaila Dewan, "Wage Premium from College Is Said to Be Up," NYT, Feb. 12, 2014, p. B3. On stationary wages in 2001-13 for bachelor's degree workers, "Where Have All the Raises Gone?" NYT, March 3, 2014, p. A22. Other statistics, Time, Oct. 27, 2014, pp. 40-41.

4) Paul Krugman, "America's Unlevel Field," NYT, Jan. 9, 2012, p. A17. Cynthia Peters, interview with Antonio Ennis on living in poverty, Z Magazine, June 2013, pp. 24-28. Paul Street, "Power Served, Millions Betrayed," Z Magazine, June 2013, p. 31. On crime/incarceration, NYT, Jan. 2, 2013, p. A19 and Feb. 28 2013, p. A12. On New York State Regents exams for New York City, Editorial, "Getting an Accurate Fix on Schools," NYT, Jan. 27, 2014, p. A16. On tax breaks for affluent college students: Josh Barro, "Who's Actually Rich? ... Asking," NYT, Jan. 29, 2015, p. A3. On college loans, Steve Cohen, "How to Make College Cheaper," NYT, Feb. 25, 2015, p. A21.

5) Helen F. Ladd and Edward B Fiske, "Class Matters. Why Don't We Admit It," NYT, Dec. 12, 2011, A21. Diane Ravitch, "Waiting for a School Miracle,"

NYT, June 11, A section. Also, Diane Ravitch, "Saving Our Public Schools," The Progressive, vol. 77, no. 10, Oct. 2013, pp. 18-21. On teenage pregnancy, Nicholas Kristoff, "Modern Family Matters," NYT, Jan. 23, 2014, p. A23. Shepard, pp. 213-217, "Poverty in America."

6) Sabine Tavernise, "Rich and Poor Further Apart in Education," NYT, Feb. 10, 2012, pp. A1 and A13. On wealthiest school districts spending as opposed to poorest ones: "Why Other Countries Teach Better," NYT, Dec. 18, 2013, p. A22. Jon M. Shepard Sociology, 5th edition (Minneapolis/St. Paul: West, 1993), p. 363 on rich advantage attending graduate school.

7) David Brooks, "Speed of Ascent," NYT, June 25, 2013, p. A21.

8) Eduardo Porter, "Dropping Out of College and Paying the Price," NYT, June 26, 2013, pp. B1 and B5.

9) Jacie Calmes, "Obama Presses Case for Health Law and Wage Increase," NYT, Dec. 5, 2013, p. A22.

10) On environment and intelligence quotient, see Patsouras, Karl Marx and Other Socialists, Ch. 8, "The Riddle of Human Nature."

Chapter 5: The Great Recession in the United States

1) Among the works consulted on the Great Recession, John Bellamy Foster and Fred Magdoff, The Great Financial Crisis, Causes and Consequence (New York: Monthly Review Press, 2009); Richard D. Wolff, Capitalism Hits the Fan: The Global Economic Meltdown and What to do About It (Northampton, Mass.: Olive Branch Press, 2010). Jack Rasmus, Epic Recession: Prelude to Global Depression (London: Pluto Press, 2010). The following three are capitalist-Keynesians: Joseph E. Stiglitz, Freefall (New York: W.W. Norton, 2010). Nouriel Roubini and Stephen Mihm Crisis Economics (New York: Penguin Press, 2010). Don Peck, Pinched (New York: Crown Publishers, 2011). Bernie Sanders, The Speech (New York: Nation Books, 2011). John Bellamy Foster and Robert W. McChesney, The Endless Crisis (New York: Monthly Review Press, 2012). Various New York Times articles.

As for articles, NYT is the principal source, many by Paul Krugman; Monthly Review (Socialist); Z Magazine (Socialist); New Left Review (Socialist); The Nation (left of center); The Progressive (left of center), Rolling Stone (left of center), even Time (centrist) were also perused. Thom Hartmann on Free Speech, a social democrat and Bill Moyers on PBS, liberal, provided invaluable information.

2) Stiglitz, Freefall, p. 20.

3) Roubini and Mihn, pp. 33, 195-98. On the $700 trillion derivatives, see Richard Duncan, "A New Global Depression," New Left Review, Sept/Oct 2012, pp. 20-31. Floyd Norris, "Wielding Derivatives As a Tool For Deceit," NYT, June 28, 2013, pp. B1 and B4. On $18 billion fines paid by banks for fraud and so forth, Peter Eavis, "Judge's...Crash," NYT, May 12, 2015, pp. A1 and B2.

4) Bill Moyers, interview with Bill Black, PBS TV, April 23, 2010. Eduardo Porter, "The Spreading Scourge of Corporate Corruption," NYT, July 11, 2012, pp. B1 and B5. On the $8 billion fine, NYT, Aug. 8, 2012, pp. B1 and B4.

5) Roubini and Mihm, pp. 111-12, NYT, June 6, 2012, p. B4.

6) Roubine and Mihm, p. 112.

1) 7) Greg Smith, "How Wall Street Is Still Rigging the Game," Time, Nov. 5, 2012, p. 18.

8) Roubini and Mihm, pp. 115 ff.

9) Ibid., pp. 162-63. Jack Rasmus, "Obama vs. Romney, Economic Programs," Z Magazine, Oct. 2012, pp. 20-21.

10) Joe Nocera, NYT, March 31, 2011.

11) John Bellamy Foster and Hannah Holleman, "The Financial Power Elite," Monthly Review, May 2010, pp. 5-6, on the perils of financialization. On the

rise of corporate profits, Jack Rasmus, "The Great Corporate Tax Shift," Z Magaine, Dec. 2013, p. 36.

12) NYT articles, Aug. 2013. For instance, Paul Krugman, "The Unsaved World," NYT, Aug. 30, 2013, p. A17; and NYT, Aug. 30, 2013, p. B3.

13) On economic concentration, see corporate/wealth concentration in Chapter 1.

14) Sanders, pp. 30-36. Jack Rasmus, "The Real Causes of Deficits and Debts," Z Magazine, Dec. 2011, p. 28. Bernie Sanders, interview by Bill Moyers, Public Broadcasting System, Sept. 9, 2012.

15) Roubine and Mihm, pp. 175-76. Jack Rasmus, "Bernanke's Bank: An Assessment," Z Magazine, Feb. 2014, pp. 21-27.

16) Nation, Dec. 26, 2011, p. 3.

17) Matt Taibbi, "The People vs. Goldman Sachs," Rolling Stone. May 26, 2011, pp. 41-46. Azam Ahmad and Ben Protess, "As Libor Fault-Finding Grows," NYT, Aug, 6, 2012, pp. A1 and A3. On trillion dollar cases, Jessica Silver-Greenberg, "Mortgage Crisis Presents Banks a New Reckoning," NYT, Dec. 10, 2012, pp. A1 and A3. On the HSBC fine, Robert Mazur, "How to Halt the Terrorist Money Train," NYT, Jan. 3, 2013, p. A19. On S&P charged with fraud, Mary Williams Walsh and Andrew Ross Sorkin, "U.S. Plans to Sue S&P..." NYT, Feb. 5, 2013, pp. A1 and B5. Jessica Silver Greenberg, "Banks to Pay $8.5 billion...," NYT, Jan. 8, 2013, p. B1.

18) Edward Wyatt, "S.E.C. Is Avoiding Tough Sanctions for Large Banks," NYT, Feb. 3, 2012, pp. A1 and A3. Peter Eavis and Ben Protess, "Considering the Fairness of JP Morgan's Deal," NYT, Oct. 22, 2013, pp. B1 and B9. Neil Barofsky, interview by Thom Hartmann, Russia Today TV, Aug. 22, 2012. On Madoff, see NYT, Sept. 27, 2013. On SAC Capital, see NYT, Nov. 5, 2013; on Johnson and Johnson, see NYT, Nov. 5, 2013. On other fines of corporations, see NYT, July 3, 2012. The "Business Day" section of the NYT duly reports business malfeasance. On the $90 billion Wall Street reimbursement on mortgages: Jessica Silver-Greenberg and Peter Eavis," Wall Street Preducts $50 Bill to Settle U.S. Mortgage Suits," NYT, Jan. 10, 2014, pp. A1 and B6. On bank fraud and failure to prosecute individual bankers, see Matt Taibbi, "The $9 Billion Witness," Rolling Stone, Nov. 20, 2014, pp. 49-55. On $100 billion fines paid by US banks, Wolfgang Streeck, "How Will Capitalism End?" New Left Review, no. 87, May/June 2014, p. 62. On the S&P fine/settlement, NYT, Jan. 22, 2015, p. B7. On HSBC bank, NYT, Feb. 11, 2015, pp. B1 and B4. On Deutsche Bank, NYT, April 24, 2015, p. B1. On the May 2013 charges against the four banks, see NYT, May 21, 2015, pp. A1 and B2.

19) Jack Rasmus, "Economic Predictions for 2012," Z Magazine, Jan. 2012, p. 21. Robin Blackburn, "Crisis 2.0," New Left Review, Nov/Dec., 2011, p. 38. Rasmus, "Bernanke's Bank."

20) Thom Hartmann, Free Speech TV, March 2 and 6, 2012. Roubini and Mihm, p. 123. Joseph P. Kennedy II, "The High Cost of Gambling on Oil," NYT,

April 11, 2012, p. A21. Senator Bernie Sanders, interview by Thom Hartmann, Free Speech TV, May 24, 2013.

21) "Big Bank Bonuses, Despite Taxpayer Help," NYT, July 31, 2009.

22) On Dodd-Frank, the Volker Rule and J.P. Morgan Chase loss: Jesse Eisinger, "The Volcker Rule Made Bloated and Weak," NYT, Feb. 23, 2012, p. B4, NYT: May 14, 2012, p. A1; May 16, 2012, pp. B1 and B3. Gar Alperovitz and Thomas M. Hanna, "Not So Wild a Dream," Nation, June 11, 2012, p. 18. NYT, May 16, 2013, p. B4. Ben Protess, "Regulators Tighten Rules on Trading Derivatives," NYT, May 16, 2013, p. B8. On final approval of The Volcker Rule, NYT, Dec. 11, 2013, pp. B1 and B5. On JP Morgan Chase's $6 billion derivatives loss, NYT, June 28, 2012. Republican wish for FDIC to cover derivatives, Thoma Hartmann, Free Speech TV, Dec. 8, 2014.

23) Roubini and Mihm, pp. 81-2 and 394. Paul Krugman, "Reagan Was A Keynesian," NYT, June 8, 2012, p. A23. On lower consumer debt in 2012, Sherle R. Schwenninger, "The Missing Economic Debate," The Nation, Oct. 29, 2012, p. 29. On slower economic growth after 2000, David Brooks, "Let's Talk About X," NYT, Nov. 28, 2012. Kozo Yamamura, "More System, Please!" New Left Review, 94, pp. 84-85. Paul Krugman, "A Permanent Slump?" NYT, Nov. 18, 2013, p. A27. Paul Krugman, "Why Inequality Matters," NYT, Dec. 16, 2013, p. A22.

24) 2011 NYT Almanac; various NYT articles. For instance, Eduardo Porter, "At the Polls...Capitalism," Oct. 31, 2012, pp. B1 and B7. On the $11 trillion US trade deficit since NAFTA, Mike Papantonio, Free Speech TV, May 7, 2015. Robert W. McChesney and John Bellamy Foster, "The Endless Crisis," Monthly Review, May 2012, pp. 24-25. NYT, March 6, 2012, p. B5. Paul Krugman, ibid., July 18, 2012. Thom Hartmann, The Big Picture, Free Speech TV, April 25, 2012. The Progressive, Nov. 2013, p. 32. Bill Press, Free Speech TV, Nov. 10, 2014. Rana Foroohar, "The 3 % Economy," Time, Oct. 6, 2014, p. 22. John Bellamy Foster and Michael D. Yates, "Piketty and the Crisis of Neoclassical Economics," Monthly Review, Nov. 2014, pp. 1-24.

25) Hacker and Pierson, p. 25, on income transfer to top 1 percent.

26) On corporate cash: James Livingston, "If companies Are People," NYT, April 15, 2013, p. A19. Jack Rasmus, "The Three Faces of the Financial Cliff," Z Magazine, Jan. 2013, pp. 38-43. On local/state governments' spending less, Eduardo Porter," In Shovels, A Remedy for Jobs and Growth," NYT, Feb. 13, 2013, pp. B1 and B8.

27) On Bain and Co. 2020 estimates: Sheila C. Bair, "Grand Old Parity," NYT, Feb. 27, 2013, p. A22.

28) Robert Pollin and Heidi Garret-Peltier, "Benefits of a Slimmer Pentagon," Nation, May 28, 2012, pp. 15-18.

29) NYT, Jan. 2, 2013, p. A20. Ursula, Huws., Labor in the Global Economy (New York: Monthly Review Press, 2014), p. 132.

30) Rasmus, "Three Faces of the Fiscal Cliff." Porter, "In Shovels, A Remedy for Jobs and Growth," Eduardo Porter, "Recession's True Cost Is Still Being Tallied," NYT, Jan. 22, 2014, pp. A1 and A6. Paul Krugman, "The Mutilated Economy," NYT, Nov. 8, 2013, p. A29.

31) Paul Krugman, "Rubio and the Zombies," NYT, Feb. 15, 2013, p. A23.

32) See, for instance, Paul Krugman, "The Excel Depression," NYT, April 19, 2013, p. A23. Katrina Vanden Heuvel, "Austerity's Grip," The Nation, May 13, 2013, p. 5.

33) Stiglitz, Freefall, pp. 135ff. Paul Krugman, "What Ailes Europe," NYT, Feb. 27, 2012, p. A17. Paul Krugman, "Years of Tragic Waste," NYT, Sept. 8, 2013, p. A19.

34) On Hayek, Kim Phillips Fein, "Mountain Views," Nation, Aug. 5/12, 2013, pp. 42-44. Paul Krugman, "Milton Friedman, Unperson," NYT, Aug. 12, 2013, p. A15. Hayek, The Road to Serfdom (1944).

35) For instance, Andrew Ross Sorkin, "A Merger Might Not Signal Optimism," NYT, June 9, 2015, pp. B1 and B3.

## Chapter 6: Unemployment

1) Foster and Magdoff, Great Financial Crisis, pp. 27-91. Many NYT articles.

2) Richard Peet, "Contradictions of Finance Capitalism," Monthly Review, Dec. 2011, p. 28. Nelson D. Schwartz, "Manufacturing's Mirage," NYT, April 2, 2013, pp. B1 and B2. Foster and McChesney, The Endless Crisis, pp. 125-54. On manufacturing GDP loss in the U.S. see Thom Hartmann, "Need to Know," Free Speech TV, Dec. 27, 2013; and Charles Kenny, "Factory Jobs Are Gone. Get Over It," Bloomberg Businessweek, Jan. 27 – Feb. 2, 2014, pp. 12-13. Fred Magdoff and John Bellamy Foster, "The Plight of the U.S. Working Class," Monthly Review, vol. 65, no. 3, Jan. 2014, pp. 1-6. On inexpensive Ethiopian labor: Bloomberg Businessweek, July 28 – August 3, 2014, pp. 11-12. On manufacturing job losses in 2000-2010, see Nelson D. Schwartz and Patricia Cohen, "Falling Wages...Middle Class," NYT, Nov. 21, 2014, pp. B1 and B6. But since 2010, they report that manufacturing has added 700,000 jobs. On Nike, see Peter Baker and Julie Hirchfield-Davis, "Obama...Trade," NYT, May 8, 2015, pp. B1 and B2.

3) Roger Bybee, "Off-Shoring," Z Magazine, July/August 2011, p. 28. David Cay Johnson, Free Speech (New York: Portfolio, 2007), pp. 49-51. John Markoff," Modest Debut of Atlas May Foreshadow Age of 'Robo Sapiens,'" NYT, July 12, 2013, p. A11. John Markoff, "Making Them More Like Us," NYT, Oct. 29, 2013, pp. D1 and D2. Clair Cain Miller, "Rise of Robot Work Force...Fears," NYT, Dec. 16, 2014, pp. A1 and A3. On greater computer capacity at work, Frank Bruni, "The Bitter Backdrop to 2016," NYT, May 13, 2015, p. A23.

4) Paul Krugman, "Sympathy for the Luddites," NYT, June 14, 2013, p. A23. Richard Wolff, Democracy at Work: A Cure for Capitalism (Chicago: Haymarket Books, 2012, Ch. 9.

5) Thomas L. Friedman, "Average Is Over," NYT, Jan. 25, 2012, p. A25. Thomas L. Friedman, "Obama's 1-2 Punch?" NYT, Jan. 16, 2013, p. A21.

6) Letter to Editor, NYT, Nov. 25, 2010. Royer Bybee, "The War on Wages," Z Magazine, Dec. 2012, p. 26. On the 600,000 jobs lost under Bush II: Sanders, p. 5. On continuing high long-term unemployed, Paul Krugman, "Writing Off the Unemployed," NYT, Feb. 19, 2014, p. A19.

7) Akron Beacon Journal, Oct. 8, 2011, p. A7. Peck, pp. 28-30. Editorial, "Women Up," Nation, April 30, 2012, p. 3. Catherine Rampell, "Weak Job Gains... Fed." Greenhouse, Big Squeeze, p. 43.

8) Kate Kahan and George Wentworth, "Out of Work and Out of Luck," Nation, Jan. 2, 2012, pp. 17-18. Paul Krugman, "End the Depression Now," Commonwealth Club of California, Link TV, June 7 and 8, 2012. Paul Krugman, "The Forgotten Millions," Dec. 7, 2012, p. A27. Fred Magdoff and John Bellamy Foster, "Class War and Labor's Declining Share," Monthly

Review, March 2013, p. 1. On unemployment benefits Annie Lowrey, "States...Jobless," NYT, Jan. 22, 2014, pp. A1 and A3. Catherine Rampell, NYT, Aug. 31, 2012, pp. B1 and B2, low wages for most new jobs, many part-time.

9) Annie Lowrey and Catherine Rampell, "Jobless and Hopeless in America," NYT, Nov. 2, 2012, pp. A1 and A4.

10) Peck, p. 19.

11) Michael Perelman, "Sado-Monetarism," Monthly Review, April 2012, pp. 31-33. Peck, pp. 19-21. David Stuckler and Sanjay Basu, "How Austerity Kills," NYT, May 13, 2013, p. A19.

12) Bob Herbert, "Long-Term Economic Pain," NYT, July 26, 2010.

13) Jackie Calmes and John Harwood, "A Close Look..." NYT, Oct. 3, 2012, p. A16. Jack Rasmus, "America's Ten Economic Crises," Z Magazine, July/August, 2012, pp. 42-43.

14) David Brooks, NYT, May 10, 2012. Paul Krugman, ibid, March 18, 2011. Paul Krugman, ibid. Aug. 5, 2011. Floyd Norris, "When Looking at Job Numbers..." NYT. Dec. 12, 2012, p. F8. Binyamen Applebaum, "As Jobs Lag..." ibid, April 30, 2013, pp. B1 and B8. Magdoff and Foster, "Plight of the U.S. Working Class," pp. 8-9. Benyamin Appelbaum, "Vanishing Male Worker," NYT, Dec. 12, 2014, pp. A1 and B8. Catherine Rampell, "Weak Job Gains...Fed," NYT, Oct. 23, 2013, pp. A1 and B4. "Making College Pay," NYT, Feb. 13, 2014, p. A22. "A Rockier Pathway to Work," NYT, April 10, 2012, p. A20. "The Road to More Jobs," NYT, July 12, 2012, p. A18. Catherine Rampell, "When Job-Creation Engines Stop at Just One," NYT, Oct. 30, 2012, pp. A1 and A3. Richard Peet, "Contradictions of Finance Capitalism," Monthly Review, Dec. 2011, pp. 25-28. Jose´ Antonio Vargas, "Not Legal," Time, June 25, 2012, pp. 36 ff. Nelson D. Schwartz, "Several Rivals Surge Past U.S. In Adding Jobs," NYT, June 8, 2013, p. A1. Paul Krugman, "The Big Shrug," NYT, June 10, 2013, p. A21. "The President on Inequality," NYT, Dec. 5, 2013, p. A30. Porter, "In Shovels a Remedy for Jobs and Growth," Greenhouse, Big Squeeze, p. 43. Colin Jenkins, "The Fight for a Living Wage is Everyone's Fight," Z Magazine, Feb. 2014, pp. 11-16. Esther Kaplan, "American Speedup," The Nation, Nov. 17, 2014, p. 29. For a government-run job program now, see Eduardo Porter, "Confronting an Old Problem May Require a New Deal," NYT, Jan. 29, 2014, pp. B1 and B8. NYT: April 3, 2012, p. B2; July 17, p. B2; Oct. 3, 2013, p. A28; on June 2015 statistics, July 3, 2015, p. B6. On foreign imports to U.S.: John Smith, "Imperialism in the Twenty-First Century," Monthly Review, July-August, 2015, p. 85.

# Chapter 7: Taxes, Budget, Politics

1) These statements are common knowledge
2) The New York Times Almanac 2011, p. 184. Z Magazine, April 2011, p. 8.
3) NYT, April 26, 2011. Eduardo Porter, "The Case for Rising Tax Rates," NYT, March 28, 2012, pp. B1 and B6. Annie Lowrey and Michael Cooper, "Romney's Anxiety Over Takers...," NYT, Sept. 19, 2012, pp. A16 and A18. "Debt Reckoning," NYT, Dec. 28, 2012, p. A15.
4) Lowrey and Cooper, "Romney's Anxiety Over Takers."
5) Paul Krugman, "Taxes at the Top," NYT, Jan. 20, 2012, p. A23. Paul Krugman, "Oligarchy, American Style," ibid, Nov. 4, 2011. Paul Krugman, "We Are the 99.9 %," ibid, Nov. 25, 2011. Nocera, "Romney and the Forbes 400," On the 2015 personal tax estimates, Patricia Cohen, "Study Finds Local Taxes Hit Lower Wage Earners Harder," NYT, Jan. 14, 2015, pp. B1 and B8.
6) Sam Pizzigati and Chuck Collins," The Great Regression," The Nation, Feb. 25, 2013, pp. 25-26 on taxes in the last hundred years. Jack Rasmus, "Income Inequality and Double Dip Recession," Z Magazine, March 2013, pp. 26-29.
7) David Kay Johnston interview, Democracy Now, Free Speech TV, March 3, 2011. Jack Rasmus, "America's Ten Economic Crises," Z Magazine, July/August 2013, p. 43.
8) NYT, August 8, 2012, pp. B1 and B2; January 21, 2013, p. A21; Jan. 31, 2013, p. A3, etc.
9) Paul Krugman, "The Soviet Contract," NYT, Sept. 23, 2011. Robert Reich, "Mitt Romney and the New Gilded Age," The Nation, July 16/23, pp. 11-14. Paul Krugman, "Mitt's Gray Areas," NYT, July 9, 2012, p. A15. Matt Taibbi, "Greed and Debt," Rolling Stone, Sept. 2012, pp. 42-50.
10) On low tax rates, see Pablo Eisenberg, "The Foundation Business," The Nation, Feb. 13, 2012, p. 35. On a fourth of corporations not paying taxes annually, Bill Moyers PBS interview with Senator Bernie Sanders, Sept. 9, 2012. Robert B. Reich, Supercapitalism (New York: Vintage Books, 20p. 140. On corporation's receiving tax write-offs when moving abroad, Thom Hartmann, Free Speech TV, March 9, 2012. On local and state subsidies to corporations, see "Race to the Bottom," NYT, Dec. 16, 2012, p. A26. On tax havens, see Nicholas Shayson, Treasure Islands; Tax Havens and the Men Who Stole the World (London: Bodley Head, 2011, pp. 8-9, for instance. On total taxes paid by large American corporations in 2012, see Nelson Schwartz, "Big Companies Paid A Fraction of Corporate Tax Rate," NYT, July 2, 2013, p. A3. On inversion, see Paul Krugman, "Corporate Artful Dodgers," NYT, July 28, 2014, p. A15. NYT, August 16, 2014. P. B2. Time, July 21, 2014, p. 14. NYT Editorial, "The Tax Dodge Goes On," Aug. 7, 2014, p. A20. Patricia Cohen, "Tax Trouble," NYT, Aug. 7, 2014, pp. B1 and B2.

On US low tax rates, Steve Rattner, "Inequality...Gets Worse," <u>NYT</u>, Nov. 17, 2014, p. A23.

11) David Leonhart, "Why Taxes Aren't as High as They Seem," <u>NYT</u>, Jan. 20, 2012, p. A13. Jack Cassidy, "How Bad Is It," <u>New Yorker</u>, Aug. 15/22, 2011, p. 29. Porter, <u>NYT</u>, March 28, 2012. Lowrey and Cooper, <u>NYT</u>, Sept. 19, 2012.

12) <u>NYT</u>, March 28, 2013, p. 24. Jack Rasmus, "The Real Causes of Deficits and Debts," <u>Z Magazine</u>, Dec. 2011, pp. 20-30.

13) Paul Krugman, "Things to Tax," <u>NYT</u>, Nov. 28, 2011.

14) See Chapter 3.

15) "Just How Much of Our Money Will Go to the Military Next Year?" American Friends Service Committee – 2012. "Where Your Income Tax Money Really Goes," <u>Z Magazine</u>, April 2011, p. 6. On Afghanistan and Iraq war costs, Giroux, p. 82. On U.S. military forces and spending, <u>Z Magazine</u>, June 2014, p. 7. On U.S. intelligence agencies, Tom Shorrock, "Put the Spies Back Under One Roof," <u>NYT</u>, June 18, 2013, p. A21; and Scott Shane, "New Leaked Document...Agencies," <u>NYT</u>, Aug. 30, 2013, p. A13. On percentage of budget on military, McChesney, <u>Blowing the Roof Off the Twenty-First Century</u>, pp. 112-19. Also, on overseas bases spending, <u>NYT</u>, July 27, 2015, p. A17.

16) Porter, "The Case for Raising Taxes."

17) Peter Lindert, "Slandering the Welfare State," <u>The Nation</u>, April 9, 2012, pp. 21-22.

18) See, for instance: Paul Krugman, "The Gullible Center," <u>NYT</u>, p. A19. Paul Krugman, "Corporate Cash Cow," <u>NYT</u>, Sept. 22, 2011. Robert Reich, "Romney and the New Gilded Age," <u>The Nation</u>, July 16/23, 2012, pp. 11-14. Various other articles in <u>NYT</u>. As example, the <u>NYT</u> Editorial, "Republican Tax Priorities," Nov. 8, 2012, p. 26. Steve Rattner, The Radical is Romney Not Ryan," <u>NYT</u>, Oct. 15, 2012, p. A23

19) Annie Lowery, "Budget Deficit Shrinks Faster Than Expected," <u>NYT</u>, May 15, 2013, pp. A1 and B2.

# Chapter 8: Left Vs. Right in the United States

1) Reading, viewing, listening: <u>NYT, The Nation, Z Magazine, The Progressive,</u> CBS, NBC, ABC, Fox, PBS, Free Speech TV, Russia Today TV, <u>Monthly Review,</u> Special Issue: <u>The Culture Apparatus of Monopoly Capital,</u> vol.65, no.3 July – August 2013. Mc Chesney, <u>Blowing the Roof of the Twenty-First Century,</u> pp 138 – 236.

2) On Lobbying in 2013, see Fang, "The Shadow Lobbying Comply," <u>The Nation,</u> March10/17, 2014, pp12-22. On lobbying, PACS and electoral campaign spending: Andy Kroll, "Follow the Dark Money," <u>Mother Jones,</u> July/August 2012, pp.17-26. John Nichols and Robert W. McChesney, "The Assault of the Super Pacs," <u>The Nation,</u> Feb 6, 2012, pp11-17.On the control of the Republican Party by the very rich who desire to privatize government:Paul Krugman, "Lobbyists, Guns and Money," <u>NYT,</u> March 26, 2012, p A23. Paul Krugman, "Plutocracy, Paralysis, Perplexity," <u>NYT,</u> May 4, 2012, p. A23, On healthcare lobbying spent, 1998-2012, see <u>Time,</u> March 4, 2013, p31. On Wall Street lobbying expenditures, "Sold Out," <u>Public Citizen,</u> March 2009. On 2012 electoral campaign expenditures by the richest 0.01 percent, Peter Stone, "Wall Street Fightn' Mad," <u>Mother Jones,</u> Sept./ Oct. 2013, p-8; On the richest 0.1 percent, Eduardo Porter, "Business Losing Clout in a G.O.P. Moving Right", <u>NYT,</u> Sept. 4, 2013, pp 1 and B2, Shepard, <u>Sociology,</u> 11<sup>th</sup> edition, pp.386-89 on PACS. On the $10 billion cost of the 2012 elections, see John Nichols and Robert W. McChesney, "Dollarocracy," <u>The Nation,</u> Sept 30, 2013, pp 22-26. On lawmakers'/lobbyists junkets, see Eric Lipton, "A loophole...Donations," <u>NYT,</u> Jan 20<sup>th</sup>, 2014, pp A1 and A10. On union spending on elections, Greenhouse, "Labor...Victories," <u>NYT,</u> Feb 20, 2014, p. A11. Mark Leibovich, <u>This Town: Two Parties and a Funeral plus Plenty of Valet Parking in America's Gilded Capital</u> (New York: blue rider press, 20for an inside look into Washington DC's politicians involved in a mad scramble for power and money, for instance, pp 161 ff. On the Gilens and Page study, see Eric Alterman, "The Power of Picketty's <u>Capital, The Nation,</u> May 12, 2014, p8. On low turnover in Congress, Frank Bruni, "Lost In America, <u>NYT,</u> Aug. 26, 2014 p A 23. On the Kochs' Jan. 2015 seminar, Nicholas Confessore," "16 Koch Budget is $889 million" <u>NYT,</u> Jan 27, 2015, pp A1 and A12. On contributions of the richest 1 percent to candidates, Eric Alterman, "Invisible Plutocracy," <u>The Nation,</u> May 18, 2015, p6. On Clinton's earning money from speeches, Philip Elliott, "Ready for Speaking Fees." <u>Time,</u> June 1, 2015, p 12. On 2008 and 2014 contributions by corporate PACs To Democrats/Republicans, <u>NYT,</u> June 30, 2015, p A14. On Buffett's quote by Stiglits, <u>The Great Divide,</u> p95. On gas, oil and coal PACS in the 2012

elections, The Nation, July 20/27, 2015, p 3. On New York State corruption, NYT, Nov, 2, 2015, ppA1 and A18.

3) On voting: McChesney, Blowing the Roof off the Twenty-First Century, pp 90 -99. Perry Anderson, "Homeland," New Left Review, no.81, May/June 2013, pp. 5-32. On Republican strength, Tim Dickinson, "How the GOP Rigs the Game," Rolling Stone, Nov. 21, 2013, pp 35 -38. On North Carolina, The Nation, March 10/17, 2014, p23. On Calvinist mindset, Charles M. Blow, "Poverty is not a State of Mind," NYT, May 19, 2014, p.A17. On dislike of Welfare, Paul Krugman, "The Insecure American," NYT, May 29, 2015, p A22. On voting restrictions, The Nation. Oct.12,2015, pp 28-29 Supreme Court Conservative decisions, The Nation, Oct 12, 2015,pp.24-25.

4) On Republican gerrymandering in Ohio, Akron Beacon Journal, Nov. 1, 2015, p.A13.
Articles in NYT, The Nation.

5) On the Democratic Socialists, articles in The Nation, NYT, Z Magazine, Dissent, The Progressive, Louis Patsouras and Jack Ray Thomas (eds,) Essays on Socialism, (Lewiston, NY: Edwin Mellon Press, 1992.

6) On the Greens and Anarchism: On the Greens, Paul Street, "Power Served, Millions Betrayed," Z Magazine, June 2013, p 29. "The Ten Key Values of the Green Party," Internet. On Anarchism, Louis Patsouras, The Anarchism of Jean Grave (Montreal: Black Rose Books, 2003.

7) On government (public) ownership, Gar Alperovitz and Thomas A. Hanna, "Socialism, American Style," NYT, July 23, 2015, p A23.

8) On education, see Monthly Review, Special Issue: Education Under Fire: the US corporate attack on students Teachers and Schools, vol. 63, No. 3 July – August 2011.

9) Sabine Tavernise, "Survey Finds Rising Strains Between Rich and Poor," NYT, Jan12, McChesney. P 224. On these polls, Nichola's D Kristoff, "Is Banking Bad," NYT, Jan 19, 2012, p A21. Alperovitz and Hanna, "Not So Wild a Dream," Andrew Ross Sorkin. "Many...Poll Shows," NYT, Dec.11,2014 pp. 131 and B11. Charles M. Blow, "Who Loves America?" NYT, Feb. 23, 2015, p A17.

10) On occupy Wall Street, articles in Z Magazine, Dec. 2011 pp15 – 25. On general discussion of American problems, see Robert McChesney, "This Isn't What Democracy Looks Like." Monthly Review, Nov. 2012, pp. 1-28. On the August 2014 Wall Street Journal/NBC Poll, Frank Bruni, "Lost in America," NYT, Aug. 26, 2014, p. A23. On the carnage in US hospitals, Thomas Moore and Steve Cohen, "Legislative Malpractice," NYT, Aug.31, 2015, p.A15. On medical expenses economically savaging the elderly, Scott Burns, "Health expenses are big monsters in room, Akron Beacon Journal, Nov.1, 2015, pp. D1 and 6. On Drug prices, Time, Oct.5, 2015, p A23; NYT, Nov.26, 2015, p. A25. On Drug shortages, NYT, Jan. 29, 2016, pp. A1 &A 20.

pA23; Nov.26 The Nation, Oct. 12, 2015, pp. 17 -18. Black downward social mobility, Richard V. Reeves, "Stuck," Esquire, Dec. -Jan., 2015/16, p.156. TPP articles NYT, Social Security/ Med.other care problems, NYT, July1, 2014, pp131 and 2; Ken Kurson, "The apology multiple," Esquire, Dec./Jan. 2015/16 pp 46-48. On basic government research leading to consumer products, Mariana Mazzucato, The Entreprenurial State:Debunking Public vs Private Sector Myths, UK: Anthem Press, 2014), pp 1-110, for instance. On twelve or so elite colleges furnishing about half of government/corporate leaders, NYT, Dec.11, 2015, p.A24. On $250 billion annual cost of US foreign bases, Peter Matthews, Dollar Democracy, (Amazon, 2015), p.195. On 2015 mergers and acquisitions; NYT. Nov.23, 2015, p A3. On tax losses in connection with corporate guilt, NYT, Dec.3, 2015,p.B3. On jail time for corporate executives, Public Citizen News, Nov./Dec.,2015,p.9 and NYT, Dec. 4, 2015, p.A16. On privatizing Freddie Mac, Social Security, etc, see NYT, Dec. 7, 2015, pp A1 and 134. On corporate stock buybacks, Tom Hartmann, RT, Dec.17, 2015. On the richest 400 paying lower taxes, NYT, Dec 30, 2015, pp. A1 and A12; ibid, Dec.31, 2015, p.B3. TNC's, Monthly Review, Jan. 2016, pp. 17 -19. On the Goldman Sacks fraud settlement, NYT, Jan. 15, 2016, pp. B1 and 136. On 2016 Oxfam Report NYT, Jan. 19. 2016, pp. B1 and 136. On the big fine in consumer technology, NYT, Jan. 21, 2016, pp. B1 and B7. On toxic food processing and chemicals, NYT, Nov. 13. 2014. p. A27 and June 4, 2015 A 23. On legislation to aid the public against corporate secrecy, NYT, Nov. 20, 2014, pA26. On FDA laxity on dangerous GMO's. Steven M. Drucker, Altered Genes, Twisted Truth (Clear River Press, 2015), pp 392 – 413. On drugs, NYT, Sept. 17, 2015, pp. A1, 31. On glysophate, Mark Bittman, "Stop Making Us Guinea Pigs," NYT, March 25, 2015, p. A25; Mark Bittman, "Trust me, Butter is Better," NYT, June 24, 2015, p. A21 on trans fats. On EPA's failure to protect the public from toxic chemicals, letter by David Roe, "Follow California's Lead", NYT May 28, 2015, p.A22. On recent higher death rates of poor whites, Editorial "Death Among Middle-aged Whites," NYT, Nov. 5, 2015, p. A24. On the homeless, Wall Street Journal, Jan.30 – 31, 2016, p. A3. Nicholas Kristof "We're Not No. 1 ! We're Not No.1 !," NYT, Ap. 3, 2013, p.A25.

# Chapter 9: American Labor's Historical Odyssey

1) Herbert G. Gutman, Founding Director, Who Built America? Working People and the Nation's Economy, Politics, Culture and Society, 2 volumes; Vol I: From Conquest to 1877, Vol. II: From the Gilded Age to the Present (New York: Pantheon Books, 1989, 1992). Howard Zinn, The Twentieth Century: A People's History (New York: Harper Colophon Books, 1984). Robert B. Reich, Supercapitalism (New York: Vintage Books, 2007). Leonard Dinnerstein and David Reimers, Ethnic Americans: A History of Immigration (New York: Harper and Row, 1988). Greenhouse, The Big Squeeze. 2011 NYT Almanac.

2) See, for instance, Tom Raum, "Most Union Members Work in Public Sector," Akron Beacon Journal, July 5, 2014, p. A5.

3) Eduardo Porter, "Unions? Past May Hold Key to Their Future," NYT, July 18, 2012, pp. B1 and B8. Adam Wasserman, "Is Momentum Shifting Back to the Labor Movement in the U.S.," Z Magazine, Jan. 2013, pp. 10-12. Richard Kim, "The Audacity of Occupy Wall Street," The Nation, Nov. 21, 2011, pp. 15-21. Sam Hanenel, "Unions Trying to Boost Numbers," Akron Beacon Journal, Aug. 11, 2013, pp. B1 and D3. Steven Greenhouse, "In New Wave of Walkouts, Fast-Food Strikers Gain Momentum," NYT, Aug. 30, 2013, p. B3. Steven Greenhouse, "Fast-Food Protests Spread Overseas," NYT, May 15, 2014, pp. B1 and B11.

4) On fast-food workers' travails, Jodi Kantor, "Starbucks…Baristas," NYT, Aug. 15, 2014, p. A11. On union busting, etc. Thom Hartmann, Free Speech TV, Aug. 22, 2014. On suing McDonald's, ibid, Aug. 7 and 8, 2014. On Danish fast-food workers, Liz Alderman and Steven Greenhouse, "Serving Up Fries, for a Living Wage," NYT, Oct. 28, 2014, pp. B1 and B8. On federal subsidies for Walmart workers, Thom Hartmann, Free Speech TV, Dec. 5, 2014. On workers' poverty, Time, August 15, 2015, p. 52. On NLRB ruling to facilitate union organizing of fast-food workers, NYT, Aug. 28, 2015, pp. A1 and A3. On industry spending to prevent unionization, Amy Goodman, Free Speech TV, April 16, 2015. On immigrant poverty, Alan Gomez, "Report…Welfare," USA Today, Sept, 2, 2015, p. 3A.

5) "On Obama's Executive Order to End Workplace Abuses," Editorial, "The Right to Cheat and Maim?" NYT, Aug. 20, 2014, p. A18. On government subsidies to low wage workers, Amy Goodman, Free Speech TV, April. 16, 2015.

6) On the workers' lawsuit, Brandon Bailey, "Apple…Lawsuit," Akron Beacon Journal, Aug. 10, 2014, p. A4. On Obama's executive order on undocumented workers, NYT, Nov. 21, 2014, pp. A1 and A11.

7) Corey Robin, "The Republican War on Workers' Rights," NYT, May 19, 2014, p. A17. Raum, p. A5. Letter by Nancy Breslow, NYT, July 8, 2014, p. A16. On

raising minimum wage not leading to higher unemployment, Paul Krugman, "Liberals and Wages," <u>NYT</u>, July 17, 2015, p. A23. On workers committees, Steven Greenhouse, "Workers...Low," <u>NYT</u>, Sept. 7, 2015, pp. B1 and B5.

8) Seven Greenhouse, "Labor Regroups in South After VW Vote," <u>NYT</u>, Feb. 10, 2014, p. B3. Tom Krisher, "UAW...Growing," <u>Akron Beacon Journal</u>, Feb. 23, 2014, p. A12.

9) On workers' ownership of industry Gar Alperovitz, "Worker-Owners of America, Unite," <u>NYT</u>, Dec. 15, 2011, Gar Alperovitz, "The New Economy Movement," <u>The Nation</u>, Dec. 9, 2013, pp. 22-30. Gar Alperovitz and Thomas M. Hanna, "Not So Wild a Dream," <u>The Nation</u>, June 11, 2012, pp. 18-23. Review, Steven Dubb, <u>Science and Society</u>, vol. 78, no. 1, January 2014, p. 138.

10) Steven Greenhouse, "Labor Leaders...Democratic Victories," <u>NYT</u>, Feb. 20, 2014, p. A11. Editorial, "The Clear Benefits of a Higher Wage," <u>ibid</u>, Feb. 20, 2014, p. A16. Tim Dickinson, "The Minimum-Wage War," <u>Rolling Stone</u>, March 13, 2014, pp. 33-36. Steven Greenhouse, "The Walls Close In," <u>NYT</u>, March 13, 2014, pp. B1 and B4. Editorial, "Germany and the Minimum Wage," <u>NYT</u>, July, 8, 2014, p. A16. <u>Time</u>, June 1, 2015, p. 13 on city hikes of the minimum wage.

11) On hours worked per year in the U.S. and other nations and so forth: Marilyn Geeway, "Supply-Siders...Labor," <u>Akron Beacon Journal</u>, Aug. 20, 1996, p. A7. Merrill Goozner, "Long Hours...Statistics," <u>Akron Beacon Journal</u>, July 5, 1998, pp. G1 and G9. Greenhouse, <u>Big Squeeze</u>, p. 6. Eduardo Porter, "America's Sinking Middle Class," <u>NYT</u>, Sept. 19, 2013, p. B4. <u>Bloomberg Businessweek</u>, Oct. 14-20, 2013, p. 21 on average annual hours of work in 2012 of nations mentioned. On the long American workweek in 2014, Jim Puzzanghera, "Poll: Average Workweek 47 hours," <u>Akron Beacon Journal</u>, Aug. 31, 2014, p. A8. On speedups, Esther Kaplan, "American Speedup," <u>The Nation</u>, Nov. 17, 2014, pp. 28-33.

12) On digital unionization, <u>NYT</u>, June 15, 2015, p. A14. On HIB workers as scabs, <u>NYT</u>, June 15 15, 2015, p. A18. On lower wages for workers, Nicholas Kristof, "The Cost of a Decline in Unions," <u>NYT</u>, Feb. 19, 2015, p. A21. On lower 2009-14 wages, Nelson D. Schwartz, "Low-Income...Paychecks," <u>NYT</u>, Sept. 3, 2015, pp. B1 and B6.

13) Unionization, a positive factor in upward social mobility, Noam Scheiber, "A Link...Prospects," <u>NYT</u>, Sept. 10, 2015, p. A23.

14) Aristotle, <u>Politics</u>, Book I, Chapter 3.

15) <u>NYT</u>, Ap. 13, 2018, p. A12, Patricia Cohen and Robert Gebeloff, "Public Servants...Middle Class," <u>ibid</u>., Ap. 23, 2018, pp. A1 and A12. Paul Krugman, "We Don't Need No Education," <u>ibid</u>, Ap. 24, 2018, p. A19, on the teacher's walkouts, Simon Romero and Julie Turkewitz, "We...Colorado," <u>ibid</u>., Ap. 27, 2018, p. A13.

# Chapter 10: Alienation in Class Society and its Causes

1) On Marx and alienation, see Erich Fromm, Marx's Concept of Man, with a translation from Marx's Economic and Philosophical Manuscripts by T.B. Bottomore (New York: Frederick Ungar, 1969), pp. 43-58. Erich Fromm, The Sane Society (New York: Holt, Rinehart, 1955), pp. 120-52. Bertell Ollman, Alienation: Marx's Concept of Man in Capitalist Society (2nd ed.; London: Cambridge Univ. Press, 1976), pp. 131-35, for instance. Patsouras, Marx in Context, Ch. 9 on alienation, includes many of the following citations.

2) Genesis 2 and 3.

3) On Rousseau, see Ernest Cassirer, The Question of Jean-Jacques Rousseau (New York: Columbia Univ. Press, 1954). Jean-Jacques Rousseau, The Social Contract and Discourses, trans. and intro. By G.D.H. Cole (New York: E.P. Dutton, 1950), pp. 234-72. On Hegel, see The Philosophy of Hegel, ed. and intro. Carl J. Friedrich (New York: Modern Library, 1954), pp. 399-445.

4) Marx and Engels, German Ideology, pp. 22 ff. Fromm, Marx's Concept of Man, pp. 24, 93-109, and 151, the last citation is the lengthy quotation.

5) K. Marx and F. Engels, The Holy Family or Critique of Critical Critique (Moscow: Foreign Language Publishing House, 1956), p. 51.

6) Marx and Engels, Communist Manifesto, pp. 15-16; Fromm, Marx's Concept of Man, pp. 93-98; the long quotation is on p. 98.

7) Capital, I, 708 for the long quotation.

8) On the long quotation, see Capital, I, 462-63. On the brief quotations, Manifesto, p. 16 and Marx and Engels, German Ideology, p. 69.

9) On "commodity fetishism," see Marx, *Capital*, I, 81-87; on "objectification" see Marx, Economic and Philosophical Manuscripts in Fromm, Concept of Man, pp. 95-97; on "reification," see Ollman, Alienation, pp. 196 ff. and 205 ff. Louis Althusser, For Marx, trans. Ben Brewster (New York: Pantheon Books, 1969), p. 230.

10) On Taylorism, labor division, and so forth, see Sudhir Kakar, Frederick Taylor: A Study in Personality and Innovation (Cambridge, MA: MIT Press, 1970); Dan Clawson, Bureaucracy and the Labor Process: The Transformation of U.S. Industry, 1860-1920 (New York: Monthly Review Press, 1980), pp. 38 ff., 71 ff., 126 ff., and 202-67.

11) On Smith, see The Wealth of Nations: Representative Selections (Indianapolis, IN: Bobbs-Merrill, 1961), pp. xvii, 3-5.

12) Daniel Singer, Whose Millennium? Theirs or Ours? (New York: Monthly Review Press, 1999), p. 163.

13) Ibid., pp. 163-64.

14) On the Swedish innovations to end the conventional assembly line, see Christian Breggren, <u>Alternative to Lean Production</u> (Ithaca, NY: ILR Cornell Univ. Press, 1992).

15) Braverman, <u>Labor and Monopoly Capital</u>, pp. 95, 194, and 241.

16) Ollman, Alienation. p. 131.

17) Simone Weil, <u>La Condition Ouvrière</u> (Paris: Gallimard, 1951), pp. 15 ff. Richard M. Pfeffer, <u>Working for Capitalism</u> (New York: Columbia Univ. Press, 1979), pp. 47-102, for instance.

18) Studs Terkel, <u>Working: People Talk About What They Do All Day and How They Feel About Their Work</u> (New York: Pantheon Books, 1974), cf., for instance, Mike Lefevre, factory worker, pp. xxxi-xxxviii, with David Bender, factory owner, pp. 393-97.

19) Barbara Garson, <u>All the Livelong Day: The Meaning and Demeaning of Routine Work</u> (Garden City, NY: Doubleday, 1975), pp. 38 ff., 58 ff., and 90 ff., for instance. Barbara Garson, <u>The Electronic Sweatshop: How Computers Are Transforming the Office of the Future into the Factory of the Past</u> (New York: Simon and Schuster, 1988), pp. 40-114, 166-71, 175-263.

20) Richard Sennett and Jonathan Cobb, <u>The Hidden Injuries of Class</u> (New York: Alfred A. Knopf, 1972), pp. 30 ff., 55 ff., 72 ff., 92 ff., 121 ff., 147 ff., 162 ff.

21) Chris Argyris, <u>Personality and Organization: The Conflict Between System and the Individual</u> (New York: Harper Torchbooks, 1970), pp. 76-122.

22) On the ILO report, see David Briscoe, "Labor force reluctant lot, report says," <u>Akron Beacon Journal,</u> March 23, 1993, p. D6; and Frank Swoboda, "Employers Recognizing What Stress Costs Them, U.N. Report Suggests," <u>Washington Post</u>, March 23, 1993, p. H2.

23) On recent downsizing and mergers of corporations, with resulting widespread layoffs of workers, coupled to overwork and higher stress of those working, and decreasing real wages, see Mitchell Lee Marks, <u>From Turmoil to Triumph: New Life after Mergers, Acquisitions, and Downsizing</u> (New York: Maxwell Macmillan International, 1994), pp. 3-28. Jeremy Rifkin, <u>The End of Work: The Decline of the Global Work Force and the Dawn of the Post-Market Era</u> (New York: G.P. Putnam's, 1995), pp. 182-90.
On increasing alienation in the family and work place, manifested by more stress and higher levels of violence, unsafe working conditions, more job insecurity, higher medical costs related to the preceding, and lower life longevity for workers relative to the rich, see Rifkin, <u>End of Work</u>, pp. 194-97. Blair Justice and Rita Justice, <u>The Abusing Family</u> (New York: Plenum Press, 1990), pp. 191-93. William Greider, <u>Who Will Tell the People: The Betrayal of American Democracy</u> (New York: Simon and Schuster, 1992), pp. 111-22. Ralph Estes, <u>Tyranny of the Bottom Line: Why Corporations Make Good People Do Bad Things</u> (San Francisco, CA: Berrett-Koehler, 1996), pp. 180-82. <u>In These Times</u>, Nov. 14-20, 1990, p. 16. The daily press is a good

source for the consequences of alienation at work and elsewhere. For instance, at work, see <u>Akron Beacon Journal</u>, Aug. 13, 1990, p. A4; Jan. 28, 1996, pp. 14, A1 and A4; July 9, 1996, p. A3. On sabotage at work, see Mary Curtius, (<u>Los Angeles Times</u>), "Employee vandalism gouging companies," <u>Akron Beacon Journal</u>, Nov. 8, 1998, pp. G1 and G8.

24) On "passive aggression," see Michael Lopez (<u>Albany Times Union</u>), "Aggression on the job: Gossip, dirty looks," <u>Akron Beacon Journal</u>, Jan. 25, 1999, p. D4. Lisa Cornwell, "Workplace violence on the rise," <u>Akron Beacon Journal</u>, Sept. 4, 1995, pp. D1 and D4. On workers competing with one another at work and its deleterious effects, see Sherwood Ross, "Competition on job is internal strife," <u>Akron Beacon Journal</u>, March 11, 1996, p. D3. On bullying at school, see Lindsey Tanner, "Bullying affects one in three, study says," <u>Akron Beacon Journal</u>, April, 25, 2001, pp. A1 and A2. On longevity of life, see "For Good Health, it Helps to Be Rich and Important," <u>New York Times</u>, June 1, 1999, pp. D1 and D9. On overworked Americans, see Diane Stafford, "Workers complain they are swamped," <u>Akron Beacon Journal</u>, May 20, 2001, p. F3.

25) On job stress and higher unemployment rates for managers, about 8 percent of the work force, see Marks, <u>From Turmoil to Triumph</u>, pp. 6-14; Michael C. Jensen, "Frustrated Middle Managers," <u>New York Times</u>, July 18, 1971, Sec. 3, p. 1. Dennis Weintraub, "Office Politics: A Deadly Game for Losers," <u>Akron Beacon Journal</u>, March 22, 1974. Earl Shorris, <u>The Oppressed Middle: Politics of Middle Management</u> (Garden City, NY: Anchor Press/Doubleday, 1981), chaps. 6 and 7. Carl Hecksher, <u>White-Collar Blues: Management Loyalties in an Age of Restructuring</u> (New York: Basic Books, 1995), pp. 3-94. On corporate waste, see David M. Gordon, <u>Fat and Mean: The Corporate Squeeze of Working Americans and the Myth of Managerial Downsizing</u>." (New York: Free Press, 1996), pp. 33-60.

26) Erik H. Erikson, <u>Identity: Youth and Crisis</u> (New York: W.W. Norton, 1968), pp. 91-141. Erich Fromm, <u>Escape from Freedom</u> (New York: Farrar and Rinehart, 1941), pp. 141-206. Erich Fromm, <u>The Sane Society</u> (New York: Holt and Rinehart, 1955), pp. 12-52. T. W. Adorno et al., <u>The Authoritarian Personality</u> (New York: Harper and Brothers, 1950), pp. 759 ff.

27) On the family (and its discontents), see John M. Shepard, <u>Sociology</u>, 5th ed. (Minneapolis/St. Paul, MN: West Publishing Co., 1993), p. 344. John Bradshaw, <u>The Family: A Revolutionary Way of Self-Discovery</u> (Deerfield, FL: Health Communications, 1988), pp. 116, 126 ff. Dennis Coon, <u>Introduction to Psychology: Exploration and Application</u> (St. Paul, MN: West Publishing Co., 1980), pp. 420-84. Judith Lewis Herman, <u>Trauma and Recovery</u> (New York: Basic Books, 1992), pp. 103, 96-114, 122, and 135. Anne Sappington and Mike Paquette, "Family Violence," <u>Akron Beacon Journal</u>, Aug. 24, 1996, p. A8 on sexually abused children. On attempted suicide by teenagers,

see <u>Akron Beacon Journal</u>, Aug. 14, 1998, p. A4. "Body-bag" journalism as daily reported on television and press presents the continuing drama/ alienation of especially the economically lowest third of the people.

28) Alex Comfort, <u>Authority and Delinquency in the Modern State</u> (London: Routledge and Kegan Paul, 1950), pp. 31-65. Harold Greenwald, "Treatment of the Psychopath," p. 364, in Harold Greenwald, ed., <u>Active Psychotherapy</u> (New York: Atherton Press, 1967). Harold D. Lassell, <u>Psychopathology and Politics</u> (New York: Viking Press, 1960), pp. 1-77. This work was first published in 1930.

29) On drugs, see Steven B. Duke and Albert C. Gross, <u>America's Longest War: Rethinking Our Tragic Crusade Against Drugs</u> (New York: Jeremy P. Tarcher/Putnam Book, 1993), pp. 23-32 on tobacco, 33-42 on alcohol, pp. 54 ff. on heroin, etc. On gambling, see Marc Cooper, "America's House of Cards," <u>The Nation</u>, Feb. 19, 1996, pp. 11-19.

30) On the Senate Judiciary Report, see <u>Akron Beacon Journal</u>, March 13, 1991, p. A6. On murder and suicide, see <u>Mother Jones</u>, Jan.-Feb., 1994, p. 40. On "Victims Costs and Consequences" report, see <u>Akron Beacon Journal</u>, April 22, 1996, p. A4. On black males and incarceration, see <u>U.S. News and World Report</u>, Oct. 16, 1995, pp. 53-54. Also, see on this and related topics, David Remnick, "Dr. Wilson's Neighborhood," <u>The New Yorker</u>, April, 29/May 6, 1996. On the number of street murders and cost of street, white-collar, and corporate crimes, see Russell Mokhiber, "Underworld U.S.A.," <u>In These Times</u>, April 1-13, 1996, pp. 14-16; Ralph Estes, "The Public Cost of Private Corporations," <u>Advances in Public Interest Accounting</u>, VI, 1995, 339-45; and Robert Sherrill, "A Year in Corporate Crime," <u>The Nation</u>, April, 7, 1997, pp. 11-20. On employee sabotage, see Mary Curtius, <u>Los Angeles Times</u>, "Employee vandalism gouging companies," <u>Akron Beacon Journal</u>, Nov. 8, 1998, pp. G1 and G8. On the costs of private anti-theft measures and the legal industry, see George Winslow, "Capital Crimes: The Political Economy of Crime in America," <u>Monthly Review</u>, Nov. 2000, pp. 38-51. On the $300 billion annually lost to tax cheating by the IRS and so fourth, see <u>Akron Beacon Journal</u>, May 14, 1978, and Curt Anderson (Associated Press), "Tax evasion scams explode on internet," <u>Akron Beacon Journal</u>, April 9, 2001, p. D5.

31) Louis Chevalier, <u>Laboring Classes and Dangerous Classes in Paris During the First Half of the Nineteenth Century</u> (New York: Howard Fertig, 1973), pp. 275 ff.

32) Ralph Estes, "The Public Cost of Private Corporations," <u>Advances in Public Interest</u>, vol. 6, pp. 337-43. Estes, <u>Tyranny of the Bottom Line</u>, pp. 171-89. Michael Satchell and Stephen J. Hedges, "The next bad beef scandal?" <u>U.S. News and World Report</u>, Sept. 1., 1997, pp. 22-24.

33) Estes, <u>Tyranny of the Bottom Line</u>, pp. 183-84, on unsafe vehicles, p. 95 on advertising.

34) Christopher Lasch, <u>The Culture of Narcissism: American Life in an Age of Diminishing Expectations</u> (New York: Warner Books, 1979), p. 396, on the quotation.

35) On unequal education in the United States, see Jonathan Kozol, <u>Savage Inequalities: Children in America's Schools</u> (New York: HarperPerennial, 1992).

# Chapter 11: American Socialism

1) Hubert Gutman, Founding Director et al., <u>Who Built America? Working People and the Nation's Economy, Politics and Society</u>. Vol. I: <u>From Conquest and Colonization Through Reconstruction and the Great Uprising of 1877</u>; Vol. ll: <u>From the Guilded Age to the Present</u> (New YorkL Pantheon Books, 1989, 1992).

Lawrence Lader, <u>Power on the Left, American Radical Movements Since 1946</u> (New York: W.W. Norton, 1979). George R. Vickers, <u>The Formation of the New Left: The Early Years</u> (Toronto: D.C. Health, 1975). Nancy Zaroulis and Gerald Sullivan, <u>Who Spoke Up? American Protest Against the War in Vietnam</u> (New York York: Hold, Rinehart and Winston, 1975). Theodore Rozak, <u>The Making of a Counter-Culture</u> (New York: Doubleday, 1969), Gart B. Nash, et al., <u>The American People: Creating a Nation and Society</u>, 3rd ed. (New York: Harper Collins, 1994). Oliver Stone and Peter Kuznick, <u>The Untold History of the United States</u> (New York: Gallery Books, 2012). Articles in <u>The New York Times, Z Magazine, The Nation, Monthly Review, New Left Review</u>

# Chapter 12: Labor, Socialism, Religion

## Reformist and Socialist Religion

1) On Catholicism: On the encyclicals mentioned, see E.E.Y. Hales, <u>The Catholic Church in the Modern World: A Survey from the French Revolution to the Present</u> (New York: Image Books, 1960), pp. 193-212 on "Rerun Novarum" and "Quadragesimo Anno." And, Michael Novak, <u>Freedom with Justice: Catholic Social Thought and Liberal Institutions</u> (San Francisco: Harper and Row, 1984), pp. 108-82, with much commentary by this conservative on Catholic social conservatism. He never once mentions Jesus of Nazareth or other Hebrew prophets. National Council of Catholic Bishops, <u>Economic Justice for All</u> (Washington DC: National Council of Catholic Bishops, 1986), pp. v-xvi, 6-33, 65-105, 147-52. Also, for some of the more recent encyclicals issued by Pope John Paul II, see <u>In These Times</u>, Aug. 21- Sept. 3, 1991, p. 2; <u>Akron Beacon Journal</u>, March 1, 1995, p. A9.

2) See Peter N. Stearns, <u>Priest and Revolutionary: Lamennais and the Dilemma of French Catholicism</u> (New York: Harper and Row, 1967). Marjorie Villiers, <u>Charles Péguy: A Study in Integrity</u> (New York: Harper and Row, 1965). Jacques Maritain, <u>True Humanism</u>, trans. M.R. Adamson (London: Geoffrey Bles: The Centenary Press, 1938), pp. 156-204 as an example of his socialism. John Hellman, <u>Emmanuel Mounier and the New Catholic Left, 1930-1950</u> (Toronto: Univ. of Toronto Press, 1981), pp. 200 ff. on sympathy for Marxism.

3) On Simone Weil, see Simone Pétrement, <u>Simone Weil: A Life</u>, trans. from French by Raymond Rosenthal (New York: Pantheon Books, 1976). See also Simone Weil, <u>Oppression and Liberty</u>, trans., from French by Arthur Wills and John Petrie (Amherst, MA: Univ. of MA Press, 1973), pp. 83-108 on her good society, basically a socialist-anarchist one. Simone Weil, <u>The Need for Roots: Prelude to a Declaration of Duties Toward Mankind,</u> trans. by Arthur Wills with a preface by T.S. Eliot (Boston: Beacon Press, 1960), pp. 34-184 on her basically socialist-anarchist society.

4) On the Catholic Worker, Dorothy Day and Peter Maurin, see Dorothy Day, <u>The Long Loneliness: The Autobiography of Dorothy Day</u> (New York Curtis Books, 1972), pp. 193-316 on her Catholic Worker experiences, including her encounters with Maurin. Dorothy Day, <u>Loaves and Fishes</u> (New York: Harper and Row, 1963), is on the journal <u>The Catholic Worker</u> and the movement in general; pp. 28-41 on "Houses of Hospitality"; pp. 42-59 on "Communitarian Farms"; pp. 103-117, on Ammon Hennacy another key member of the movement. Arthur Sheehan, Peter Maurin: Gay Believer (Garden City, NY: Hanover House, 1959), pp. 90 ff on his meeting Day and so forth.

5) Gustavo Gutierrez, A Theology of Liberation (Maryknoll, NY: Orbis Books, 1973), pp. 111 ff on necessity for socialism in Latin America; pp. 236-37 on Guevara; 272 ff. on the class struggle; 265 ff. on the Church being part of the traditional power structure; 175 ff. on sin; pp. 287 ff. on Bible's denouncing wealth, power, and privilege of the few at the expense of the many. Also, see the brilliant work of José Porfiro Miranda, Communism in the Bible (Maryknoll, NY: Orbis Books, 1987), pp. 1-85. For a Protestant view similar to Gutierrez's and Miranda's see C.M. Kempton Kewitt, "The Marxist Jesus of Nazareth," in Louis Patsouras and Jack Ray Thomas, eds., Essays on Socialism (San Francisco: Mellen Research Univ. Press, 1992), pp. 299-343. See also William K. Tabb, ed., Churches in Struggle: Liberation Theologies and Social Change in North America (New York: Monthly Review Press, 1986), with its many excellent articles, in which the similarity of interests between Marxism and religious socialism is evident.

6) See O.J. Brose, Frederick Denison Maurice, Rebellious Conformist (Athens, OH: Ohio Univ. Press, 1971). Brenda Colloms, Charles Kingsley, The Lion of Eversley (London: Constable, 1975). Peter N. Stearns, Priest and Revolutionary: Lamennais, and the Dilemma of French Catholicism (New York: Harper and Row, 1967).

7) See Donald Gorrell, The Age of Social Responsibility: The Social Gospel in the Progressive Era (Macon, GA: Mercer Univ. Press, 1988).

8) Robert T. Handy, ed., The Social Gospel in America: Gladden, Ely, Rauschenbusch (New York: Oxford Univ. Press, 1966), pp. 33-169, on Gladden; pp. 184-250 on Ely.

9) On Rauschenbusch, see Dores R. Sharpe, Walter Rauschenbusch (New York: Macmillan, 1942). See, for instance, His Christianity and the Social Crisis (New York: Macmillan, 1914), pp. 44-92, in which Jesus of Nazareth is portrayed as a socialist.

10) On Niebuhr, see Gabriel Fackre, The Promise of Reinhold Niebuhr (Philadelphia: J.B. Lippincott, 1970), pp. 20-21. June Bingham, Courage to Change: An Introduction to the Life and Thought of Reinhold Niebuhr (New York: Charles Scribner's, 1961), pp. 163 ff.

11) On Thomas, see W.A. Swanberg, Norman Thomas: The Last Idealist (New York: Scribner's Sons, 1976), pp. 43-179, for instance.

12) See National Council of Churches of Christ in the United States of America, A Policy Statement (1966), 5 pp.

13) On Karl Barth, see Thomas C. Oden, The Promise of Barth: The Ethics of Freedom (Philadelphia: J.B. Lippincott, 1969), pp. 25 ff. on his socialism. On Paul Tillich, see his The Socialist Decision, trans. Franklin Sherman from German, intro. John Stumme (New York: Harper and Row, 19710, pp. 61 ff., 117 ff., and 157 ff. Wilhelm and Marion Pauck, Paul Tillich: His Life and Thought (New York: Harper and Row, 1976), I, 67, ff., on Tillich's socialism.

14) Henri Troyat, Tolstoy, trans. from French by Nancy Amphoux (New York: Doubleday, 1965), especially pp. 373-584 on Tolstoy's religious/anarchist quest.

15) Nicolas Berdyaev, Dream and Reality: An Essay in Autobiography (New York: Macmillan, 1951). Nicolas Berdyaev, The Realm of Spirit and the Realm of Freedom, trans. Donald A. Lowerie (New York: Harper and Brothers, 1952), pp. 57-63 on socialism. Nicolas Berdyaev, Slavery and Freedom, trans. from Russian by R.M. French (New York: Charles Scribner's Sons, 1944), pp. 200-22 on his socialism.

16) Laurence J. Silberstein, Martin Buber's Social and Religious Thought: Alienation and Quest for Meaning (New York: New York Univ. Press, 1989), pp. 193-98 on Buber's religious/socialist decentralized society. Also, see Martin Buber, Paths in Utopia, trans. R.F.C. Hall, intro. Ephraim Fischoff (Boston: Beacon Press, 1958), pp. 7 ff., 24 ff., 38 ff., 46 ff., and 139-49. For proper human relations, see Martin Buber, I and Thou, trans. and prologue by Walter Kaufmann (New York: Charles Scribner's Sons, 1970), pp. 92-100.

17) Mohandas K. Gandhi, An Autobiography: The Story of My Experiments with Truth (Boston: Beacon Press, 1957), p. 137, on his being "overwhelmed" by Tolstoy's The Kingdom of God Is Within You. C.F. Andrews, Mahatma Gandhi's Ideas: Including Selections from His Writings, intro. Horace G. Alexander (London: George Allen and Unwin, 1949), pp. 202-17 on Tolstoy Farm. Louis Fischer, The Life of Mahatma Gandhi (New York: Harper and Row, 1964).

18) For an excellent view of the various currents of Islamic or Arab socialism, see John Obert Voll, Islam: Continuity and Change in the Modern World (Syracuse, NY: Syracuse Univ. Press, 1994), for instance, pp. 173 ff., 289-373; 313 for the brief quotations. On the Arab left, socialists and communists, the former being particularly important in Arab life, see Albert Hourani, A History of the Arab Peoples (New York: MJF Books, 1991), pp. 397-410; and John L. Esposito, Islam: The Straight Path (New York: Oxford Univ. Press, 1991), pp. 156-86 on Islamic socialism. On Qaddafi and the Libyan Islamic Socialist Revolution, see David Blundy and Andrew Lycett, Qaddafi and the Libyan Revolution (Boston: Little, Brown, and Co., 1987), pp. 57-68, 84-129. Dirk Vanderwalle, ed., Qadhafi's Libya, 1969-1994 (New York: St. Martin's Press, 1995). The various articles by well-known writers in the field are excellent. On the Green Book, see Muammar al-Qadhafi, Part II: The Solution of the Economic Problem, Socialism (London: Martin Brian and O'Keefe, 1978), pp. 19-20 on the quotations. On the Iranian Islamic Revolution, including its extensive nationalizations, banks, large industry, insurance companies, and so forth, see Martin Kramer, ed., Sh'ism, Resistance and Revolution (Boulder, CO: Westview Press, 1987): articles by Marvin Zunis and Daniel Brumberg, "Shi'ism as Interpreted by Khomeini: An Ideology of Revolutionary Violence," pp. 47-66; Mangol Bayat, "Mahmud Taleqani and the Iranian Revolution," pp.

67-94; Shaul Bakhash, "Islam and Social Justice," in Iran," pp. 95-116. On Ali Shariati, see Esposito, Islam, pp. 178 ff.

19) For a general view of Buddhism, see Richard H. Robinson and Willard R. Johnson, with assistance from others, The Buddhist Religion: A Historical Introduction, 4th ed. (Belmont, CA: Wadsworth Publishing Co., 1997), pp. 218-19, 238-40, 301-09, on Buddhism's social activism, with new emphases on changing the present world. Edward J. Thomas, The History of Buddhist Thought (New York: Barnes and Noble, 1967), is excellent; pp. 11-26, for instance, on "The Ascetic Ideal," the Sangha life-style. Peter A. Pardue, Buddhism: A Historical Introduction to Buddhist Values and the Social and Political Forms They Have Assumed in Asia (New York: Macmillan, 1968), indicates the complex interplay between Buddhism and political and social forces; for instance, pp. 27-30, on asceticism for lay Buddhists, while economically exploiting others, including slaves, although slave-trading is prohibited. Larson, Religion of the Occident, pp. 126-54, presents the best short description of the Buddha's socioeconomic and other views that I know. On Buddhist Socialism and the differences and similarities between Marxism (and 20th century Communism) and Buddhism, see Ernst Benz, Buddhism or Communism: Which Holds the Future of Asia? (London: George Allen and Unwin, 1966), pp. 95-124. on the "Social and Political Teachings of Buddhism," is of great interest. The quotation from U Nu is from here. "The Buddhist Critique of Communism," pp. 217-34, is a masterpiece; it features Vijayavardhana's The Revolt in the Temple.

20) On traditional religion's general decline, although it appears to be slightly gaining in Eastern Europe and the former Soviet Union with the fall of Communism, with statistics, see Time, Aug. 9, 1976 (Gallup Poll); David Briggs, "Religion Enjoys a Revival," Akron Beacon Journal, May 22, 1995, p. A6; P. Ehrensaft and A. Etzioni, Anatomies of America: Sociological Perspectives (New York: Macmillan, 1969), pp. 272-85. Gordon Wright, France in Modern Times: 1760 to the Present (Chicago: Rand McNally, 1960), p. 557, "The Dechristianization of Rural France." H. Stuart Hughes, Contemporary Europe: A History (Englewood Cliffs, NJ: Prentice-Hall, 1976), p. 290, on Communism's destruction of Orthodox Christianity in Russia. Akron Beacon Journal, Jan. 16, 1998, p. A9 – a recent poll in Russia has 46 percent of respondents as atheists.

21) On Christian conservatism in America, see Sara Diamond, Not by Politics Alone: The Enduring Influence of the Christian Right (New York: Guilford Press, 1998). Clark Morphew, "Conservative Christians back Bush," Akron Beacon Journal, Jan. 13, 2001, pp. A14 and A16. On the democratic socialist Martin Luther King Jr. see David J. Garrow, Bearing the Cross: Martin Luther King Jr. and the Southern Christian Leadership Conference (New York: William Morrow, 1986).

# Postscript on Religion

1) On religious support for clean energy, see Religion Chapter and <u>Yes!</u>, Spring 2016, p. 21. On contraception, <u>NYT</u>, Feb. 19, 2016, p. A12. Naomi Oreskes and Erik M. Conway, <u>The Collapse of Western Civilization: A View from the Future</u> (New York: Columbia University Press, 2014), pp. 89, Pope Francis I, <u>Laudato Si (On Care for Our Common Home)</u> Encyclical Letter, Vatican City: Libreria Editrice Vaticana, 2015. On Jacobson/Delucci Plan, see Louis Bergeon, "The World Can Be Powered by Alternative Energy," <u>Stanford Report</u>, Jan. 26, 2011 (4 pp.).

## Chapter 13: Ecology and A Proper Socialism

1) Bill McKibben, <u>NYT</u>, Dec. 14, 2015, p. A23. <u>NYT</u>, Dec. 6, 2015, p. A6. Robert Pollin, "The New Green Economy," <u>The Nation</u>, Nov. 16, 2015, pp. 13-18. <u>NYT</u>, Oct. 2, 2015, p. A 6 on India and fossil fuel pollution. <u>NYT</u> Dec. 15, 2015, p. A30. <u>NYT</u> Oct 2, 2015, p. A6. Mark Hertsgaard, "Breakthrough in Paris," <u>The Nation</u>, Jan. 4, 2016, pp. 4-7. <u>NYT</u> Oct. 27, 2015, p. A8. <u>NYT</u>, Feb., 2016, p. A23. <u>Z Magazine</u>, March 2016, p. 18. <u>Yes!</u>, Spring 2016 articles on a post-carbon society. <u>Monthly Review</u>, Feb. 2016, front and back inside covers on techno-utopia proposals. On religious support for clean energy, see Religion Chapter and <u>Yes!</u>, Spring 2016, p. 21. On contraception, <u>NYT</u>, Feb. 19, 2016, p. A12. Naomi Klein, <u>This Changes Everything: Capitalism vs. The Climate</u> (New York: Simon and Schuster, 2014), pp. 1-119. Naomi Oreskes and Erik M. Conway, <u>The Collapse of Western Civilization: A View from the Future</u> (New York: Columbia University Press, 2014), pp. 89. The principal influences on my socialist views: Karl Marx, Eugene V. Debs, Peter Kropotkin and Jean Grave.

# Chapter 14: The 2016 Election and its Candidates

1) <u>The New York Times</u> Nov. – Dec., 2016; <u>The Nation</u>, Nov. 25, 2016 and "The Obama Years," <u>Z Magazine</u>, Dec. 2016 and Jan. 2017, various articles.

# Chapter 15: 2016 Election Results and the Early Trump Presidency

1) The material in this chapter is generally common knowledge which I have gleaned from The New York Times, Akron Beacon Journal, The Nation, Time, Z Magazine, Monthly Review, New Left Review and television, including CBS and NBC evening news, Free Speech TV and RT TV. On Postel, see RT TV, April 12, 2017 and Professor Noam Chomsky on Democracy Now, Free Speech TV, April 26, 2017. On normally aggressive US foreign policy, see Noam Chomsky, Who Rules the World? (New York: Metropolitan Books, 2016), pp. 19-20, 108-10, 132-34, among others. Also, for instance, see "Trump's Twisted Budget," The Nation, pp. 3-4, March 20, 2017. Articles by Mike Davis, JoAnn Wypijewski, Dylan Riley, Alexander Zevin and Perry Anderson in New Left Review, 103, Jan. and Feb. 2017.

Jack Rasmus (a leftist economist teaching at St. Mary's College, CA), "The Trump- Goldman Sachs Cut for the Rich," Z Magazine, Nov. 2017, pp. 40-44. Jack Rasmus, "A Letter of Thanks to Our Wealthiest 1 Percent," ibid, Jan. 2018, pp. 27-30. New York Times articles, 2017 – March. 2018. Tom Hartman and others, Free Speech TV, 2017 – 2018.

Michael Wolff, Fire and Fury: Inside the Trump White House, New York: Henry Holt and Company, 2018, pp. 186 and 233, for instance.

# Conclusion

1) Chris Hedges, <u>America: The Farewell Tour</u> (New York: Simon and Schuster, 2018), pp. 46-51.
2) On U.S. debt and so forth, Jack Rasmus, "Comparing Crises: 1929 with 2008 and the Next," <u>Z Magazine</u>, Dec. 2018, pp. 36-41. On bond yields, Richard Wolff, Thom Hartmann, Free Speech TV, Dec. 7-8, 2018.

Printed in the United States
By Bookmasters